Freemasonry, Politics and Rijeka (Fiume) (1785-1944)

Also from Westphalia Press

westphaliapress.org

Freemasonry, Politics and Rijeka (Fiume) (1785-1944)

by
Ljubinka Toševa Karpowicz

WESTPHALIA PRESS
An imprint of Policy Studies Organization

Freemasonry, Politics and Rijeka (Fiume) (1785-1944)
All Rights Reserved © 2017 by Policy Studies Organization

Original edition: Masoneria, politika i Rijeka (1785-1944), Rijeka, Državni arhiv Rijeka, 2015.

Westphalia Press
An imprint of Policy Studies Organization
1527 New Hampshire Ave., NW
Washington, D.C. 20036
info@ipsonet.org

ISBN-13: 978-1-63391-528-2
ISBN-10: 1-63391-528-X

Daniel Gutierrez-Sandoval, Executive Director
PSO and Westphalia Press

Cover design by Robert Krančić
http://www.grafik.hr/
Cover page: Detail of patent from April 23, 1779, assigning to Rijeka status of
corpus separatum (with the seal), Državni arhiv Rijeka, Rijeka.
Edited by Maria Theresa.

Updated material and comments on this edition
can be found at the Westphalia Press website:
www.westphaliapress.org

For Izabela Karpowicz

FOREWORD

POLITICS AND FREEMASONRY: RESEARCH ISSUES

Freemasonry is the oldest, most widespread and most diverse international fraternity in the world. According to the majority of authors advocating Freemasonry,, who rely mainly on the Bible, the fraternity was first established among Egyptian colonists, in order for it to spread to all continents to this day.

Independent of the author's attitude to Freemasonry, there is no doubt that the passage of time and disjuncture of the fraternity influenced on various forms of Masonic ritual, while the blueprint, practice and organization of Freemasonry within various historical circumstances also influenced the emergence of various (emulated) Masonic associations and practices.

Authors today mention by name the existence and emergence of some of the forty-eight recognized rituals, while the number of variants of emulated Masonic associations and unrecognized rituals and associations is uncountable.[1]

However, even the briefest history of Freemasonry implicitly suggests that, from its infancy until today, it has been associated with politics. Researching the link between Freemasonry and politics poses numerous difficulties.

---

[1] The Ritual (ceremony) is a formal act of service based on Masonic law or practice or habit. This is a symbolic ceremony and means of presenting ideas. Freemasonry is structurally rigid in terms of its principles and general rules. However, it expresses itself by employing various methods that are called rituals.

The main problem lies in the fundamental Masonic principle—adherence to the principle of *secrecy*. [2]

Modern Freemasonry began in 1717 when *the Grand Lodge of England* (Grand Lodge—the mother of the world) was constituted, but it was only in 1723, once the regulations and charges of the Masons had been laid down and codification completed, that Freemasonry began developing into a system. At the same time, England witnessed the unification of four lodges at national level and the degree of importance of Masonic information, which ought to be protected under the principle of *secrecy*, was established.

The result of strict adherence to the principle of *secrecy* is that an independent researcher only rarely, if ever, succeeds in obtaining access to firsthand Masonic documents at national level, or those at the level of individual lodges. This is made all the more impossible given that the documents are usually housed in archives belonging to the Freemasonry or in the private archives of high-ranking members of the Masonic hierarchy (where Freemasonry is concerned, this was the case until its unification at the national level). From that point on, only high-ranking members were given access, which usually resulted in works extolling Freemasonry.

Another aggravating factor for researchers lies in the fact that different state and political systems ranging from „democracies" to „dictatorships" not only favor or hinder making documents that are stored in the archives available, but also affect the assessment of the level and various forms of *secrecy* attached thereto. Therefore, familiarity with a given society and political milieu at an exact moment in history emerges as a key hypothesis for conducting research comprehensively and, subsequently, drawing logical conclusions therefrom.

---

[2] According to Masonic doctrine, the Masonic notion of *secrecy* (a secret) has its foundations in the Divine Order of Nature where all that is „grand and beautiful and useful is born of night and mystery." God himself is environed with shadows, „clouds and darkness are around about his throne." So Freemasonry works in secrecy, but its benignant fruits are visible in all lands. Besides, this principle of secrecy furnishes a mysterious bond of unity and strength, which can be found nowhere else. Therefore, meetings of Masons are held at night.
Definition according to the American author Robert Macoy, 1815-1895. The book was published shortly before his death: *A Dictionary of Freemasonry*, New York, reprint in 2000 p.647-648 and p.345

With respect to the relationship between Freemasonry, politics, and state and political systems, besides the *Order of the Grand Lodge of Britain* (the so-called Anglo-Saxon Freemasonry), which historically gave rise to numerous lodges that were constituted by national lodges of this order, when researching one should underscore the difference between this order and the Order of the *Grand Orient of France.*

This order, on the eve of the revolution in 1789, managed to assemble six hundred lodges, three hundred of which were of another obedience, and so the *Grand Orient of France was* constituted. This was an order that was, at once, declaratively, publicly and covertly politically active.

The *Grand Orient of France* expanded territorially and numerically on the back of Napoleon's conquests and „national lodges" were established in the conquered lands. The *Grand Orient of France* was based on principles other than Anglo-Saxon Masonry. It did not, for instance, recognize God, was opposed to religion and the Church, was markedly political, and therefore the Anglo-Saxon Freemasonry did not recognize it.

In the Austrian Empire (which is covered by this research), an empire ruled by the staunchly Catholic Habsburg dynasty /House of Habsburg/ Freemasonry has a peculiar history.

At the beginning of enlightened absolutism, Masons in the Habsburg monarchy were associates of enlightened ruler Joseph II, only to be later outlawed by him. After suppression it was far more difficult to control Freemasonry in the Hungarian part of the Habsburg Empire, and even more so in the Military Frontier. In these parts of the Empire, although outlawed, Freemasonry operated semi-publicly.

In addition, the main feature of Hungarian Freemasonry during the enlightenment lay in its almost exclusive attachment to the militarized and politicized *Order of Strict Observance*, whose written records in Hungary disappeared during the war in 1941, i.e. they are unavailable.

Due to the division of the Austrian Empire into two entities, Austria and Hungary (February 17, 1867), the position of Freemasonry became disparate, considering that each of the components of the Dual Monarchy engaged in separate internal politics.

In the Hungarian part of the Dual Monarchy, officially called the *Lands of the Crown of St. Stephen*, the environment was favorable for Freemasonry, while in the western part, Freemasonry was prohibited. Masons congregated in lodges in the eastern part of the Empire, which contributed to the myriad of Masonic lodges. The *Lands of the Crown of St. Stephen* included Croatia and Slavonia and Rijeka (Fiume) as a *corpus separatum*.

Constituting and operating lodges in any of these lands was subject to obedience to the Hungarian (mother) Lodge—which oversaw their work.

RIJEKA (FIUME) AND RESEARCHING THE RELATIONSHIP BETWEEN FREEMASONRY AND POLITICS

G iven that Fiume, (nowadays) Rijeka, having the status of *corpus sepa-ratum*, became part of the *Lands of the Crown of St. Stephen* with the right to elect representatives to both the Croatian Diet and the Diet in Budapest, it thereby gained a standing in the system of political decision-making, albeit a modest one. Although it had the right to elect only one representative to the Diet in Budapest, and considering its economic role as Hungary's only port, enterprising coalitions of political interest groups formed around the representative for Rijeka.

On the other hand, the same fact—the election of representatives to parliament—prompted local politicians, organized into similar interest groups and political parties at state (Hungarian) level, to monitor political developments in the capital keenly, while bidding to play the decisions of the central authorities to their advantage by way of the city's „autonomous" institutions.

This spirited approach by Rijeka's „autonomous authorities" to the politics being directed from the capital of the country, but also from Zagreb, lasted until the end of the Dual Monarchy when these same seasoned Rijeka politicians, and even ordinary citizens—citizens of Hungary—had to turn their attention to events at the Paris Peace Conference (1919), both in the neighboring Kingdom of Italy, and to the immediate east, in the newly formed Kingdom of Serbs, Croats and Slovenes.

Information from the „brethren" of any national lodge was now particularly valuable.

Given its policy of expressing continual loyalty to the political system of their home country, any shift in borders, even within countries, proved tumultuous for the Freemasonry. The problem of Freemasonry, considering that it is, in essence, a political organization, is rooted in the fact that, within the state, it operated to the letter of the law and was at a loss as to how to act if incentives had their roots outside national borders and the „brethren" within

9

countries were opposed, having conflicting political goals.[3]

An example of a change of political objective in such cases manifested itself in the „Rijeka question" following the collapse of the Dual Monarchy. Namely, the protracted resolution of the „Rijeka question" proved not only disquieting for the Rijeka Hungarian *Sirius* Lodge but acted as a stimulus for both Masonic orders of Italy, the *Grand Lodge of Italy* (Piazza del Gesù) and the *Grand Orient of Italy* (Palazzo Giustiniani), to concern themselves with its resolution, along the lines of political interest groups in Italy itself, organized into national lodges of a strictly determined order.[4]

Were the question to arise as to which aspects of public law played a role in the emergence of the Rijeka *corpus separatum* as the quintessential paradigm for exploring the relationship between Freemasonry and politics, the responses would read as follows:

- First of all, Rijeka is a historically defined area (less than 20 km²).
- Secondly, prominent persons in this area knew each other, or at least, recognized each other; hence, the possibility *of secrecy,* both in terms of membership of the Freemasonry, and in terms of its activity, was almost impossible.
- Thirdly, given the fact that the *corpus separatum* during the period 1785-1944 belonged to various public law entities, the official standing of Freemasonry varied.
- Fourthly, as Rijeka was not the center of national (state) level Masonry,Freemasonry activity in this area was transmissionary, but also subject to adaptation, or the dictates of local circumstances.
- Fifthly, given the fact that Rijeka was a port city easily accessible by sea and by land, both lawful national Masonic fraternities, as well as

[3] This was clearly evident following the annexation of Bosnia and Herzegovina in 1908, when the Serbian Freemasonry broke from the obedience of the *Symbolic Grand Lodge of Hungary* and founded its own independent Freemasonry, not to mention that the assassination in Sarajevo took place shortly afterwards, followed by the outbreak of World War I, an event—according to some Masonic authors—that is not without its links to Freemasonry.

[4] Further reading: Ljubinka Toševa Karpowicz, D' Annunzio u Rijeci. Mase, mitovi i uloga masonerije (*D'Annunzio in Rijeka. Masses, Myths and the Role of Freemasonry,* Rijeka, *2007.*

emulated Masonic associations, were at work, i.e. ones that „foreign national Freemasonry" secretly supported as their own in situ political apparatus.

The perennial politicization of the community of Rijeka was rooted in Rijeka's primary function as a port for maritime trade. The importance of the port changed over time in line with the economic policy of the region, and therefore also in line with policy in the narrow sense of the word.[5]

It all started with the mercantilist policies of the Habsburg rulers, in which the port of Rijeka played an important, economically stimulating role, first for the Austrian Empire, and, from 1779 onwards, for Hungary.

This policy coincided with the ascension of Ferdinand I to the Hungarian-Croatian throne in 1527. His policy centered on conquering the maritime trade routes in the eastern Adriatic. In furtherance of this policy, Rijeka was granted new privileges. As Rijeka became inextricably linked to the policy pursued by the Crown, from 1593-1728 it had to swear allegiance to the ruler, (and from 1599 to each archduke of Austria in particular) which generated an awareness among the public and the nobility of its special position.

In a move that was most probably linked to his desire for continuity of economic policy, Emperor Leopold I, by way of the edict of June 9, 1659, bestowed a new coat of arms on Rijeka, which became the first city to adopt the motto INDEFICIENTER (Inexhaustible). From that point forward, the coat of arms was included on the flag representing the political hinterland of Rijeka, and this shift reflects not only public law changes in the hinterland of the city, but also its status therein.[6]

Various other acts of Habsburg rulers point to Rijeka's important status: the proclamation of Rijeka (and Trieste) as free ports in 1719, its written con-

---

[5] Ljubinka Toševa Karpowicz, " Važnost riječke luke u političkoj povijesti grada Rijeke 1786-1924"(„The Importance of the Port in the Political History of the City of Rijeka 1786-1924,"), Luka Rijeka(The Port of Rijeka), Rijeka, 2001, pp. 241–250.

[6] Chronologica synopsis jurium et privilegorum fedelissimae, maritimae, commercialis urbis, liberi portus, districtuaque Fluminensis. Flumine, Typius Fratrum Karletzky, 1825.

sent to the provisions of the Pragmatic Sanction, the appointment of *a cap-tain-general* (1437-1751), membership of *Intendanza* (based in Trieste), giving it direct ties to Vienna. These economic reforms remained in force until 1776, when *Severin County* was established.

With the establishment of *Severin County,* Rijeka's patriciate and the governor himself were compelled by the *Hungarian Regency Council* to communicate through the *Croatian Regency Council.* When it was dissolved in 1787, the handling of Rijeka's affairs was transferred to the *Hungarian Governor's Council*, resulting in Rijeka being designated *corpus separatum.* At the same time, by way of an act abolishing *Severin County*, the districts of Rijeka, Bakar and Vinodol were united as a separate administrative unit called the *Hungarian Littoral.* This unit was directly subordinated to the *Gubernium.*

With this an entirely new administrative body—the *Gubernium* of *Hungarian Regency Council.*Rijeka—was established in Rijeka. The head of the *Gubernium* was the governor, appointed by the emperor through the *Hungarian Royal Chamber* in the capacity of the Hungarian government, based in Vienna. The *Gubernium* organized the entire functioning of the demarcated territory, while the governor and his office gave the city the semblance of a capital by the sea.

As with every capital, Rijeka too, being „a capital by the sea," was inhabited by numerous nationalities divided by class:

1. At the top of the ladder were the governors and staff of the governors' offices. Persons appointed as governors of Rijeka were archetypal in nature.

Governors of Rijeka belonged to the Hungarian *gentry* class. They often belonged to nations of Eastern Hungary, and more often than from *Transylvania.*

Another social group in Rijeka were the patricians of the „free city." They belonged to the same social class as the governor and were on an equal footing with him.

The first member of the Hungarian *gentry* to rule Rijeka was a member of the common noblesse, as opposed to a member of the Hungarian nobility (magnates). *Gentry* were the heirs of former imperial army officers, whose number began to grow rapidly during the wars with Turkey in the seventeenth and eighteenth centuries. At that time, Hungarian kings and Transylvanian princes guaranteed individuals and even entire communities exemptions from feudal obligations, in return for an army permanently on stand-by.

As a result, after the Turkish wars in 1787, the number of common nobles reached 389,146 members, and was estimated at 617,521 in 1839, representing some 5% of the population of the country. In the early nineteenth century they personified the typical middle-class element of *Transylvania* and started calling themselves the gentry, in Hungarian *dzsentri*.[7]

The high numbers of *gentry*, following the expulsion of the Turks from Hungary, found themselves left to defend the status of the *gentry* and commenced to do business, finding employment within the civil service, or studying and specializing in administration. The gentry worked in government institutions of the Empire, acted as imperial advisers and associates, and very often were at the same time affiliated with Freemasonry. It was these members of the *gentry*, those in the employ of the civil service of the Empire, that most often became governors in Rijeka. Information on the first Masonic lodges in Rijeka shows that, except in the factories (both sugar refineries) which were operated by Dutch manufacturers, Rijeka governors opened lodges or were members of the Freemasons. Thus, for example, János Péter Szapáry, Governor (1788– 1791) and Sándor Pászthory, Governor (1791–1798), were members of the later prohibited Masonic order known as *Strict Observance*.[8]

Given the fact that they belonged to the select educated Hungarian class, on completion of service in Rijeka they went on to work in the Austrian civil service.

---

[7] Andrew C. Janos, *The Politics of Backwardness in Hungary, 1825–1945*, New Jersey, Princeton, 1982, pp. 18-19.

[8] In 1763, at the convent in Altenberg, near Jena, the *Order of Templar Strict Observance* was founded. At that convent, Europe, according to the ancient structure of the (Masonic) Temple, was divided into nations and languages, provinces (province), Grand priories and priories, prefectures, perceptories etc. Luigi Troisi, *La Massoneria. Profilo storico–cronologico*, Foggia, 1990, p. 26.

2. Citizens of Rijeka belonged to a class that also enjoyed privileges, since cities were considered corporations and were legal entities enjoying aristocratic privileges.

In Hungary in 1787 there were seventy privileged settlements with 498,000 inhabitants. Over time, some cities were afforded new privileges, as, for example, parliamentary representation, autonomy, and—to draw a distinction between the earlier status of „free"—the status of „imperial city" was often awarded. Rijeka did not hold imperial city status.

The privileges enjoyed by some cities were awarded because they provided specific services to the Crown. In the eighteenth and nineteenth century, the percentage of people who inhabited those cities did not exceed 13.5 percent.[9]

Unlike the *gentry* and high nobility, free cities paid taxes and supplied the Empire with an army, and were opponents of the feudal order, later becoming centers of an anti-authoritarian political culture and strongholds for opposition parties.

This book takes the year 1785 as a starting point for several reasons:

•   The census conducted in the Empire between 1784 and 1787 shows that in 1785 Rijeka was a bordered urban center holding the status of a municipality with attributes of an administrative center of the Empire.

•   Rijeka was inhabited by entrepreneurial-minded citizens from various parts of the vast Empire whose social status was based on trade rather than land ownership.

•   Those appointed as governors of Rijeka were mainly members of the impoverished nobility of the eastern part of the Empire who actively and in their own way dealt with the economic and other reforms of the Habsburg rulers.

In 1850 the City of Rijeka—then a part of Croatia—had 4,515 residents, with around 617 inhabitants living in the surrounding area. Most numerous was the urban patrician class, with 49 patrician families of Italian, German,

---

[9] Andrew C. Janos, op. cit. pp. 20-22.

Croatian and French origin, numerous clerics of all faiths, and wholesalers (16) and retailers (52)[10]. They were all members of the middle class.

The connection with Austria and Rijeka's special legal and political position gave a considerable boost—primarily economic, but also to the social life of the city—right until the division of the Austrian Empire into two parts under the Austro-Hungarian Compromise. However, this in itself put Rijeka in a very intriguing legal position and afforded it a prominent economic, and therefore political role.

The end of the First World War and the break-up of the Austro-Hungarian Empire signaled the end of the „Hungarian" part of the city's history.

Nevertheless, Rijeka remained in the limelight on the international stage mainly due to the lengthy efforts to resolve the issue of its status at the international conference in Paris, followed by the dawn of Fascism brought about by the coup mounted against the government of Riccardo Zanella.

This book aims to show the connection between politics and Freemasonry in Rijeka in the period from 1785 to 1944, with the exception of D'Annunzio's occupation of Rijeka (September 12, 1919 - January 3, 1921) and the part played by the Freemasonry, which the author has already discussed in a separate book.

---

[10] Franz Rački, *Fiume gegenüber Croatien,* Agram, 1869, p. 8.

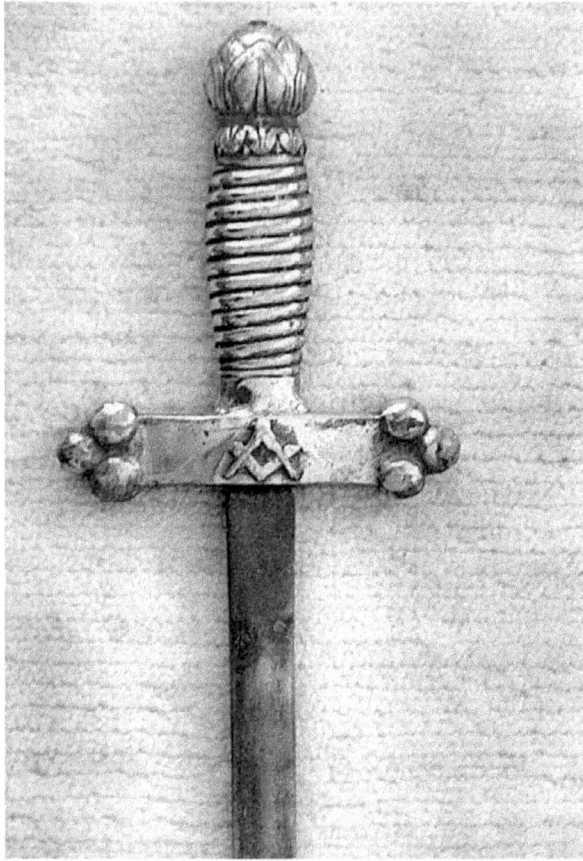

The hilt of a ceremonial Freemason sword (private collection, Rijeka)

1

ENLIGHTENED ABSOLUTISM IN AUSTRIA

1. JOSEPHINISM AND FREEMASONRY

The protracted, expensive and unsuccessful War of the Austrian Succession (1740–1748) which Maria Theresa (1740–1780) led against Frederick II, King of Prussia, then the Seven Years' War (1756–1763), left the Austrian Empire economically destitute.

Given that the Hungarian magnates supported the empress in these wars, they succeeded in preserving their fundamental feudal privileges, in particular the right to tax exemptions, as reward therefor. This led to an economic situation where the western part of the Monarchy developed industrially, while the Hungarian part remained agricultural. The after-effect of this was a state at odds economically. Its eastern, Hungarian part was characterized by large estates (latifundia) in the hands of a small number of owners, agricultural exports and a sparse population.

At the beginning of the Enlightenment reforms, namely from 1765 to 1772, Maria Theresa herself, as ruler, was the chief advocate of enlightened absolutism, only to be joined after 1772 in her endeavor by the classes of the Empire. However, such was the political involvement of the classes that they were difficult to control, given both the size of the Empire, and given their ethnic, cultural and religious differences. The demands of the Hungarian classes ranged from demands for reform of the feudal system, to demands for secession of some parts of the Empire, and to independence (Jacobins).

Frederick II (or Frederick the Great), King of Prussia (1740–1786), the prominent advocate of Prussian prosperity in the "Germanic spirit," enjoyed an enviable reputation among the Hungarian nobility viewed him not only as an economic, but also a political model. Being a very dynamic Mason, his success was partly attributed to his ideals, but also to his international Masonic affiliations. [1]

Maria Theresa, as a model Catholic, was openly opposed to Freemasonry. It is believed that she did not know that her husband Francis Stephen of Lorraine (1708–1765), whom she married in 1736, was a Mason, initiated in 1751 at a special lodge in The Hague. Given that she, as a woman, could not be at the head of the Holy Roman Empire, she appointed her husband in that capacity. Owing to his position, Freemasonry in the Austrian Empire prospered under his guardianship.

Thanks to his intermediation, under the auspices of the Grand Lodge of England, the first lodge in Vienna was constituted in 1742. At first the lodge was called the *Three Firing Glasses,* only to change its name soon thereafter to the *Three Cannons.*

Given the fact that the empress's co-regent was master of the lodge, the nobility of the vast Empire hastened to join and in the space of twenty weeks of opening, fifty-six candidates had been initiated. Among its members were non-Germanic representatives - Croats, for example Count Đivo Gundulić from Dubrovnik and Baron Kazimir Drašković from Croatia. Members of eminent noble families of Hungary became Masons also—Hoyos, Apponyi,

---

[1] Frederick The Great (1712–1786) was an active and prominent Mason. He was initiated on the night between August 14–15, 1738 at a special lodge in Brunswick. He later invited Baron von Oberg and, with four other „brethren," founded a lodge, and on June 20, 1740 Frederick the Great became its master. The seat of the lodge was in Charlottenburg. He also initiated his brothers and associates into the lodge. He placed the lodge under the protection of the *National Grand Lodge of Germany,* when it was officially recognized by the *Grand Lodge of England.* As king, Frederick the Great was patron to Voltaire (a Mason), and held George Washington and the American Revolution in high esteem. He authored numerous works, which were published in thirty volumes. He waged war against Maria Theresa (1740–1748) and seized Silesia from her. During the war, she demonstrated great resourcefulness and courage, even without the support of her husband Francis I also a Mason. William R. Denslow, *10,000 Famous Freemasons,* 2012, Vol. II p. 86. Kuess-Scheilcherbauer, *Zweihundert Jahre Freimaurerei in Österreich,* Wien, 1959.

Bánffy, Kaunitz, Batthyány, Esterházy, Festetics, Pálffy, Szapáry and Teleki. Italians—the Marquis Doria, for example—, the Jews—Ludwig (1721–1780) and Karl (1739–1813) Zinzendorf and senior Empire officials became members of the lodge.[2]

In 1764, Maria Theresa issued an edict banning Freemasonry in the Austrian Empire. Enforcing the ban on Freemasonry in the vast empire proved challenging, especially in the Hungarian part, where Freemasonry continued to operate independently with the help and intermediation of the German, Polish and, later, the French Freemasonry.

The most notable support came from the German Freemasonry. The reason was not only linguistic closeness, but also the social composition of the members. Germany's Freemasonry was composed mainly of officers and its supporters mostly resided in the eastern parts of the Austrian Empire. In light of the ongoing war with the Turks, officer numbers were particularly high in that area. Thus, in 1749, the first military lodge was opened in Transylvania. It belonged to the Order of *Strict Observance*.[3]

---

[2] Kues-Scheichelbauer, op. cit., 1959, Domokos Kosáry, „Aufgeklärter Absolutismus – aufgeklärte Ständepolitik. Zur Geschichte Ungarns im 18. Jahrhundert." *Südost-Forschungen,* 39/1980, pp. 210-219. *Ludwig und Karl grafen und Herren von Zinzendorf, Minister unter Maria Theresia, Josif II, Leopold II. und Franz I. Ihre Selbstbiographien nebst einer kurzen Geschichte des Hauses Zinzendorf, herausgegeben von Ed,. Gaston Grafen von Pettenegg.* Wien, 1879. The author states that in 1742 the following were initiated in summary proceedings to the *Zu den drei Kannon lodge*: Kazimir Drašković of Trakošćan (then aged twenty-seven), a major in the *Forgács* regiment, "a brave warrior who has contributed 24 ducats," with the same amount given by the Dubrovnik prince Gondola. Jozsef Riga, an orientalist, also became a member, then Count Johann Ernest Hoyos (aged twenty-five) contributed 60 ducats, and the Prince of Hesse 200 ducats. The lodge was attended by Maria Theresa and other women, but they were dressed in men's attire. Teodor Merzdorf, *Keiser Franz I. als Freimeurer,* Wien, 1877.

[3] There is little in the way of information about the *Order of Strict Observance,* and what does exist varies from author to author. This order holds particular significance in terms of the influence of the Freemasons on Joseph II and for understanding the prosperity, tenability and policies of Freemasonry in the Hungarian part of the Monarchy. The most extensive writings on this topic were by the famous author of Templar Freemasonry René le Forestier, *La Franc-maçonnerie templière et occultiste aux XVIII et XIX siècles*, Paris, Louvain, 1970.
The most accomplished historian of Freemasonry in Hungary, where this order held prominence, is the Hungarian historian Ludwig Abaffy. In writing the history of Hungarian Freemasonry in the eighteenth century he availed of its archive, which was kept in the castle at Lake Balaton, and was owned by the Festeticz family. The archive comprised 10,000 documents covering 115 volumes.

Officers' chamber in castle Trakošćan, owned by the Drašković family. Portraits of the officers suggest that they may be members of the Viennese Lodge „Zu den drei Kannon" which Kazimir Drašković became a member of in 1742 or members of the Order „Strict Observance" of Ivan Drašković (the „Zur Kriegsfreundschaft" lodge)

Based on documents from this archive, Abaffy published five books between 1890–1899. The archive was destroyed in 1945. Copies of some documents are now in the possession of the *Grand Lodge of Hungary*. A fifth, unfinished volume by the same author covers the period up to 1875.

According to the author of one article on *Strict Observance*, meetings of members of this order often had nothing to do with Freemasonry. The goal of the association, according to the same author, was relocation to North America and the colonization of Labrador. Masons were active in the recruitment of supporters, with lodges merely a place for collecting money. Astrid Krönig, „Die Kommmunikation der Strikten Observanz. Die Konvent von Kohlo, Wiesbaden und Wilhelmsbad." *Zeitschrift für Internationalen Freimaurerei-Forschung.* 2004, p. 9-67.

She has made this claim, in our opinion, based only on the work of the German (Germanic) part of the order, without taking into account the part of the order that operated in the lands of the Provincial Lodge of Hungary.

The order Freemasonry of Freedom (Freimaurerei der Freiheit—*Latomia Libertatis sub Corona Hungariae in Provinciam redacta)* was founded on October 22-24, 1775 in Brezovica castle near Zagreb. The order was founded by Count Ivan Drašković (1740–1787), named „Jacobus," and Count Stjepan Niczky (1747–1777), named „Hieronimus." After the death of Count Niczky, the order was named *Drašković's Observance.* The founders sought to affranchise from the lodges in Prague and Vienna, and establish a new eclectic system based on „old duty" which would, in addition, be more suited to Hungarian-Croatian Freemasonry. The working language of the order was Latin. The seat of Count Niczky's order was in Varaždin, while the seat of Drašković's order was in Zagreb and Glina (Military

This order was established by a German, Karl Gotthelf, Baron von Hund (1722–1776). He introduced the new Scottish rite into Germany and gave it the name "Rectified Masonry." After 1764 the order was named *Strict Observance*. Considering that the order insisted on German national pride as a sentiment, it attracted those who did not belong to the nobility, or were members of a lower class of nobility.

The order was led by „unknown superiors," and dealt with the reorganization of Freemasonry in order to eliminate occult mastery (science), which had been previously practiced in lodges. In addition, the order's doctrine emphasized the need to establish harmony and homogeneity in Freemasonry by intensifying strict discipline and subordination to its rules.

The German wing of *Strict Observance* eventually began to digress from its sister order in Hungary. This parting of ways is particularly evident in the constitution of *Draškovič's Observance*, as *Strict Observance* was renamed in 1778 by its reformer.

---

frontier). The new system had six degrees. According to René le Forestier, the new order came to being by separating from German Freemasonry and unification with Hungarian Freemasonry in 1775. The new order supported the reforms of Joseph II. It united with Hungarian Freemasonry in 1775 and thus Draškovič's new order came to being. A year later, Adam Weishaupt, modeled on *Draškovič's Observance*, established the *Illuminaten*. René le Forestier, op. cit. pp. 126-151. Norbert Schindler, "Der Geheimbund der Illumniaten-Aufklärung, Geheimnis und Politik.". In: Helmut Reinhalter, ed. *Freimaurer und Geheimbunde im 18. Jahrhundert in Mitteleuropa*, 1986. 2nd edition. The author emphasizes the importance of the *Illuminaten* in understanding the German Enlightenment, but also the methodological necessity of examining the role of Freemasonry in politics in an empirical and interdisciplinary manner: sociologically and historically.

According to the British author, who lists the members of *Strict Observance*, but not the name of the order, the order was influenced by Scottish and British Freemasonry. Nicholas Parsons, "Scottish and English Influences on Hungary in the reform Age," The Hungarian Quarterly, vol. 39, Winter 1998, p. 112. He cites the following Masons as having separatist leanings: Draskovich, Erdödy, Festetics, Batthyany, Podmaniczky, Csáky, Széchenyi.

Ivan Mužić states, according to the author Reinhalter, that in the early 80s of the eighteenth century *Draškovič's Observance* had eight lodges: *Zur Freiheit* in Varaždin, *Zur Klugheit* in Zagreb, *Zur Kriegfreundungschaft* in Glina, *L'Invincible aux bras armes* (military lodge of the *Lička frontier regiment*), *Zur Grossmuth* in Pešta, *Zur Wachzamkeit* in Sisak, *Zur Verschwiegenheit* in Bratislava, *Zu den Drei weissen Lillien* in Timişoara, *Zum grünen Löwen* in Prague. Ivan Mužić, *Masonstvo u Hrvata, (Masonry in Croatia*),VIII ed.), Split, 2005, p. 20.

According to Drašković, all men are equal by birth, therefore he demanded the liberation of serfs. These rules were "revolutionary" for their time, not only because of the demand for the abolition of serfdom, but also because the level of class hierarchy for Freemasons of this order was less important. Since its inception in 1764, the German wing of *Strict Observance* grew so fast that it became the largest and most influential Masonic organization in the German lands. In 1768, the order numbered forty lodges, but was disbanded in 1782.

There are a number of hypotheses for this.

At its height in Germany, the order had around 6,000, at most 6,500, members. There were 1,375 members of renown, 227 of whom belonged to the high nobility, 496 to the lower, and 41 members were from the ruling houses. The order followed a different course of development in the Austrian lands compared with the German lands. *Strict Observance* began in Vienna. In 1771 the order opened a lodge under the name *Three Eagles*.[4] Then another German Rite was established – the Rite of Zinnendorf. This Rite opened two lodges in the same city—in 1771 and 1775.

In Prague, in 1776, four lodges were founded. The following year the *Zinnendorf Rite* established the *Provincial Grand Lodge of Austria* in Vienna and by 1784 there were already forty-five lodges in the Austrian Empire. Representatives of lodges from Bohemia, Hungary and Transylvania decided at a meeting in Vienna on April 22, 1784 to establish *Grosse Landesloge von Österreich (Grand Country Lodge of Austria)* as a mother lodge.

To this national lodge, from the English mother lodge, was granted the right to minister seven provincial districts: (The Provincial Lodge of Austria, the Provincial Lodge of the Bohemia, the Provincial Lodge of Galicia, the Provincial Lodge of Lombardy, the Provincial Lodge of Transylvania, the Provincial Lodge of Hungary and the Provincial Lodge of the Austrian Netherlands).

---

[4] Ludwig Abaffy, *Geschichte der Freimaurerai in Oesterreich-Ungarn*, Fünfter Band, Budapest, 1899, pp. 162-161.

Among the provincial Masonic districts, the *Provincial Lodge of Austria* had the largest number of lodges under its control. This provincial lodge, among others, belonged to the lodge in Trieste, founded in 1775, under the name *For Harmony and Common Unity* (*Zur Harmonie und allgemeine Eintracht*). The Trieste lodge consisted of twenty-seven members, more than double the average number of members. The lodge was prohibited in 1795 because it had joined the outlawed *Strict Observance Oreder of Count Hund*.[5]

Crest of Strict Observance in Hungary

The Provincial Lodge of Galicia had lodges in three cities: Timişoara, Lviv and Tarnovo.

The Provincial Lodge of Transylvania, due to its territorial standing, was one of the most important and boasted the best educated members. One of its prominent members, Georg Bánffy (1747–1822), was initiated as a Freemason in 1777 at the *Andreas zu den drei Seeblätter Lodge* in Sibiu. In 1788 he became governor of Transylvania. That same year he became a member of the *High Chapter* in St. Pölten, and in 1781 Grand Master of the *Provincial Lodge of Transylvania*.

Having become a close acquaintance of Joseph II during his travels through *Transylvania*, the Emperor appointed him Court Chancellor in 1781 and, in doing so, Bánffy—one of the best-known magnates of his time— joined the innermost circle of his advisors.[6]

The second largest lodge after the *Provincial Lodge of Austria*, which boasted seventeen lodges in different cities, was the Provincial Lodge of Hungary, which had twelve lodges. It included, among others, *K mudrosti Lodge* (Wisdom) from Zagreb, the *Savršeno jedinstvo Lodge* (Perfect Unity) from Varaždin and the *K hrabrosti Lodge* (Courage) from Karlovac.

---

[5] Kuess-Scheichelbauer, *200 Jahre Freimaurerei in Österreich*, Vienna, 1959.

[6] Von Lenning, *Allgemeines Handbuch der Freimaurerei. Encyclopädie der Freimaurerei*, Leipzig, 1901, Band. I, p. 68.

In 1777, seven lodges – two of which were from Hungary – united and established the first Grand Lodge: *U provinciji slobode* (In the Province of Freedom), later named *Drašković's Observance*. In 1778, Count Ivan Drašković was Grand Master of the Lodge.

In 1779, members of the lodge decided to quit their "splendid isolation" and join one of the larger orders. After the lodges accepted Drašković's eight conditions for unification, they were united on 21 September, 1781, and it was thus that *Drašković's Observance* joined the *Grand Lodge of Vienna* in 1781. In the same year, the national lodge of Pest was visited by the future Emperor of Russia, Paul I, which bestowed prestige on the Hungarian Freemasonry.

Count Károly Pálffy was elected Grand Master of the Freemasonry Province of Hungary. However, the lodge was not operational before 1784, given that efforts to revive the *Provincial Lodge of Hungary* dragged on for four years. However, it was then that Count Pálffy was elected the Grand National Master, i.e. the Master at the level of the entire Austrian Empire.

Following the election, Count Pálffy immediately convened a conference to legalize his new appointment on May 28, 1784. Lenhoff-Posner states that it is not known when persons were elected to the various bodies, but Count Pálffy was comfortably confirmed as the Grand Master of the Province. Count Joseph Splény was elected his deputy, Pászthory (no first name stated) as the Provincial Secretary. [7]

When Joseph II began to rule independently, following the death of his mother in 1780, he embarked on political, ownership and religious reforms intended to improve the Empire, homogenize the state administration, bolster the country's economic and cultural development and fill the empty state coffers.

Unlike the reign of his mother, who made a deal with the Hungarians, the first years of Joseph II's reign were marked by active support from the Hungarian pro-Masonic Catholic nobility, even though the ruler—the son of a

---

[7] Eugen Lennhoff/ Oskar Posner, *Internationales Freimaurerlexikon*, Zürich, Leipzig, Wien, 1932, p. 1614.

Freemason father—was not a Freemason himself. A number of Masonic lodges burgeoned under his auspices, and there was not a large town in the monarchy without a lodge. These lodges were sometimes in surreptitious and sometimes even in overt conflict.

The importance of Masonic support lay not only in their numbers, but also in the fact that the Masonic ranks included the most educated, and the most enlightened part of Hungarian society. The extent of Masonic support is clear considering that in 1780, which was the first year of Joseph's independent reign, there were about nine hundred Freemasons in Hungary operating within thirty lodges.[8]

---

[8] Joseph II issued a series of documents introducing reforms along the lines of the Masonic concept of Enlightenment, thus confirming that he was an enlightened autocrat. First, in his *Patent* dated December 31, 1780 he abolished the committee that was tasked with protecting the Catholic faith, depriving it of its privileged status. Next, on March 31, 1781, he prohibited the forced religious conversion of heretics in some parts of Transylvania and in some restless regions of Hungary, thus removing the crux of the religious disputes. On June 16, 1781, he repealed the religious patent dated August 27, 1778, legalizing the purchase of citizenship provided a subject declare themselves Catholic as confirmed by a Catholic priest, entailing the right to purchase land, and finally in a "normative regulation" dated October 13, 1778, he made all churches equal. He abolished the German language as the state language, the Latin language was once again declared the language of diplomacy and he abolished the Hungarian language in Hungary. In doing so, he essentially abolished Hungary's status as an independent kingdom, unlike the Germanized central administration in Vienna. Hans Riegelmann, *Die europäischen Dynastien und ihrem Verhältniss zur Freimaurerei,* Berlin, 1943. Riegelmann states that Joseph II was the ruler who, at the beginning of his reign, surrounded himself with Freemasons and offered them the most important departments in his administation, given that they were the most educated people of their time—Prince Dietrichstein, Franz dem Paula von, Count Cobenenz, Born, Ignaz Edler von, Zinzendorf Karl von, Sinnenfels Josef von (Jew) et al. Joseph II used Freemasons to propagandize his reforms and to win over the Freemasonry itself in favor of the reforms, p. 103, Anonymous Author (Gothic characters): *Die Ungarische Freimaurerei und das k.u. k. Heer, dritte Auflage,*Wien, 1889. Hans Wagner, *Freimaurer um Joseph II. Die Loge Zur wahren Eintracht,* Berlin, 1980. Fran Zwitter,"Francuske revolucionarne ideje u zapadnim jugoslovenskim zemljama u vreme francuske revolucije I Napoleona I.("French Revolutionary Ideas in the Western Yugoslav Countries at the Time of the French Revolution and Napoleon I"),Otisak iz zbornika radova : *Jugoslovenska zemlje I Rusija za vreme Prvog srpskog ustanka 1804/1814.*in (*Collection of papers: The Yugoslav Countries and Russia During the First Serbian Uprising (1804-1814)).* Belgrade, 1983. pp. 65-88. „Die Freimaurerei unter Kaiser Joseph II (1780-1790)."L. Lewis, *Geschichte der Freimaurerei in* Österreich *im allgemeinen,*Wien, 1861. Robin Okey, *The Habsburg Monarchy,* 2001. pp. 47-67.

Apart from this, since the Freemasons were among the most educated people in Hungary, they advocated the principles of the Enlightenment through the press, celebrated the reforms implemented and the Emperor as an enlightened monarch. Some of Joseph II's most important associates were, for example, Count Károly Zichy, the Governor of Transylvania until 1782, and Károly Pálffy, the unified Hungarian-Transylvanian Administrator between 1783 and 1787.

In addition to the civil servants who were Freemasons, the "brotherhood" included senior military officers in Vienna and Buda, as well as the leading members of the Empire's society, upper and middle landed *gentry*, teachers and church officials—even though the Catholic Church forbade them from being members—and the Jews. All of them were high-ranking members of a system of a complex bureaucracy that was large in numbers, employed by Joseph II to rule and implement reforms.[9]

The conflict between Hungarian magnates and Freemasons began when Joseph II denied the request made by the former to abolish positive discrimination favoring Austrian economic interests, practiced by Count Karl Zinzendorf's Commission for Taxation of Reformers (and Freemasons) and their simultaneous request to direct the investments and loans to the Hungarian part of the Monarchy. However, in time, the overwhelming and covert separatist activities of the Hungarians, triggered by the policy of widespread Germanization and centralization, made Joseph II enact the so-called *Freimaurerpatent* in 1785.

In it he ordered that Freemasonry must be recognized by the state, which implied that the entire entity (including its membership) be registered, and that it be put under police surveillance.

---

[9] Kálman Benda, „Probleme des Josephinismus in den Habsburgischen Monarchie," in *Südostforschungen*, XXV/1966, pp. 38-71. Stephan Tull, *Die politische Zielforstehungen der Wiener Freimaurerei und Wiener Jakobiner im 18. Jahrhundert*, Wien, 1993. The author states (p. 183) that the reformist Freemasons held discussions in their private apartments. At the time, "Josephinism" was a political concept referring to those persons who supported the revolutionary or at least reformist movement that criticized the form of state government, the King, and the privileges of the nobility and clergy due to the situation that existed. There were several similar connected groups at the time in Vienna, made up of civil servants, former supporters of Joseph's reforms, doctors, professors, judges, merchants and writers.

This led to a reduction in the number of lodges, and for some it spelt the end.[10]

The conflict between the Hungarian magnates and Joseph II was further intensified in the fall of 1788, when the Hungarian county Assemblies cancelled their participation in talks about their increased participation in the war against the Turks. Furthermore, Joseph II refused to be crowned King of Hungary, carried out comprehensive *Germanization*—both linguistic and administrative—and thus the conflict spilled over into all spheres of the German-Hungarian relationship.

There was also opposition to *Germanization* in the Netherlands, where the conflict between the Austrian state and local administration took a dramatic form. However, the success of Joseph II's reforms was evident in Bohemia, Moravia, Austria and Slovakia and these parts of the vast Monarchy were given the role of promoter of economic prosperity.

The French Revolution of 1789, which took place during the second attempt at reforms made by Joseph II, not only alarmed the autocratic Central European and Eastern European sovereigns, but also led to a conflict between the members of the reformist nobility. On one side there were reformists, and on the other the revolutionaries, the so-called Jacobins.

During the years of absolutism 1791–1793, which is to say after the sudden death of Joseph II (February 20, 1790), the politicization of classes reached its zenith. Apart from reformist demands, the most radical political demands were made. This particularly referred to the Hungarian enlightened nobility.

The revolutionaries were small in number. Their program was republican, modelled on the French bourgeois revolution. They sought to achieve full independence, establishing an independent Hungarian state. These were the

---

[10] Domokos Kosary, „Aufgeklärter Absolutismus—aufgeklärte Ständepolitik. Zur Geschichte Ungarns im 18. Jahrhundert," in *Südostforschungen,* XXXIX/1980, pp. 210-219. Paul Lendvai states that the Emperor Joseph II was a Freemason himself and that in 1780 there were about thirty lodges in Hungary with about eight to nine hundred members. Ref: *The Hungarians,* in the chapter titled *The Fight against "Hatted King,"* 1809, pp. 177-182. Lendvai's book is a compendium, and he used a wide range of literature of his time. Horst Haselsteiner, "Cooperation and Confrontation Between Rulers and the Noble States: 1711-1790," pp. 138-164. George BARANY, "The age of royal absolutism, 1790-1848," pp. 175-208, Peter F. SU- GAR, ed.: *A history of Hungary,* 2004.

Hungarian Jacobins, whose progressive ideas remained alive until 1830.[11]

Leopold II came to the throne at the time when France was engulfed in revolutionary unrest. To prevent an alliance between the rebel Hungarians and the Prussians and Turks, at the urging of his secret advisors, Leopold II renewed the ideas of enlightened centralism of Maria Theresa and, striving for reconciliation with the rebel Hungarians, he agreed that the Diet of Hungary, which had not convened since 1765, may now do so.

During the 1790/91 session of the Diet of Hungary in Pressburg (nowadays Bratislava), a compromise was reached which was imposed on the Emperor by the feudal Hungarian opposition. Under the pretext that Joseph II, having refused to be crowned King of Hungary, had actually renounced his right to the Habsburg succession, the Crown of Hungary was offered to Frederick William II (1744-1797), the King of Prussia (1787-1797), as a reward for Prussian help against the Habsburg dynasty. This, understandably, frightened Leopold II to death, and he had to agree to the Hungarian terms.

The Diet passed a number of bills, guaranteeing to the next two generations a free and independent state of Hungary with its own legislature, to be governed by the Diet and the King in accordance with its laws, and not by patents and orders, and that Saint Stephen's Crown—which had been taken to Vienna by Joseph II—would be returned to Buda, that the Diet would convene every three years, that secondary education would be delivered in the Hungarian language, but that official communication would be in Latin. Furthermore, it was decided that a traditional coronation of the King of Hungary would take place.

Under compulsion, Leopold II agreed to the terms of the Hungarian nobility, but he was simultaneously working on a secret plan—to crush their resistance—in which he was ultimately successful.[12]

---

[11] Vaso Bogdanov, "Hrvatska revolucionarna pjesma od 1794 i učešće Srba i Hrvata u zavjeri Martinović " ("Croatian Revolutionary Song from 1794 and the Participation of Serbs and Croats in Martinovic's Jacobin plot,") in *Starine JAZU*, Book 46, pp. 350-366. The same, (*The Jacobin Plot of Ignjat Martinovic,"*) Zagreb, 1960. Vaso Bogdanov describes Hajnóczy as a collaborator of Ignjat Martinovic, pp. 47-54. In 1781, Martinovic was admitted to the secret society of the Illuminati. Walter Markov, „I Giacobini dei paesi asburgici," *Studi storici*, Roma, 3/1962, pp. 493-525, Fran Zwitter, "French revolutionary ideas in the Western Yugoslav countries at the time of the French Revolution and Napoleon I" op. cit., pp. 65-88.

[12] Denis Silagi, *Ungarn und die geheime Mitarbeiterkreis Kaiser Leopolds II*, München, 1961. Robin Okey, op. cit., p. 53.

2. RIJEKA DURING THE REIGN OF ENLIGHTENED MONARCHS (1785/86 CENSUS)

Rijeka developed into an important trade center of the northern Adriatic, owing to the fact that on March 18, 1719, together with Trieste, it was declared a free port.

Maria Theresa, the daughter of Charles VI, continued her father's policy and in 1745 merged the administration of both ports in Trieste in the *Supreme Commercial Intendance*. This institution remained in charge until Rijeka was annexed to Hungary in 1776. In the meantime, a very important patent was enacted in 1750 concerning flags of long-voyage ships, and a bit later, more precisely on October 17, 1764, an order was made to separate the main ports (Trieste and Rijeka) from ancillary ports (Bakar, Karlobag and Senj).

An Edict (*Edictum politicum*) dated April 25, 1774 was key to the development of maritime traffic, both for Trieste and for Rijeka, regulating the duties and rights of sea captains, naval officers and other maritime officers. It resolved all outstanding issues regarding maritime traffic.

In 1776, the administration of Rijeka was handed over to Croatia, but on April 23, 1779, it was separated from Croatian lands and handed over to Hungary as a *corpus separatum*. Joseph II started implementing more consistent reforms than those of his mother. He first familiarized himself with the works dealing with the rights and obligations of serfs and feudal lords, then he familiarized himself with their authors and only then did he address the reform of agricultural production, and agro-economic and similar relationships in *Cisleithnia* and *Transleithania*.

To obtain support from the lower classes for his reforms, he issued the *Patent on Religious Tolerance* of October 13, 1781, he abolished serfdom on November 1, 1781 in Bohemia, Moravia and Silesia, and in 1782 in Carinthia, Styria and Inner Austria. Finally, in 1785, he abolished serfdom in Hungary.

Joseph II's reforms encountered stiff opposition from the privileged classes, and he was forced to repeal all reforms on January 28, 1790. Only the Patent on Religious Tolerance remained in force, and partially, the patent abolishing serfdom.

Joseph II died soon thereafter, and what followed was a return to the previous organization of the economy and counties.

The wave of vandalism that followed Joseph II's death saw the destruction of all the land registers throughout *Transleithania*, so as to ensure there would be no means of assessing taxes. All that remained was the land register for the city of Rijeka, and that for the trading district and the surrounding area (Gemeinde Fiume).

This 1785/86 census in the municipality of Rijeka represents unique material evidence of the ideas and efforts of one enlightened ruler to modernize public administration. The census for the municipality of Rijeka is more than that, being also a comprehensive document that reveals not only the economic and other entities of the late feudal municipality of Rijeka, but also its economic strength.[13]

The census was to be carried out not only accurately but also in a uniform manner. Hence, *Instructions for Entering Records into the Land Registry* were issued on April 12, 1785, and then a form was prescribed to be completed by a commission of seven representatives set up for such purposes. The commission's work was supervised by three auditors.

The completed forms were bound together and this is how Land Registers (*Katasterbuch*) were compiled, which served as the basis for the regulation and payment of taxes and for determining the amount of produce that was to be kept by the producer, i.e. the serf.

Immediately prior to the census, Joseph II divided Hungary, Croatia and Slavonia into ten districts, and on March 30, 1787, he abolished *Severin County*, thus creating the *Hungarian-Croatian Littoral*. This unit consisted of three districts: Rijeka, Bakar and Vinodol. It was overseen by a governor. The remainder of the Croatian lands were linked to Zagreb.

Following the abolition of *Severin County*, Rijeka was divided into two jurisdictions: *Gubernium* and *Magistrat*. The *Gubernium* had responsibility for trade and health affairs, while the *Magistrat* was subordinated through the governor to the Royal Hungarian Regency Council.

---

[13] Ivan Erceg, *Jozefinski popis grada Rijeke i njegove okolicwe (1785-87)*, (*Josephinian Land Registry of the City of Rijeka and its Immediate Surroundings (1785/87)*, Zagreb, 1998, Book II, DAR Rijeka.

Under the decisions of July 19 and October 11, 1787, the *Gubernium* gained the status of a separate political body with its own jurisdiction, independent even of the royal commissioner in Zagreb. It was subordinated to the governor, who was reliant on the *Royal Hungarian Regency Council,* as the highest secular body.

Apart from the governor, as the chairman of the new governing body of Rijeka, there were two vice-chairmen, two secretaries, one clerk in charge of protocol (recording clerk) and support staff.

Following these administrative changes, all three ports of the Hungarian littoral gained prominence in commercial trade.

In 1789, turnover from imports and exports was 3,874,787 guldens, whereas turnover increased to 4,692.227 guldens in 1790. [14]

The Josephinian Census of Rijeka describes the territory of the Municipality of Rijeka. It included Sušak, Trsat, Kalvarija, Plase, Krasica, Brgud and Mlaka. According to the census, Rijeka (then known as Fiume) included the Commercial District of Fiume (Fiumaner Commercial District), Dominion of Fiume (Herrschaft Fiume) and the Municipality of Fiume (Gemeinde Fiume).

At the end of eighteenth century, the city of Rijeka itself had 4,515 inhabitants, whereas 617 inhabitants lived in its inner-city area. The status of Rijeka guaranteed that it would be the seat of state bureaucracy, municipal and city administration, and entrepreneurial-minded nobility.

In 1776, forty-nine patrician families of various ethnic origins lived in Rijeka, but they were not members of the nobility. [15]

---

[14] Moriz von Engel, *Die Freihafengebiete in* Österreich-Ungarn, mit *anschliessenden Behandlungen der Freihafen des Deutschen Reiches und anderen Staaten,* Wien, 1906, p. 83.

[15] In 1776, the following patrician families lived in Rijeka: Zanchi de Catto und Linkenberg, who were ennobled in 1566, Sabbatini-Rossi in 1567, Giacomini 1567, Diminić 1567, Celebrini 1593, Urbani 1594, Bardarini de Kusselstein 1594, Bono 1602, Barčić 1602, Buratelli 1610, Tudorović 1610, Spogliati 1617, de Steinberg 1627, Marchisetti 1628, Tranquilli 1635, Gaus de Honberg 1637 count A Petazzi 1645, Monaldi 1647, Vitnić 1682, bar. Ab Argento 1687, Rastelli 1696, bar. A. Leo 1696, Bono de Mariani 1696, Franul de Weissenthurm 1696, de Marburg 1698, de Danano 1699, de Orlando 1703, de Zandonati 1716, de Marotti 1717, Svilokosi 1717, de Benzoni 1724, Rafaelis 1727, Lumaga 1728, de Terzi 1737, baron a Keil 1739, de Geliczi 1751, Jakob 1762, Troyer de Aufkirchen 1764, Verneda 1764, Buzzi 1764, Peri 1766, de Munier 1766, Mordax de Dax-

At the time of the Josephinian Land Survey, Rijeka was the most urbanized and the largest town, on a par with eight free royal towns in Croatia.

"That aside, according to the land registry entries, Rijeka had all the features of a developed administrative and commercial center.

The city housed numerous religious institutions (churches, convents, religious associations, fraternities). Since the city's status was that of a *Gubernium*, the governor was the head of the executive authority. He was appointed by the emperor and the king. He answered to the emperor, but in matters of governance he was tied to Buda town. As a *Gubernium*, Rijeka was at the same time the seat of government institutions of the (Hungarian) Kingdom, i.e. *Transleithania*.

Only numbers referring to the land plots are specified in the land register of the Municipality of Rijeka. Hence, today it is difficult to determine where a certain census plot used to be. It is assumed that the institutions of the Kingdom were located in the center of the city and that land plots marked with numbers starting with 500 were located in the center. For example, the office located on land plot number 537 was that of the governor of Rijeka, whereas the governor's residence was built right next to the office. The building was located on land plot number 535.

At the time of the census, Count Pál Almásy (1749–1821) served as governor from 1783–1788. He took office from Joseph Mayláth (de Székely), the first governor of Severin County and Rijeka (1776–1783).[16]

The governor's main task was to promote trade, the precondition for which was the construction of a road between the port of Rijeka and the hinterland.

---

enfeld 1766, count Theodor Batthyany 1776. This makes for forty-nine patrician families of Italian, German, Croatian and French origin. Franz Rački, op.cit., p. 8.

[16] Count Jószef Mayláth de Székely was a typical civil servant of the enlightened absolutism era. He was Chamberlain Court Counsellor in Vienna in 1776, and subsequently appointed governor of Rijeka in 1776 and Grand Prefect of Severin County in 1777. In 1783, he became Chairman of the Hungarian Court Chamber, in 1784 he became Grand Prefect of Pest County, Hungarian Court Vice Chancellor, Vice Chairman of the Viennese Court Chamber, from 1794–1795, the trustee and deputy of the governor of Galicia, in 1797, Court Secretary of Galicia, from 1802-1809 he was State Minister, and he retired in 1809. Eva Faber, "Imperial Economic Policy on the Adriatic," in: *Luka*, Rijeka, 2001, p. 85, note 100.

This road was built during Pál Almásy's administration and it was commissioned in August 1785. Information about the construction of the road between Rijeka and the hinterland show that the *Municipality of Rijeka (Gemeinde)* had great importance as a trade district and an important economic entity.

As Rijeka was an export-import port, it housed the *Royal Customs Service* (das Königliche Mautamt). The customs service was housed in two buildings with a courtyard (land plot numbers 476 and 477), with the *Royal Infirmary* (das Königliche Sanität) right next to it (land plot number 475).

Going on the proximity of the census entries, one may conclude that the services of the Kingdom were located next

Count József Mayláth, the Governor of Rijeka and the Hungarian coast 1776–1783

(Governor portraits in this book come from: *Testimonies of an Edifice*, Rijeka, 1996.)

to one another, all next to the city gates facing the sea. The *Royal Provisions Office* (Königliches Proviand Hauss), was probably in charge of supplying ships' stores. It was a building with a courtyard, and going by the topographic layout, it appears to have been located outside the city (land lot number 7).

The Castle (*Kaštel*) of Rijeka, which dominated Rijeka's skyline, also bore the "royal" attribute. There was a wine cellar next to it, with two buildings, one of which had a courtyard (land plot numbers 397, 398 and 399).

Save for those in state or royal ownership, the town held title to offices and buildings. One of them was the city infirmary. It was located in the area known as "pod gornjem Gomilom," and it included a garden with fertile land on which vegetable and vine could be cultivated.

The Municipality of Rijeka (Gemeinde) owned a large swath of fertile land—meadows, wine cellars, a coal dump, roads, houses, the bridge over the River Rječina, a wheat market, vine cellar and the a communal "laundry area." The

Assembly building (land plot number 130) also belonged to the Municipality, along with a timber market.

An ambiguous census entry reads: "state property belongs to the authorities" (*Aerarum gehörig Obrigkeit*), as it is unclear to which authority the term „Obrigkeit" refers. This entry covered the part of the city called „kod Potoka od Lazareta" and „s druge strane od Potoka." Buildings and warehouses (land plots 630 and 631) belonged to this legal entity.

Military property was also attributed to "Obrigkeit". This census entry referred to quarters for sailors in the service of the navy, also housing the gunpowder magazine (land plot number 445).

An important business entity was that under the name of "Compagnie." It was probably the *Trieste-Rijeka Privileged Company*, whose main business activity was sugar refining.

The sugar refinery was established in 1750 by the Dutch and the Germans, with capital of over one million forints, which was a substantial amount of capital in those days. The capital invested in the refinery was divided into 1364 shares. The shares were held by 231 shareholders, whereas the refinery itself owned 13 shares. The most affluent shareholder was Count Moritz de Fries (Vienna 1777–Paris 1826), who held 256 shares, and the Empress herself was given thirteen shares as a gift.

The factory processed sugar flour into sixteen kinds of refined sugar, and made various syrups. Its business operations made it one of the largest manufacturers in the Habsburg Monarchy. The company collapsed during the French occupation of Rijeka, and all efforts to recommission it failed. [17]

According to the land survey, "Compagnie", or the sugar refinery, owned a mill (plot 638), fifteen buildings, one with a courtyard (629, 628, 627, 626, 623, 622, 621, 607, 606, 604, 603, 601, 600, 599 and 596), eight warehous-

---

[17] Ljubinka Toševa Karpowicz, "Pokušaj obnove rada Rafinerije šećera u doba francuske vlasti (1809)", ("An Attempt to Recommission the Sugar Refinery under French Authority (1809),"), *Rijeka*,1-2-/2002, pp. 105-113. Viktor Hofmann"Tršćansko-riječka privilegirana kompanija 1775-1804" ("Trieste-Rijeka Privileged Company 1775-1804") in *Doba modernizacije, (An Era of Modernization=*, Rijeka, 2006., pp. 45-75

es—three within the plot number 629, one warehouse with a stable (plot 622) and four more plots (numbers 608, 605, 598 and 597), a factory with a courtyard and a house with a vineyard behind it, making a total of twenty adjacent land plots. It was an independent manufacturing and storage complex, by definition.

Another important company included in the land survey was the potash (potassium carbonate) factory. It was not built by raising share capital, rather it was wholly-owned. It seems to have been situated in "Brajda", according to the specification. There was also an orchard and a vineyard at the same location. Everything was owned by Pactan Cavalli (land plot number 574).

Count Pál Almásy, Governor of Rijeka and the Hungarian Littoral 1783–1788

Significant economic activity in Rijeka was generated by the association of mills, which mostly processed wheat brought from the continent by orthodox merchants, according to the available archival sources.[18]

The mill company also owned buildings next to the mills, which were probably used to store flour. The mills and buildings were located on the following land plots: 596, 599, 600, 601, 603, 604, 605, 606, 607, 608, 609, 621, 622, 623, 626, 627, 628, 629 and 638 (a mill, a building and a courtyard). It is assumed that the mills were built along the River Rječina (in italian *Fiumara*), adjacent to one another. A deductive conclusion may be drawn about the layout of the land plots thanks to the knowledge that the entries starting in or around the number 600 were located along the River Fiumara.

---

[18] Ljubinka Toševa Karpowicz, Pravoslavna opština u Rijeci(1720- 1868), (*Ortodox Municipality in Rijeka (1720-1868),* Belgrade-Rijeka 2002

According to the land survey, Rijeka's emergence as the seat of manufacturing and administration was complemented by numerous churches, convents, seats of various religious orders, religious associations and fraternities.

According to the land survey, there were six churches in Rijeka: the Church of St. Vitus, the Church of St. Michael, the Church of St. Barbara, the Church of St. Sebastian, the Church of the Holy Three Kings, the Church of St. Andrew, the Church of St. Bernadine and the Church of St. Augusta, i.e. the Augustinian convent and one chapel at the graveyard.

There is data about the Church of St. Michael in the books. It was a small church in the old town, close to the Church of St. Vitus. It seems that the small church had been destroyed on the orders of Joseph II, when other churches were also destroyed (1787), but it was reconstructed in 1793.[19]

Orthodox real estate was also registered during the land survey (three land plots bearing the same number).

The Orthodox was a census entry termed „denen Grüchen" (the Greeks). They owned one building in "Zagrad", surrounded by an orchard occupying two-thirds of the land, while one-third was under grapevine (land plot 506). A part of "Zagrad" called „zad Kuchium" is in the same census unit, along with a church with a yard and a garden, out of which three-fifths was for the garden and two-fifths was for the vineyard (all on land plot number 506). The land was purchased from Ignazio Zanchi.

Apart from the churches listed, there were three convents in Rijeka. One of them was a nunnery (land plot 324). There was also the Convent of Capuchins with a courtyard (land plot 571). Judging by the topography of the city, the nunnery and the convent were situated in Brajda.

The Augustinian convent with a courtyard and two vineyards with a pasture were close to the Augustinian church (land plot 203). In 1788, the convent was disbanded, and its property became state property.

The census entry "Kapitulo," or the capitol, was a religious association. The Capitol owned three houses. The Augustinians were the richest order

---

[19]   Giovanni Kobler, *Memorie per la storia della liburnica Città di Rijeka,* Rijeka, 1896, Book II, p. 142.

in Rijeka until its abolition. The church was located on land plot 203, and there were buildings or houses next to it, some of them with a vineyard. The Augustinians owned fifteen houses at different locations in Rijeka (land plots 204, 210, 258, 260, 332, 291, 370, 55, 162, 142, 114, 189, 194, 390 and 301).

There were two bakeries on land plots 194 and 132, whereas the convent with a courtyard, a church and a vineyard were located on land plot number 203. This land plot was subject to control by a special commission, following which it was entered in the land terrier as a convent with a courtyard, a church and a vineyard, calculated as a one-acre garden. The seat of the *Jesuit Collegium* was situated on land plot number 168.

Certain churches had their fraternities, i.e. communities of the faithful that lived by certain rules. For example, the *Church of St. Sebastian* had a fraternity of the same name, owning two dwellings (land plots 374 and 379).

The Church of St. Michael had a fraternity too. It also owned two dwellings. The fraternity of the Brotherhood of the Reverend (Bruderschaft von hochwürdigen Gut) also owned two dwellings (land plot 57; the other dwelling had no land plot number assigned). There is an unclear entry in the land survey—"szemenario," at times "semenarium." We translated it as "seminary." The "seminary" owned a large estate: arable land, meadows and houses.

The entire property was located on land plot number 194, in the part of the town called "nad Žezlinom" and in Brajda, as well as on land plots 444, 182, 180 and 84. The items of information contained in the Josephinian Census show that in the final years prior to Joseph II's abolition of most convents and confiscation of their property, ownership of property in Rijeka was largely by various religious institutions and associations. Under Joseph II's policy of Enlightenment, the property of religious institutions was under threat of closure and expropriation; hence, the anti-Enlightenment opposition turned it into inherited property, trusts and foundations, and only a small portion became state property. This is how "state" property emerged. One such was the estate of (Erbe) Franz Monaldi. It consisted of a dwelling and two more dwellings with a garden and a vineyard. All of the foregoing was situated in an area called „pod perilo" (land plots 101 and 202).

The Rossi estate is also recorded in the land survey. It consisted of three dwellings (land plots 5, 6 and 10), then the Tudorović estate—one dwelling (land plot 272), Poglaÿen estate—one dwelling (land plot 211), Joseph Giustini's estate (land plots 153, 148 and 529), Renaldi inheritance—two dwellings with a courtyard (land plots 393 and 394), Tranquilli inheritance— a dwelling with a courtyard (land plot 74), Stjepan Jakobin inheritance—a dwelling (land plot 63), Munier inheritance—a dwelling with a courtyard (land plot 244) and Pelozi inheritance—a dwelling (land plot 266). Such a large number of estates is surprising.

Kobler writes that when the convents were closed, members and priests were given pensions and estates. Apart from the names listed, Kobler names Carl Sambsa as the owner of four dwellings (land plots 675, 674, 564, and 311).[20]

It is our assumption that only the title holder of the confiscated property was changed, that they formally stopped being convent and church property through conveyance to another title holder, but that everything remained the same, which probably happened soon after Joseph II died.

Apart from those already mentioned, the remaining dwellings and various buildings, accounting for 730 of the plots surveyed, belonged to citizens of Rijeka of a relatively similar social class.

Among the private individuals, the wealthiest owner was Antun Vito Barčić, sometimes also recorded as "Parčić." According to Riccardo Gigante, the Barčić family was a patrician family from Rijeka, having been granted that status as early as 1602. The coat of arms was described by Riccardo Gigante in his book.[21]

The property census states that Antun Vito Barčić owned only "dwellings," so it may be concluded that he owned exclusively residential property. Antun Barčić owned twenty dwellings, mostly located in the part of Rijeka marked 500, maybe in the center of the city (land plots 581, 583, 584, 585,

---

[20] Carlo Sambsa was a prior of the Augustinian convent. ISTI, op.cit., vol. 1, p. 99.

[21] Riccardo Gigante, „Blasonario fiumano,“ *Rijeka, XII-XIX/1935-1936, p. 110*

586, 587, 588, 589, 590, 591, 592, 593, 594 and 595). It therefore seems that Antun Barčić owned Rijeka's entire city center. One of his dwellings with an orchard was separated from the rest and was situated in Brajda (land plot 458), and there were two more detached dwellings (land plots 218 and 313).

Considering that state, municipal, city property and property belonging to churches, convents, factories and various estates accounted for approximately one hundred of the land plots, we can conclude that Antun Vito Barčić's wealth stood at one-fifth of that of all owners listed, based on the number of land plots.

It is noteworthy that women were frequently owners of one, two or more dwellings. They owned ninety-four dwellings in total.

The wealthiest among them was Ursula Spingarolli, owner of four dwellings, and Maria Diminić, owner of three dwellings. Both owners came from nobility, and the dwellings were probably family inheritance. Ursula Spingarolli de Dessa came from a patrician family from Rijeka that was also of Hungarian nobility, dating back to 1291. The family appeared in the 1664 Rijeka Census. The family coat of arms was described by Riccardo Gigante.[22][23]

Anna Steinberg came from nobility. She owned a dwelling on land plot number 49. The family coat of arms was described by Riccardo Gigante.[24]

Several women owned two dwellings. They were: Katarina Korošac, Helena Veronese, Helena Franković, Frana Fumulo, Margareta Mauro, Maria Bašić, Tonka Salvini and Maria Trikuppa. One among them was Helena Franković de Bersez, of Venetian nobility, recognized as such as early as the sixteenth century. The Franković family were also knights of the Austrian Empire as of 1879. The family coat of arms was described by Riccardo Gigante.[25]

Marija Trikuppa, owner of two dwellings, was Orthodox and as a ktetor she donated 1,000 forints towards the construction of the Temple of St. Nich-

---

[22] Ibid, op.cit., p. 115
[23] Ibid, p. 122
[24] Ibid, p. 157
[25] Ibid, p. 126

olas in Rijeka, which was one of the largest donations.[26]

Mathias Paravich was among the owners of a large estate registered under a single land register unit (638). He owned a vineyard, an orchard, a dwelling, a meadow and arable land on that plot, so it may be assumed that his land became part of the city environs due to urban growth and expansion of the city beyond the narrow town walls, all the more so as Paravich was neither of a patriciate or noble background.

A similar conclusion can be drawn about another significant property owner, Mathias Studenaz, on plot 265, on which there was a dwelling, a garden, a vineyard, arable land, etc.

Some historical names, or even historical families, are included on the list of property owners. These are Felix and Joseph Gerliczy, probably related.

Each of them owned one plot with a dwelling (plots 568 and 569). The Gerliczy family (formerly Gerlicich) had been Austrian nobility since 1747.

Joseph Felix de Gerliczy was born in Rijeka in 1715. He came from an old Bosnian family that fled to Hungary from the Turks in the fifteenth century. During Charles VI's final war with the Turks (1737–1739), he was the Imperial Trustee in Transylvania. In 1747, he became Captain Administrator of Rijeka, Bakar and Trsat. He remained in that position until 1752, i.e. until the abolishment of Intendance in Trieste and the establishment of Severin County in 1776.

Joseph de Gerliczy's contribution to the establishment of trade relations with the north-east part of the Monarchy, Transylvania in particular, was enormous and he was awarded the title of Baron in 1774. In 1777, he was awarded the title of Hungarian Baron. When Joseph Mayláth de Székely was governor of Rijeka, Joseph de Gerliczy was in charge of trade affairs, and in that capacity, he issued a report on the financial standing of Rijeka's Orthodox merchants, in order to present evidence supporting their application to obtain a permit for the construction of an Orthodox church. Joseph Gerliczy owned one building with a courtyard housing a theatre— which was a Free-

[26] record in the gate of the Temple of St. Nicholas in Rijeka

mason custom (land plot number 510). The coat of arms of the de Gerliczy family was described by Riccardo Gigante.[27]

The Tudorovich family is also a historical family associated with Rijeka. They were Hungarian nobility, recognized as of 1627.

Nicoló Andrea Tudorovich (1694–1751), born in Rijeka, was a prebendary and then Archdeacon of Rijeka, and in 1729, he was an apostolic prothonotary and an abbot. He interceded with Emperor Charles VI not to allow members of the Orthodox Church into Rijeka and to prohibit the construction of their church. After the death of the last family member, the dwelling passed into the hands of the Augustinians (plot 272). The coat of arms was described by Riccardo Gigante.[28]

Zanchi de Cato e Lincherberg was also one of the great historical and noble families of Rijeka. They were ennobled in 1556. The Zanchis were: Anton, Ignaz, Joseph and Margareta.

A wholesaler and a nobleman named Arsenije Jovanović (ot) Šakabent (1746–1796) also lived in Rijeka, and he was related to the Serbian Patriarch Arsenije Jovanović Šakabenta (IV). He owned a dwelling on land plot number 46. In our opinion, the dwelling was on the far outskirts of the town.

A Serbian noble family which was related to the Šakabent family was made up of three brothers: Sava, Teodor (plot 441) and Aleksije Vukovich. At the time of the Josephinian Land Survey, the oldest brother (Sava) had already moved to Novi Sad, while Aleksije Vukovich had just moved to Rijeka, but had not purchased a dwelling yet.

Even a superficial analysis of data from the Josephinian Land Survey confirms that Rijeka was a trade, administrative and religious center. The city was home to various state, municipal and religious institutions, a multi-religious and multi-ethnic, noble, civil, urban community, rich and literate, and as such, useful both in terms of economy and politics. It was therefore neither affected by the anti-reform nor the separatist movement. This is what made the preservation of the 1785/87 land survey possible.

---

[27] Gigante, op.cit., p. 127
[28] Ibid, Op.cit., p. 163.

However, Rijeka was not exclusively a port. In the final years of the eighteenth century, numerous manufactories and industries operated in Rijeka. That is why a guide published in 1804 (*Beschreibung der Handlung und des Industriefleißes der K. K. Seestädte und Freihafen Triest und Rijeka*), which was supposed to be used as a handbook for aspiring entrepreneurs, is of great informative value.

According to the information in that handbook, the following manufactories and factories existed in Rijeka:

1. Hat manufactory, owned by Giuseppe Fulvie;
2. Private leather processing and button-making factory, established in 1771. Its owners were Odenigo Minussi and Francesco Rubinić, while Giovanni Battista was director. This factory's products were more expensive than other factories' products on the market, but the owners justified this by the fact that the raw materials were imported from far-away lands;
3. Stone dishes manufactory, owned by Giuseppe Pessi;
4. Rope factory owned by the heirs of Orlando and Canton and Cantarelli, for which material was transported from Venetia and Romania;
5. Wax factory, owned by Giuseppe Pessi. The factory was bought by the Dutch and they made a project for construction of the sugar refinery, and were completely successful in it. The company then sold the refinery to a private owner. According to the handbook, the factory produced high quality sugar;
6. Sugar factory in Rijeka and Trieste. According to the handbook, the abundance of water in Rijeka compared to Trieste was of particular convenience. It was a key factor in the Dutch deciding to build the sugar refinery there. They were also granted privileges from the state for the next twenty-five years. Following a few years in business, the privileges were discontinued, but owing to previous results, the company continued to operate successfully;
7. Wool processing factory. The wool was brought in from Croatia;
8. In 1780, the factory for potash processing was founded and it was granted privileges for a period of eight years, with the right to export

its goods to Pest and across the sea. The factory was owned by Pactan Cavalli. It was situated in Brajda. It was surrounded by a vineyard, one-third of the harvest of which was used for wine production. There was an orchard there, too, all on land plot number 574.

The aforementioned 1804 handbook lists the names of fifty-two wholesale merchants and ten brokers and consuls (the names of which will be given in the German original).

Orthodox merchants featured prominently on the list of wholesalers (Risto Circovich, Lazarus Illich, Simon Krilovich, Dimitrije Mauricij, Georg Melissino and Francesco Pregl, Teodoro Manasteriotti, Alessio Ostoich, Giovanni (Jovan) Ostoich, heirs of Petar Ostojich, heirs of Triffun Petrovich, Risto Petrovich, Gavra Rajovich and Ignaz Rajovich). All of them, according to information from other sources, imported wheat from Vojvodina.[29]

There are also wholesalers of Rijeka, known to us from other sources, on the census list—Andrea Lodovic Adamich, Jozeph David, Oswald David and Paolo Scarpa.

At the end of the eighteenth century, the following countries had consulates in Rijeka: Great Britain (Vice-Consul Franz Kragnez), Denmark (Franz de Tommassich), the Netherlands (Vice-Consul Joseph de Tomasich), Tuscany (Giuseppe de Orlando), the Kingdom of Naples (Vice-Consul Paolo Scarpa), Malta (Marquis Ladevege), Spain (Vice-Consul Jozef David) and the Dubrovnik Republic (agent Carlo Barcich).

Rijeka and the Hungarian littoral were, in economic terms, the most developed areas in the Hungarian part of the Monarchy. The remaining part of Hungary consisted of large latifundia in the hands of a small number of noble families, and that part of the Empire exemplified the remainder of a typically late feudal state.

---

[29] *Beschreibung der Handlung und des Industriefleisses der K. K. Seestädte und Freihafen Triest und Rijeka,* Leipzig und Triest, 1804, p. 95

3. BEGINNINGS OF FREEMASONRY IN RIJEKA

The beginnings of Freemasonry in Rijeka and the composition of its members were influenced by a range of factors, both across the Empire, and locally.

The social and religious (national) makeup of members had significant impact on the diversity and numbers of Freemasons and their order in the Habsburg Monarchy. The Freemasons in the military hierarchy usually adhered to the order of *Strict Observance*, i.e. the reformed Freemasonry ritual of Hungary as their own, and not the ritual established by the *Grand Lodge of England*.

In the non-military area of Austria, Freemasons were members of high and middle nobility, and part of the system of English Lodges, which together with their members constituted the cornerstone of the Habsburg Monarchy feudal system. The lodges were, therefore, meeting places for their classes, and as such they contributed to upholding the existing order.

At the far reaches of the Habsburg Monarchy and in the Military Frontier, lodges were centers of Enlightenment and the struggle for Hungary's independence from the Habsburgs.[30]

Due to the religious (ethnic) and social composition of the population and due to its distance from the administrative seat and the system of military hierarchy, in the period of enlightened absolutism, Rijeka remained untouched by its ideas, which is to say untouched by the movements that sprang from it. Apart from that, it was far from the Military Frontier as well, so the separatist ideas of the oppressed peoples of the Monarchy could not reach it. In other words, it was an island on a (turbulent) mainland!

---

[30] The first Croatian lodge was probably founded by Count Ivan Drašković in Varaždin in 1772, then lodges in Osijek (1773) and Otočac (Lika, 1777) were formed. In 1775, the statute and the ritual of *Drašković's Observance* was established. The following year, Ivan Drašković became the Grand Master. On 28 February 1784, at the convention in Pest, the *Grand Lodge in Vienna* was established, and Count Károly Pálffy became the Grand Master of the Hungarian and Croatian lodges. Ivan MUŽIĆ, op.cit., pp. 19-21

Other factors also contributed to the Freemasons' abiding interest in Rijeka, however indirectly and sporadically.

Although it was one of the most developed industrial cities in the Monarchy, a hub of capital investment in several branches, the town in which many international citizens, mostly from the protestant Netherlands, worked and traded, the presence of numerous churches and orders and other religious institutions was a contributing factor to the constant presence of anti-reformist and anti-Freemasonry forces. Their activities were primarily orchestrated by the local, Catholic clergy that, by defending their religious and therefore proprietary domination at the level of *corpus separatum*, simultaneously defended the power of the Catholic dynasty of the Habsburgs.

The years-long endeavor by the wealthy Orthodox merchants to obtain a permit to construct an Orthodox church in the town and to have their right to publicly practice their religion recognized may serve as a telling example. Although, for example, Empress Maria Theresa continued the politics of her father, Charles VI, and reached an accord with the Serbian Patriarch Arsenije IV Šakabenta, affirming the Serbian privileges on three occasions (April 24, May 18 and June 4, 1743), this agreement, and even the *Patent on Religious Tolerance*, was not binding on the local Catholic clergy in Rijeka.[31]

Ethnic and proprietary qualities of the citizens of Rijeka are also key to understanding how the Freemasons operated on the territory of *corpus separatum* over an extended period.

Actions taken by the replaceable clerks of the Empire on orders taken from the governor and his subordinate associates, both at his office, and at the level of the *Guberniums*, particularly the *Magistrat,* as the highest local authority, played a very significant role in this.

There was yet another significant factor: territorial origin, or the place from which someone came and invested their capital, regardless of whether it was invested in industry or trade. This factor played an important role, together

---

[31] Ljubinka Toševa Karpowicz,"Problemi izgradnje Pravoslavne crkve u Rijeci 1717-1746", in *Artefakti, n. 11/2010. pp.17-33*

with the relatively economically independent position of entrepreneurs from the current constellation of the Empire's and Kingdom's political forces.

The fact that numerous churches and other religious institutions existed in Rijeka resulted in natural opposition to the concept of the Enlightenment in all its instances. The entirety and long-lasting circumstances on the ground made Freemasonry in this city specific, both on the level of its (local) organization, and in terms of the traits of its members.

Information on the first Masonic lodges in Rijeka was published by Attilio Tamaro.[32] Danni's original records, which were employed by Attilio Tamaro for the purpose of his article, were kept at the archives of the *Ministry of Internal Affairs* of Austria. They were partially destroyed in 1927.

The oldest information on the existence of a lodge in Rijeka dates to December 2, 1769. The lodge was within the former sugar refinery (established in 1750). Members of the lodge were made up of French and Belgian refinery workers. Filippo de Courten was master of the lodge. He subsequently went to Trieste and became master of the local lodge. Following the previous master's departure, Laurens was appointed as the new master. J. A. Lederer was the Treasurer, P. Everard—Senior Warden, T. E. Terrdez— Junior Warden, F. C. Charres—Secretary, and J. B. Rönenkampf—"The Fearsome One."

Attilio Tamaro claims that he found these names, and the information related thereto, on a diploma privately owned by Mario Alberti, an Italian writer and irredentist political activist.[33]

The lodge within the sugar refinery operated under the name of *l'Ami Solitaire Inconnu* à *l'Oriente de Fiume*. This would suggest that the first lodge in Rijeka (1769) had been constituted during the reign of Maria Theresa – (1745-1780), and before she separated Rijeka from the union of hereditary lands. Accordingly, the lodges were constituted by the Dutch and the French originating from the Austrian Netherlands (1713–1794), who were shareholders or employees in the sugar refinery in Rijeka.

---

[32] Attilio Tamaro, Origini della massoneria a Rijeka, in *Archeografo Triestino*, vol. XIV-XV, 1948, pp. 355-369.

[33] Ibid.

Since there was active political opposition to Austrian administration in the Austrian Netherlands (and later a rebellion in 1788), it may be assumed that the Lodge of Rijeka did not stand idly by, which may be the reason why there were no written records about it. Namely, lodges in the Austrian Netherlands and Luxemburg that were part of Austria between 1713 and 1794 had no connection whatsoever to the rest of the Freemasonry in the Monarchy. Joseph II disbanded them in 1784 since they operated independently. Eleven lodges were disbanded out of seventeen in various Dutch towns—four operated secretly until 1876, when all of them were disbanded.

Two hundred and forty workers were employed in the sugar refinery, mold factory and warehouses in Rijeka. Forty-two of these were foreigners. Among them were twenty-one Lutherans from Hamburg, with twenty-one Lutherans from the Netherlands. It is assumed that the Dutch, in their efforts to resist the Habsburgs, constituted a lodge in Rijeka. [34]

Italian author Attilio Tamaro writes that Danni's article contains no information on the lodge referred to in the diploma owned by Mario Alberti. The first mention in Danni's article about a lodge within a sugar refinery refers to a lodge constituted in another refinery established by the *Imperial Privileged Company* in 1775, in Trieste and in Rijeka at the same time.

Tamaro cites that the first lodge in Rijeka was the lodge within the Trieste-Rijeka Privileged Company (1775–1804). The refinery in Rijeka was commissioned in 1755. This factory was built by the Dutch, who were also its directors. In 1777, Peter de Vierendeels (? – 1803) became its first director.[35]

The lodge operated exclusively within the factory and held no private meetings. The refinery's interim directors were: Ignatz Verpoten, Striker and Toussaint de Baque, then Reinhow, who was master of the factory, and tobacco factory owners Blondin and Detret from Dunkirk. Members of the lodge

---

[34] ibid.

[35] Ludwig Abaffy states that lodges in the Austrian Netherlands and Luxemburg, which were part of Austria from 1713 to 1794, had no connection whatsoever to the rest of Freemasonry in the Monarchy. In 1784, Joseph II disbanded them, since they operated independently. Eleven lodges out of seventeen in various Dutch towns were disbanded—four operated secretly until 1876, when all of them were disbanded. *Geschichte der Freimaurerei*, Fünfter Band, Budapest, 1899, pp. 376-381.

from Rijeka included Paravić, an advocate, and Alois Peretti, a commercial court recording clerk.

Danni's article states that all individuals mentioned were known Freemasons. The lodge held no public meetings until the rebellion of 1788 in the Netherlands.

During the Dutch Rebellion, two new lodges opened in Rijeka. One of them was located in a vineyard owned by Franz Müller, a landowner (land plots 97 and 120), which is to say far outside the city.

The lodge on Franz Müller's property (who was probably Belgian) was situated in the part of Rijeka named "Luke pod perilom." It had its own archive and emblem—the revolutionary lions of Belgium, and members met on a weekly basis and organized festivities. This lodge included, according to Danni, important but "the most crooked" („lüderliche") people in Rijeka. The most important among them was the Gubernium Counsellor Marco de Sussani, who was a patrician from Senj, Secretary of the *Gubernium* in Zadar Ludwig Henry, and Anton Brumoro, a doctor.[36]

This lodge ceased to exist in peculiar circumstances. One night, the room in which it was housed caught fire. The lodge was the target of public disapproval, and the group ceased their Masonic practices. Judging by the "attributes" of the members of this lodge, and by its organization (archive) and symbols, it was probably a lodge that was part of the rebel or revolutionary anti-Habsburg Dutch and Belgian separatist movements and associated with the French Bourgeois Revolution. The fact that its members were not nobility, but rather members of the general public and liberal professionals, may serve as additional explanation, while members of the lodge in Rijeka were considered liberals and enemies of Austria.[37]

---

[36] Attilio Tamaro, op.cit.

[37] Marco Susanni later took part in the 1790 -91 Diet of Hungary in Pressburg (Prague), together with Sava Vuković, a representative of the Rijeka *Orthodox Municipality* " Adamić *i Mihanović na Saboru u Požunu*", (Adamić and Mihanović at the Diet in Pressburg", *Adamićevo doba 1780-1830,(The Age of Adamić,)* Rijeka, 2005, pp. 187-221.

There was another lodge housed within the Capuchin monastery, in a dwelling enclosed by a garden on land plot 571, which was comparatively close to Franz Müller's dwelling.

According to Danni's article, this lodge included "children who still deserved to be flogged," which may mean that its members were young (both as people and as Masons).

Citing Danni's article that this lodge was "attended by the Church and people," it can be concluded that its work was public and authorized, only to be subsequently disbanded out of "despair" (Verzweiflung), according to Danni, and banished from Pest. It was probably temporarily disbanded due to the provisions of *Freimaurerpatent* of 1785, i.e. the order for members to register so as to facilitate police surveillance. Since it operated from a Capuchin convent, and the period during which it operated is unknown, it may be assumed that it was the Templar Freemasonry Lodge, to which members of the famous Szapáry family belonged.

Following its registration, the lodge was probably reinstated by the then governor, Count János Péter Szapáry, when he came to office in the *Gubernium* of Rijeka, i.e. became governor (1788-1791). He rented a garden in "Brajdica", and displayed Masonic emblems in a room intended for Masonic ritual (Temple). The lodge remained operational for the duration of Szapáry's tenture as governor of Rijeka, more exactly until 1791, and was closed when Count Klobusicki succeeded him as governor.

Count János Péter Szapáry, governor of Rijeka, who reinstated the lodge in 1788, was a member of the great and extensive old aristocratic Szapáry family, with its first known ancestor dating back to 1560. The first known Freemason member of the Szapáry family was linked with the establishment of the first lodge of Vienna in 1742. Another two family members were Freemasons of *Drašković's order of Strict Observance*.

These were: Count Paul Szapáry and Count Joszef Szapáry, both members of the *Unity* (Zur Vereinigung) lodge that had its seat first in Pressburg, present-day Bratislava, and was then moved to Pest.[38]

Count Paul Szapáry, Imperial and Royal Chamberlain, took part in the 1782 Congress of Wilhelmsbad as Hungary's representative, and prior to the lodge being constituted, was initiated into the order of Templar nobility by Count Karl von Hessen-Kassel so that he could attend the Congress.[39]

The Hungarian branch of *Strict Observance* came to life and continued operating in Rijeka thanks to those members of the Szapáry family who ruled Rijeka as governors (Count János Péter Szapáry, Governor 1788–1791, Count Géza Szapáry, Governor 1873–1883, Count Lászlo Szapáry, Governor 1898–1903), even when the order was prohibited. This piece of information is key to understanding the political history of Rijeka, not only in the era of enlightened absolutism, but also in the years that followed.

Eva Balász, a Hungarian historian, presented information that the order continued to operate in Rijeka after it had been formally prohibited.

---

[38] René le Forestier, op.cit., pp. 126-151.

[39] Together with other Freemasons, Paul Szapáry, from the *Zur Grossmut* Lodge of Pest, was a close associate of Joseph II's. Karl von Zinzendorf was also a close acquaintance. Zinzendorf belonged to the Teutonic order, but later became a Catholic. In 1771, he visited Rijeka and Trieste. In 1766, he became a member of the *Concordia Lodge* from Strasburg. He knew all members of *Drašković's Observance* and was a frequent guest of Batthyány, and was friends for some ten years with Count Teleky from Transylvania. Apart from Count Paul Szapáry, the following individuals are stated as visiting members from other Masonic lodges in the protocol of the *Zur wahren Eintracht* Lodge that was the closest to Joseph II: Antoine Batthyány *(Zum goldenen Rad),* Georg Bánffy *St. Andreas zu den drei Seeblätern* from the Sibiu lodge. Nicholas T. Parsons, "Custodians of the Future. Scottish and English Influences on Hungary in the Reform Age," in *The Hungarian Quarterly*, vol. 39, 1998, pp. 96 -112. Count Alois Batthyány appears as a member of *Minerva* Lodge in Sadagora (Transylvania). Par sons states that Drašković, Festetics, Erdödy, Batthyány, Podmartniczky, Csáky and Szécheny were reformist Freemasons., Éva H. Balázs, "Freimaurer, Reformpolitiker, Girondisten," in *Beförderer der Aufklärung in Mittel- und Osteuropa, Freimaurer, Gesellschaften und Clubs,* Berlin 1979. ISTA: *Les Lumiers en Europe centrale et orientale: L' ere des Lumiers et les Josephinist en Hongrie,* Budapest, 1971. ISTA, *Karl von Zinzendorf et ses relations avec l'Hongrie à l'époque de l'absolutisme* éclaire, Budapest, 1975.

She writes that the order of *Draškov-ić's Observance* operated in Rijeka, as the so-called Freemasonry of Freedom (*Freimaurerei der Freiheit—Latomia Libertatis sub Corona Hungariae in Provinciam redacta*), established between October 22 and 24, 1775 in Brezovica castle near Zagreb, which will be discussed in the next chapter.

Following the sudden death of Joseph II, his heir and younger brother Leopold II suppressed Freemasonry gradually and moderately. When he too died suddenly, he was succeeded by his son Francis I. He devoted himself to suppressing the secret societies that had, as a backlash against absolutism, become widespread through-

Count János Péter Szapáry, Governor of Rijeka and the Hungarian Littoral (1788-1791)

out the Habsburg Monarchy. A reinforced police force kept a watchful eye on all secret societies, and all members of these societies were considered revolutionaries and Jacobins, and consequently, enemies of Austria. Lodges were outlawed and disbanded on May 18, 1794. From that point on, publicly active and organized Freemasonry in Hungary was not to be seen for seventy years. Hungarians became Freemasons abroad—in Italy, Great Britain, and the US, for example—until Freemasonry returned to Hungary in 1868.[40]

Based on the foregoing, i.e. on the modest information about the first lodges in Rijeka, it may be concluded that:

- membership thereof was exclusive,
- they operated behind closed doors,
- their members were mostly foreigners, but that the lodges were connected to or were parts of various "centers" of Freemasonry, which is why they had varying political agendas.

---

[40] Eugen Lennhoff/ Oskar Posner, op.cit., pp. 1614-1615.

In 1794, the first Austrian era of Freemasonry came to a close, both in Austria and in Rijeka. The Dutch and Hungarian branches were active in Rijeka. Both branches were revolutionary in terms of political action, albeit availing of different means. The Dutch branch was made up of entrepreneurs and their employees, which is to say, the citizenry. They supported the ideas of the French Revolution: equality, fraternity and liberty.

Members of the Hungarian branch that by and large adhered to the independent order of *Strict Observance,* more precisely to Drašković's version of it, were members of the Hungarian nobility and court officials, church dignitaries and army officers.

They mostly came from Transylvania, less frequently from the Military Frontier and Croatia-Slavonia. Their political agenda was: **the return of constitutionalism, abolishment of the imperial absolutism of the Habsburgs, return of the Hungarian crown—a symbol of Hungary's statehood (the Holy Crown of St. Stephen)—to Buda and exclusive use of the Hungarian language.**

Rijeka was unaffected by the ban on Freemasonry in Hungary. Hungarian and Dutch Freemasonry was soon replaced by French Freemasonry, which had completely different characteristics.

4. LEOPOLD II'S SECRET POLICY AND RIJEKA IN *PROJECTUM ARTICULI* BY AN ANONYMOUS AUTHOR

The Hungarian nobility's dissatisfaction with the reforms carried out by Joseph II as of 1785—with the aim of taxing the nobility—mounted in subsequent years.

The fact that all religions were afforded equal rights, as well as the enormous increase in costs during the disastrous Russo-Turkish War, which Joseph II entered on February 9, 1788 to help Catherine II of Russia, fanned the flames of their resistance.

Catholic-Masons were among the most vocal opponents, particularly of equal rights for all religions. They were the most numerous and best-qualified. In 1780, there were around 900 Freemasons within thirty lodges scattered throughout the Empire. Furthermore, they occupied the most important positions in the state or were the wealthiest landowners.

The following were among those who lost faith in Joseph II: Count Károly Zichy, Chancellor of Transylvania until 1782, and Károly Pálffy.[41]

The fact that Count Károl Pálffy (1735-1816) lost faith was particularly detrimental. He entered into state service during the reign of Maria Theresa in 1762, rose through the ranks steadily and in 1776 became Acting Secretary of the *Royal Chamber of Hungary*. It is known that in 1781, i.e. in the service of Joseph II, he became Knight of the *Order of the Golden Fleece*.

It is not known when Pálffy became a member of *Draškovic´'s Observance;* perhaps it was at its founding in 1772. However, in its session held on September 21, 1782 in Pest, when seven lodges of *Draškovic´'s Observance* were united in an attempt to break away from the Berlin lodge, he was elected Grand Master of the *Provincial Lodge of Hungary*. The following areas came under the jurisdiction of that lodge: Hungary, Slavonia and Dalmatia, Transylvania, and later Bukovina.

---

[41] Robin Okay, The Habsburg Monarchy, 2001, p. 50.

Before Ivan Drašković became Grand Master, he set out his stall, and only accepted the position once the members acceded to his demands. The most important of these demands referred to so-called "Hungarian Liberalism," which meant Hungary's independence from the imperial house of Habsburg and opposition to the Germanization orchestrated by the Habsburgs.

In 1783, Pálffy became Chancellor of both Hungary and Transylvania. He remained in that position until 1787. Pálffy began his work as Grand Master of the Provincial Lodge of Hungary in earnest in 1784 because of attempts by Joseph II, due to his contempt for Freemasonry, to hamper its legalization. For all intents and purposes he outlawed it the following year.

Pálffy used the name of "Jacobus" to correspond with his "brother" Sándor Pásztory during his time as governor of Rijeka (1791-1798), regarding some of Count Ivan Drašković's property in Croatia and the Military Frontier. Pálffy had no qualms about asking Pásztory for assistance, given that he and Drašković and another fourteen "brethren" were founders of the Freedom Lodge on March 10, 1774. Futhermore, Pásztory was Drašković's brother in law. [42]

In the history of Hungarian Freemasonry, information often differs or overlaps, which is one of the consequences of the destruction of the main Masonic archives housed in Count Gyorgy Festetics' castle in Dégh near Siofok Sol. It is not known when the members of the Templar order of *Strict Observance* decided to deposit their collection of documents in Dégh. The archive contained documents of both the Hungarian part of the *Templar order of the Knights* of the *Rosy Cross* and the *Asian Brothers order*. [43]

[42] Ludwig Abaffy, „Die ungarische Provozial-Loge," in *Hajnal*, br.271883, pp. 24-19.

[43] The Asian System or *Asian Brothers* was a Masonic sect characterized by mystical theory that emerged in Germany in 1780. This sect interpreted Masonic rituals and symbols in its own unique manner. Within the order, there are several degrees that are more or less the same as those of the *Knights of the Rosy Cross* and Hermetic Freemasonry. According to Robert Macoy (1815-1895), *A Dictionary of Freemasonry*, New York, reprint 2000, p.93.

Reconstruction of the palace of Count György Festetics in Dég. The castle was razed to the ground in a fire in 1945, and with it a rich Masonic archive. A third of the documents that survived the blaze was transferred to the National Archives of Hungary

For that same reason, it is unknown when the order of *Drašković's Observance* was abolished or abandoned or whether it simply "coalesced" into the *Provincial Lodge of Hungary*, given that they had the same Grand Master.[44]

Josephinism did not die with Joseph II (February 24, 1790). His brother Leopold, the Grand Duke of Tuscany, himself a proponent of Enlightenment and a Freemason, persecuted Freemasons when he came to the throne.[45]

[44] Ludwig Abaffy, „Die ungarische Provinzial-Loge!" In *Hajnal,* No 2/1882, pp. 24-29.

[45] Harry S. Truman (ed), *10,000 Famous Freemasons,* vol. III, 2002, p.45.

During his brief reign (1790-1792) over the Habsburg monarchy, through various public concessions and secret strategies, he sought to preserve, at least partially, the enlightened work of his brother, whom he had to denounce on his deathbed.

As soon as he came to the throne, he had to tame the general chaos that Joseph II had left in his wake. Crushing the Hungarians' resistance and thwarting their secessionist movement was of paramount importance.

Lodge emblem
The three white lilies

Considering that the Hungarians, following the lead of the French, demanded a constitution, Leopold II had to accede to the convening of their diet. A proclamation convening the Diet of Hungary was issued on March 15, 1790. The emperor ordered the court chancellor at the time, Count Károly Pálffy, to extend an invitation to the diet to the Orthodox clergy, but not prominent members of the Illyrian nation.[46]

Both assenting to the Diet of Hungary and the cherry-picking of representatives of the *Illyrian nation* to invite to the diet were part of a secret strategy employed by Leopold II. He courted allies that were against the Hungarian nobility among the opponents of the feudal order—Ignjat Martinović, József Hajnóczy, and Professor Karol Kopi—, while simultaneously encouraging the non-Hungarians in the Hungarian part of the Empire to make a stand for their rights at the expense of the Hungarians.

Among the many opponents were the Serbs and Romanians in Transylvania, numbers of whom had increased after the victorious battle against the Turks. In Transylvania, their number grew to about 500,000 subjects.

In addition, approximately 700,000 subjects—non-Hungarians—lived in the Military Frontier; hence, Leopold II could count on a considerable

---

[46] Manojlo Grbić, *Karlovačko vladičanstvo (The Diocese of Karlovac)*, 1990 (reprint of 1890 edition), p.112.

number of opponents of the Hungarians. Leopold's initial strategy of inviting only Orthodox clergy to the Diet of Hungary bore fruit.

By engaging the Orthodox clergy, the emperor permitted the convocation of the "National Church" congress in Timisoara. In doing so, writes Robin Okey, he played the *divide et impera* (divide and rule) card to the detriment of the Hungarians." [47]

It is not known whose decision it was for the "National Church" Assembly to be held in Timisoara, but Károly Pálffy most probably had an important hand in it, either as Grand Master of the Provincial Lodge of Hungary, or as chancellor at the court of Leopold II.

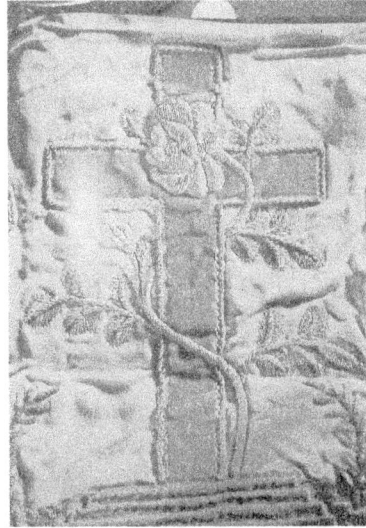

Cover of the Bible of the Knights of Rose Order

Also located in Timisoara was the Templar and occultist, i.e. military only lodge, and, after the ban of 1785, also the secret Masonic Lodge of the Order of *Draškovič's Observance—Three White Lilies*. The lodge was constituted in 1776 in amity with an Order of the Golden and Rosy Cross, and, as with every military lodge membership, was exclusive to military personnel.[48]

---

[47] Robin Okey, *op. cit,* p. 53

[48] It is noteworthy that circa 1787 in Timisoara a branch of the "Rosen-Orden" (Rose Order) was founded, a branch of a secret society whose members included officials, and also members of the Orthodox clergy. Members of the society included Petar Petrović, Bishop of Timisoara, Jovan Jovanović Šakabenta, Metropolitan of Vršac, Gerasim Adamović, Bishop in Bezdan and Pavle Vukovid-Branković, a priest in Cenad. This order permitted women members. After 1789, there is no more information on the order. On October 3, 1883, Ludwig Abaffy gave a lecture about the order at the headquarters of *The Historical Society* in Budapest, a report on which was published in the *Hajnal* No. 17/1883, pp. 125-126.
Zoran Nenzić claims also that the Šakabents were Masons but does not mention the *Rose Order*. American author Robert Macoy claims that the Masonic orders of the rose flourished during the eighteenth century in Germany. Their author was a priest. They prospered under the influence of Baron de Prinz, until they were replaced by the Templar *Order of Strict Observance*. Op. cit., p. 329

There is no firsthand information about the lodge, nor about the Order of *Draškovic's Observance*, but it can be assumed that debates in and the work of the *Timişoara Diet* were consistent with proposals that were received directly from Vienna by military personnel, as the primary proponents of different solutions, as well as by the imperial commissioner, all of whom were swayed by Leopold II's secret policy. Besides Robin Okey, this policy, the aim of which was to fan the flames of hostility between the Hungarian nobility and the Catholic clergy and Orthodox clergy and nobility, has been written about by Denis Silagi and Robert Schwicker.

Both authors emphasize that the demand by some of the participants in the *Timişoara Diet* for expropriation of the Banat region from the jurisdiction of the Hungarian counties, and the demand that this area, as an autonomous area, be directly subordinate to the Crown, was "excessive" and "dangerous."[49]

It stands to reason that Leopold II rejected the demand for expropriation of the Banat, as his only concern was intimidation of the Hungarians, not legalizing territorial autonomy for the Orthodox faithful.

A draft of the demand for secession of the Banat was most likely prepared by someone from the *Court Chancellery* at the emperor's request, perhaps in fact by Count Károl Pálffy, who played a multifaceted role in matters of the *Timisoara Diet*.

---

[49] Denis Silagi, *Ungarn und der geheime Mitarbeiuterkreis Kaiser Leopolds II.* München, 1951. Robert Schwicker, *Die politische Geschichte der Serben in Ungarn,* Budapest, 1880, pp. 377-378. J.H. Robert Schwicker wrote in detail about the *Demands and Appeals* that the members of the *Timişoara Diet* furnished on November 4 to the imperial commissioner, and emphasizes that the demands for a separate territory and the establishment of an *Illyrian Court Chancellery* were particularly perilous. The establishment of a separate *Illyrian Corps* would be a particular danger, he says, because it would threaten the integrity of the country, and eventually may lead to the complete disintegration of the territory on the southern frontier of the country. In addition, this "Illyrian province" would be in complete contradiction to the interests of the Hungarian nation. Furthermore, in the Banat, according to the census of 1772, "Rašani" (Serbs) were a minority. It lists the following figures: 78,780 "Rašani" (Serbs), 43,200 Germans, Italians and French, while the majority, namely Romanians, numbered 151,639. p. 378-379.

The conflict between the emperor and the Hungarians was, for the most part, overcome with the coronation of Leopold as King of Hungary on November 15, 1790 in Pressburg (nowadays Bratislava, Slovakia). A few days later, precisely on November 28, after the end of *Timişoara Diet-* November 15., all three Banat counties were legally united and given a voice in the Diet of Hungary, but albeit now continued its work on addressing matters of improving (maritime) trade.

Sava Vuković, a member of the Timisoara Diet and the Diet of Hungary

In early 1791, various sessions of this Diet were attended by two delegates from Rijeka. These were Marco de Susanni and the newly-appointed nobleman Sava Vuković. Later in 1791, two more delegates joined the Diet—Louis Adamić and Antun Mihanović.

Marco de Susanni presented a study to the Diet in which he listed barriers to the development of maritime trade. The study was accompanied by a map. Hungarian historian Imre Ress also writes about the participation of Marco Susanni, along with Adamić, in the Diet of Hungary in Pressburg, and references the study and the map.[50]

---

[50] The Mason Marco de Susanni was one of six children of Nicolò de Susanni, who are mentioned by name in 1751 as holders of their father's hereditary peerage. In 1776, Marco Susanni is mentioned as a patriciate of Senj and the largest ship-owner in Rijeka. The following year his name appears on the list of the largest maritime traders in Karlovac. It is not known when he became advisor to the Governor of Rijeka, Count Pászthory. However, in one motion, sent by way of the Governor to the *Royal Hungarian Regency* in Pest on May 27, 1791, Marco Susanni proposed measures to increase maritime trade for Hungary. Lajos HORVÁTH, "Riječki zastupnik u madžarskom državnom saboru", (Fiume's Representative in the Diet of Hungary 1848-49,), *Vjesnik HAR,* volume XLI- XLII, 2000, pp. 127-153.

The other delegate from Rijeka—Sava Vuković—actually lived in Novi Sad. He was made a nobleman in 1791 thanks to the Serbian Metropolitan and Mason Stevan Stratimirović. He attended the Diet of Hungary as a Hungarian. He too presented a study in which he stressed the need to build a new road to Rijeka, in addition to the existing *Karolina* and *Josephina roads*, and the need to passing new laws on duty-free zones along the Danube, Tisa, Sava, etc.[51]

The Diet was also attended by the Governor of Rijeka (1788 - 1791), the Mason János Péter Szapáry (? - 1815) who was appointed to the Diet as one of the ten members of the *Trade Committee* (deputatio regnicolaris in commercialibus)

Probably owing to him, the issue of legalizing Rijeka's position as part of the Hungarian Holy Crown was raised in the Diet of Hungary, by way of a memorandum. At the same time, the Diet of Croatia demanded the return of Rijeka to Croatia.

Among the documents published by Gavrilović-Petrović regarding the Timişoara Diet, as well as some documents after the dissolution thereof, there is one study by an anonymous author bearing the title *Projectum Articuli* dated January 13, 1791, which was presented in Vienna.[52]

It is unclear what purpose this document was to serve, perhaps as a proposal for commission by the *Illyrian Court Chancellery*, or perhaps as an item on the agenda of the Diet of Hungary in Pressburg.

[51] Isztvan Soos, "Rijeka u središtu i8nteresa mađarske politike ",("Fiume as a Center of Interests of Hungarian Politics,"), *Temelji moderne Rijeke, ibid.(Foundations of Modern Fiume 1780-1830)*, Rijeka, 2006, pp. 179-191. It is interesting that the author mentions the demand made by the "citizens of Fiume" but fails to name who was the delegate to the Diet of Hungary. The representative was the then (Hungarian) Governor of Rijeka (Fiume), János Péter Szapáry. Having served as Governor of Rijeka, he became President of the Chamber and in this capacity, the President of the *Commission for the Reincorporation of Rijeka into Hungary* on July 31, 1822.

[52] Vladan Gavrilović, *Temišvarski sabor i Ilirska dvorska kancelarija 1790-1792.(Timisoara Diet and Illyrian Court Chancellery 1790 to 179),*, Novi Sad, 2005, pp. 257-258. It is interesting that the preamble of this document uses the term "Banate of Temes" ("Banatus Temessiensis"), while the German text uses the term "Banat of Temeswar." Manojlo Grbić also used the term "Banat of Temes."

It is probable that the document entitled *Projectum Articuli* was intended to convey the Hungarian and Croatian demand at the Diet in Pressburg with regard to resolving the status of Rijeka. In addition, from some of the wording it appears that the demand for an exchange of territory—Rijeka for the Banat—was a continuation of the meddling from within the *Timisoara Diet.*

It is, in many ways, an intriguing document.

It is, above all, an intriguing question as to why a substitute solution was offered for the Banate of Temes to the "Illyrian na-

Count Alexander, Sandor, Pászthory, Governor of Rijeka and the Hungarian Littoral, 1791-1798

tion" in mid-January 1791, on the basis of Law 18 of 1741 and Law 24 of 1751—laws which discuss the reincorporation of the Banate of Temes (as in the original in Latin!) into the Hungarian Kingdom after the peace with Turkey. Instead, a territory in the northern Adriatic was offered, where a small group of members of the "Illyrian nation" had lived of late.

In other words, why did the question of a replacement territory in the northern Adriatic even arise, if the question of the status of the "Illyrian nation" had been solved by way of their recognition as equal subjects of the Hungarian Kingdom?

The author of the study was also asked this.

If we carefully analyze this study, it is evident that:

1. Assuming the study was intended for the purposes of consulting the emperor, it is obvious that the author personally knew Leopold II as he wrote to him in the first person, without revealing the institution to which he belongs.

2. The author's name has been omitted, perhaps due to the proposal of January 13 serving merely as an explanation of the proposal submitted on January 11 of that year.

3. This confirms that between the afor ementioned dates the author was in Vienna, and supplemented the second proposal there, perhaps at the behest of the sponsor.
4. The study shows that the author is an expert in law and is well versed in all administrative and legal changes in the northern Adriatic adopted during the reign of Joseph II (specific mention is made of the abolition of *Severin County* by the royal edict of March 20, 1786 and its incorporation into Zagreb County).
5. It is obvious that he is au fait with the mentality of Rijeka's patriciate ("not one to engage in trade"), which may be down to personal experience.

The study, in our opinion, was a draft work program for the *Illyrian Court Chancellery* in Vienna. It was submitted at a time when the emperor had already proposed an amendment to the bill of January 8, 1791, pursuant to which those of Eastern Orthodox faith were guaranteed full civil rights, including the right to purchase property.

The bill mentions that the initial bill was submitted on January 11, 1791, and that the bill of January 13 was simply a clarification thereof.

The Croatians, as pointed out by Manojlo Grbić, demanded that the bill of 11 January in this sense be amended to prevent the Protestants being given the right to purchase property (Law 46 of 1741), with the bill, as amended to that effect, being accepted by the Hungarians on January 26, 1791.[53]

Vladan Gavrilović believes the anonymous author of the study to be Prince Kaunitz. Our hypothesis is that the author could be one of the Governors of Rijeka - or Jánosz Péter Szapáry, a delegate from Rijeka in the Diet of Hungary and the Governor of Rijeka from 1788-1791, or Sándor Pászthory, Governor of Rijeka from 1791-1798. Interestingly, in the spirit of restoration that was to follow, Sándor Pászthory in the official portrait of him as Governor of Rijeka, is depicted resting on Hungarian legislation presented in two volumes of the book *Corpus Juris Hungarici.*

---

[53] Manojlo Grbić, op. cit., p.143 etc.

Both hypotheses hold the same weight.

Supporting the hypothesis that the author is Jánosz Péter Szapáry is the fact that Leopold II, in passing through Rijeka, had to have met with the governor.

According to the diary of Karl von Zinzendorf (1739-1813), Leopold II, as Grand Duke of Tuscany, before he became emperor in March 1790, often passed through Rijeka. Zinzendorf's diary shows that he and the now Emperor

Leopold II met in Rijeka on September 15, 1790, during a session of the Diet of Hungary and immediately before the final session of the *Timisoara Diet*—therefore during the emperor's journey from Tuscany to Vienna. The diary shows that on September 17, Zinzendorf presented the emperor with a study on the cost of "our mercury", at which time he learned of his appointment as president of the imperial chamber.

Count Karl von Zinzendorf

Zinzendorf also states that Leopold II, on his way to Pressburg, where he was to be crowned King of Hungary, again passed through Rijeka (November 9, 1790) and returned via Rijeka to Tuscany on November 20 of the same year.[54]

A more likely assumption is that the author of the study was Sandor Pászthory, who according to Abaffy was not only Károl Pálffy's right hand, but also his head, as he was viewed by his contemporaries.

In Abaffy's opinion, Pászthory was also one of the defining personalities of his time. Both high-ranking state officials (Pászthory and Pálffy), both members of *Drašković's Observance*, conspired to put an end to "Josephinism", return the Hungarian crown to Budapest and strengthen the Hungarians economically.

---

[54] Karl Graf von Zinzendorf, *Wien von Maria Theresia bis zu Franzosenzeit:aus den Ta- gebüchern des Grafen Karl von Zinzendorf,* selected writings, translated from French with commentary by Hans Wagner, Vienna, 1972.

It is plausible that Pálffy, having relinquished the role of master of the *Provincial Lodge of Hungary*, found himself in the role of royal court secretary, where we again encounter him entrusted with the important task of maintaining contact with the Orthodox clergy throughout the territory under the jurisdiction of the lodge of his order on matters concerning the organization of the *Timisoara Diet*.

Regardless of the authorship of this study, author Eva H. Balász presents a very significant fact.[55]

She writes that all three persons with a connection to Rijeka at the time of the *Timisoara Diet* were members of *Draskovic's Observance* and embodied the same economic, and thus political ideals.

She points out that during "Josephinism", Masons from the eastern provinces of Hungary (Transylvania, Wallachia) settled in regions south of the Danube in Croatia, in particular Rijeka; regions, therefore, that due to their commercial advantages were key to economic reform in Hungary, and in turn the reason that Rijeka was once the center of *Draškovic's Observance* (*"Latomia Libertatis sub corona Hungarie in provinciam redactae"*), an exclusively Hungarian system which was completely independent of Freemasonry in the rest of the Empire.

In Rijeka, the "brethren" primarily busied themselves with matters of Hungarian trade, the position of the peasantry and issues of modernization through constitutionalism. She writes that later, the "brethren" moved from this region to settle in Pest and Buda.

Furthermore, E. Balász notes that the lack of information, and therefore writings about the role of Freemasonry in Hungary in general, and in particular about the *Order of Strict Observance*, stems from the fact that the documents are deposited in private archives, with only some held in the National Széchényi Library (*Széchenyi Bibliothek*), in manuscripts of the *Ungarische Akademie der Wissenschaften,* with some documents kept in Slovakia.

---

[55] Éva H. Balázs, "Freimaurer, Reformpolitiker, Girondisten", in *Beförderer der Aufklärung in Mittel-und Osteuropa, Freimaurer, Gesellschaften, Clubs,* Berlin, 1979, pp. 127-140.

In addition, E. Balász points out that Karl Zinzendorf during a months-long study tour through Hungary and Transylvania in 1772 significantly contributed to the lodge's program in Croatia and Rijeka, which were lands central to *Draškovic's Observance*. In addition, in 1775, a separate, independent order, *Latomia Libertatis sub Corona Hungarie*, was constituted from the reformed *Order of Strict Observance*. E. Balász writes that the Hungarian Freemasons sought advice from Zinzendorf not only while he was Governor of Trieste, but also after his move to take up office in Vienna.

Ignjat Josip Martinović

According to E. Balász, Zinzendorf's Freemason friends included: Nikola Škerlecz of Lomnica, József Podmaniczky, Pál Almásy (Governor of Rijeka from 1783-1788) and József Szapáry (Governor of Rijeka from 1788-1791).

The circle of high-ranking officials—Masons that were active in Rijeka, she says, saw this city occupy a prominent place in the history of Freemasonry in central Europe and beyond. In Rijeka, and southern Hungary too, this circle acquitted itself not only in practical terms, but also its representatives were the founders and authors of Hungarian literature on agriculture. Published works influenced public opinion in Hungary and raised awareness of the need for modernization. Their works were central to sparking discussion around the need for modernization in the Diet of Hungary.

E. Balász goes on to say that during the Diet of Hungary of 1790/91, it transpired that exponents of *Draškovic's Observance* from the eastern provinces had planned to overthrow the dynasty and presented their anti-Habsburg program to the Diet (of Hungary). In addition, the author points out that in Timisoara itself, one lodge of the Order of *Strict Observance* was active although the order's headquarters was in Buda and Pest.[56]

Some members of the *Order of Strict Observance* took their demands one step further, writes the author, and thus a splinter-group of so-called "Hungarian Jacobins" was formed, led by Ignat Martinović [57]

Coming back to the proposal of the unknown author of the project of the independent territory, the question remains of what is required in order to implement an administrative reorganization of the northern Adriatic arises. What is the premise for establishing a commercial district in the northern Adriatic?

The condition, says the author, is if the **demand** by the Hungarians for the Banat of Temeşwar is met, then the **request** of the "Illyrian nation"— which had been of great service to the state —should be met, offering it, if possible, other "lands" (in the original) as an equivalent replacement.

The unnamed author mentions the "lands" that could be offered to the "Illyrian nation" in exchange for the Banat of Temeşwar.

---

[56] Èva H. Balázs states that Count Szapáry, having retired to Buda from the office of Governor of Rieka, opened a reading room (Leserkabinett) in 1792 in Buda, in which the nobility congregated to read the latest newspapers and books and hold discussions. Ibid, op. cit., p. 134-135. Eugen Lennhoff/ Oskar Posner, *Internationales Freimaurerlexikon,* Zürich, Leipzig, Vienna, 1931, p. 1614. Ivan Mužić, *Freemasonry in Croatia,* Split, 2005, p. 20.

[57] In 1781 in Bukovina (Černovic), Ignjat Martinovic made the acquaintance of Count Potocki, one of the leaders of the Polish revolution and Poland's foreign minister. He spent twelve to fourteen months traveling with him through Switzerland, France, Belgium, the Netherlands and Germany, finally ending up in Lviv. From Lviv he went to Russia in 1782. Two years later the Lviv Academy was transformed into a university. Ignat Martinović became dean in 1791. Leopold II appointed him as court chemist. He was sentenced to death in 1795 for treason. Vaso Bogdanov, "Hrvatska revolucionarna pjesma iz godine 1794 i učešće Hrvata i Srba u zavjeri Martrinovićevih jakobinaca", (Croatian revolutionary song from 1794 and the involvement of Serbs and Croats in the conspiracy of Martinović's Jacobins) in *Starine JAZU,* book 46. pp. 350-366. IBID, *Ignat Martinović's Jacobin conspiracy,* Zagreb, 1960. Vaso Bodganov describes Hajnóczy as an accomplice of Ignjat Martinović, pp. 47-54. In 1781, Martinović was inducted into the secret society of the *Illuminati*. Walter Markov, "I Giacobini dei paesi asburgici," in *Studi storici,* Roma, 3/1962. pp. 493-525, Fran Zwitter, "Francuske revolucionarne ideje u zapadnim jugoslovenskim zemljama u vreme francuske revolucije Napoleona I", (French revolutionary ideals in the western Yugoslav lands during the French Revolution of Napoleon I), op. cit., p. 65-88.

This would be the coastal city of Rijeka, "which never belonged to Hungary, which, consequently, should not be allowed to secede from itself". However, if the estates ("Land-Stände" - without specifying whose, most probably the *Illyrian* estates) were appeased, the cities and ports of Bakar and Kraljevica should be incorporated into Rijeka, which once belonged to the abolished *Severin County*, and which are now subject to Rijeka's commercial authorities. Furthermore, a small stretch of road connecting the minute *Severin municipality* to Karlovac, i.e. a section of the *Karolina road*, should be incorporated into Rijeka also.

The cities of Senj and Karlobag, under the same proposal, were to remain under the jurisdiction of the military, frontier judiciary; however, at the wish of the "Illyrian parties" (*Illyrischen Partheyen*) they were to enjoy the right to protection at the *Illyrian Court Chancellery*.

This part of the proposal suggests that the proposal of January 11 was concerned with the future work of the *Illyrian Court Chancellery*, while the bill of January 13 served simply to clarify the previous bill.

Contemporary monument to the Hungarian Jacobins at a cemetery in Budapest

The clarification contained seven points, the seventh of which had three sub-items. The bill addressed these topics as follows:

1. if the trading district (or administrative district) remained independent of the other provinces, this would, first and foremost, make a return to the original dynasty impossible, while at the same time overcoming a slight misunderstanding, which would

2. give it justification in Hungary's eyes because (the "Illyrian nation"), that was inhabiting Hungary, would be represented through its representative office at the court; this would also allow

3. Hungary to realize its much desired annexation of the Banat, and thus

4. his Majesty would placate both the Hungarians and *Illyrians*, and

5. trade would flourish, because the nearby Dalmatians, Albanians, inhabitants of Dubrovnik, Montenegrins, Turks, and Venetians, who mostly belong to this religion and nation (!), would be afforded their own country and protection through representation at the court, and would thus bolster links between their states. In doing so, continues the author,

6. the patriciate of Rijeka, who, through farming, expected labor assistance from the Hungarian-born proletariat, would have a workforce pool from other provinces, which would, through its connections with the hinterland, make a significant contribution to the importance of trade for the city;

7. extending the trading district to Karlovac would see Karlovac become an important center of trade,
   a) considering that the local *Illyrians* held sway over trade there,
   b) through them, to Croatia, Carinthia, Styria, Hungary and via
   c) the river Kupa to Karlovac to the Danube all the way to the Turkish lands, through them to European Turkey and parts of Asia, all the way to the Black Sea, and across to Russia, where this nation and its religion would be "at home."

The final part of the project explains the reasons for the inclusion of individual elements in the study (Karlovac, Rijeka, *Severin County*, the *Karolina road*), and states that the demand by the bishop to move to Karlovac should be met, which, in turn, would attract many families to move to the area.

The study titled *Projectum Articuli* is an expert and enthusiastic proposal for developing a commercial district for Rijeka and its environs. Alongside the evident enthusiasm, there is a clear and positive attitude towards the Orthodox faithful, if

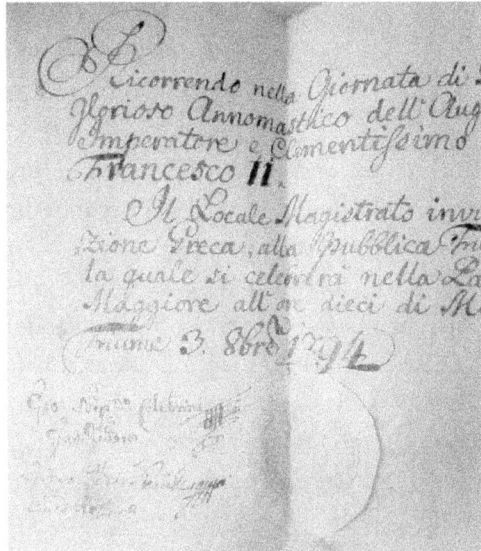

Invitation to the Orthodox faithful to celebrate the inauguration of Emperor Francis II. Archive SPCO

not entirely, then at least towards those in Rijeka and Karlovac. There is also evidence of a liberal attitude towards the commercial (and other) integration of nations and states "from Rijeka, across the Black Sea to Russia."

Looking at these points of the proposal in the study, one might think that the author is a Serbian noblemen, jurist and diplomat, a member of the family which founded city of Arad, Sava Tekelija (1761-1842). However, we doubt that he personally met with Leopold II, or was familiar with the tendencies of Rijeka's patricians. In addition, he advocated annexation of the Banat in the *Timisoara Diet* and urged the "Illyrians" to opt for civil rights. Furthermore, for president of *Illyrian Court Chancellery* had already been appointed count Balaša, so hence that hypothesis has no foundation.

The concept of a Rijeka-emporium as the nexus of a vast territory stretching to the Black Sea and Russia, after its first mention in this study, will appear again later.

For us the almost identical proposal put forward by Rijeka patrician Erasmus Barčić 1860 in his book *La Voce di un patriots* holds the greatest significance.[58]

After the end of the Diet, as with Hungarian estates as well as the Timişoara D*iet*, a period of reaction began. All ideas reminiscent of the revolution were labeled dangerous. Only the Jacobin movements in Trieste, Zagreb and Transylvania remained active. Police apparatus numbers were increased and the death penalty for treason was introduced.

Nobility from throughout the vast Empire, both in the East and the West, were involved in the opposition movements of 1794/95 that sought liberation from Austria. However, this was an independent movement, independent of events in France. Reformists, secret societies and Freemasons went to ground in 1795. For the next seventy years, Freemasonry in Hungary was either well-hidden or it vanished.

During that time, Freemasonry would come to prominence in France.

---

[58] Erasmus Barčić, *La Voce di un patriota*, Fiume, 1860.

2

FREEMASONRY IN RIJEKA DURING THE *ILLYRIAN PROVINCES* AND THE RESTORATION

1. FRENCH FREEMASONRY AND THE FREEMASONS OF RIJEKA DURING THE *ILLYRIAN PROVINCES*

The French came close to the Northern Adriatic several times, invaded Trieste on several occasions and eventually established their adminis- tration there. However, the political, cultural and social changes in- troduced by the French Revolution were only felt after the fall of the *Venetian Republic* in 1797. [59]

At the time, Rijeka was alternately governed by the Austrians and the French.

French troops made inroads into Croatian territory in the Adriatic coastal region for the first time in the spring of 1796. It was then that the French army entered the affluent merchant city of Rijeka, which was the first time its citizens had come face to face with the French. From that moment on, for the next four years, Rijeka was, intermittently, under French administration: from April 1797, from December 1805 to February 1806, from May 1809 and November 1809 to August 1813.

---

[59] Almerigo Apollonio, "Trieste tra guerra e pace", in *Archeografo Triestino*, 1995 p. 194-342. : The French captured Trieste several times: March 23, 1792, May 24, 1797, November 9, 1805, March 4, 1806, May 18, 1809, and October 14, 1813.

In December 1810, the Hungarian governor, Count József Klobusiczky, handed the city over to the French and retreated to his estate in Transylvania. Klobusiczky was the last of the "enlightened" Freemasons.

Administrative changes that would have long-lasting effects were introduced thereafter.[60]

At the end of 1805, when the Peace of Pressburg was signed, the situation in the Adriatic changed significantly, particularly in its southern parts. At the time, Rijeka was occupied by French troops who used the port for several months as its starting point for transport toward Dalmatia.

Under the Treaty of Schönbrunn (14 October 1809), the Austrian Emperor Franz I ceded a large part of his territory where Napoleon founded the state of *Illyria*, i.e. the *Illyrian Provinces of the French Empire*, with its capital in Ljubljana.

No battles were waged in Rijeka, and it became part of the *Illyrian Provinces* with the signing of the Treaty of Schönbrunn. The city's municipal administration was informed thereof on November 11, 1809, and three days later the French general Clauzel asked the citizens to be cordial to the French soldiers and promised that the soldiers would maintain civil order. An interim local government body was formed, headed by Giovanni Andrea de Marochino, Giuseppe de Zanchy and Giovanni de Beniczky, whereas Saverio Tranquilli was appointed judicial administrator of the city administration.

On 16 December 1809, Chassenon was appointed Intendant of Rijeka, and Contades as Intendant of Civil Croatia. Marco de Byrde joined this body as provisional intendant and was tasked, among other things, with replacing the Austrian state symbols with French ones.

In 1809, when the French takeover of the administration from the Austrians began, the French army remained in Rijeka for around fifteen days. Intendant Marco de Byrde issued an order that a war contribution of 135,700

---

[60] Count Jószef Klobusciczky (?-1826) was a member of the Budapest *Die Grossmuth* lodge. Before he became Governor of Rijeka, he held the office of Imperial and Royal Chamberlain, was a member of the secret Economic Council, and a member of secret Imperial Council. Ludwig Abaffy, *Geschichte der Freimaurerei in* Österreich-Ungarn, op. cit., vol. III, p. 385.

forints be collected in Rijeka to raise funds not only for the army's supplies but also for its upkeep.

The list of contributors included the names of 1,087 individuals and institutions. The highest amounts were to be paid by Andrija Ludovik Adamić, Cristifor Luppi, and the Tarabocchia brothers.

The contribution was determined based on the Rijeka merchants' financial standing. Adamić was well known to the French owing to his cooperation with the French authorities (as well as with the British via Malta) and the smuggling of colonial and other goods to the continental hinterland, to the detriment of French interests.[61]

In the end, on May 30, 1809, Rijeka paid a contribution (460,000 forints) that was three times the amount it had paid three and a half years earlier.[62]

In public law terms, the *Illyrian Provinces* were just one of the French departments, although they had a certain degree of independence and separate citizenship. All provincial authorities were accountable to the government in Paris and the Supreme Court of France.

In early April 1809, when Napoleon declared war on Austria, the French troops in Dalmatia passed through Rijeka to rendezvous with the rest of the

---

[61] Numerous articles and a special memoir have been penned about the life and times of Andrija Ludovik Adamić. The oldest, albeit short, but comprehensive biography of Adamić was published by Riccardo Gigante. Adamić (1767–1828) was born in Rijeka and graduated in practical commerce in Vienna. After graduating, he returned to Rijeka, where his father owned a tobacco shop. He became wealthy as a merchant trading throughout a wide area and invested in the construction of a theater (1805), a glass factory in Mrzle Vodice, and a paper mill in Rijeka that was made world famous by Smith and Meynier. He was involved in the construction of the *Luisiana road*. In 1808, he became a member of the Patrician Council, Rijeka representative to the Diet in Pressburg in 1825-26, and was, until his death, representative of Rijeka for trade in Budapest from 1827 to 1828. During the French occupation of Rijeka he rendered key services to Austria. At the time, he was a member of the French Freemasonry. In addition to owning a theatre, a glass factory and a paper mill, he owned numerous luxurious villas in Rijeka and its surrounding areas, and the beautiful "Capricio" villa on the island of Cres. See: Irvin Lukezic, "Životopis Andrije Ljudevita Adamića",("Biography of Andrija Ljudevit Adamić"), in *Adamićevo doba*, (*The Adamić Era 1780-1830*), (Editor-in-Chief Ervin Dubrovic), Rijeka, 2005. pp. 15-75, Silvino Gigante, "Stralcio delle corrispondenza di Lodovico Andrea Adamich col tenente maresciallo Laval Nugent", *Fiume*, XVIII/1940, p. 131-171.

[62] Nevio Setic, "L'Istrie et Rijeka sous l'administration française et le blocus anglais de la côte adriatique," in *Croatian Illyrian Provinces*, Zagreb, 2010, p. 283-302.

French troops. This is why General Marmont, Commander of Dalmatia, stayed in Rijeka from May 28 to 30, 1809.

The French conquest was accompanied by felicitous propaganda, much of it owing to the French Freemasonry. Although it is believed that Napoleon was not a Freemason, he never confirmed nor denied it. The Freemasons claim that he was initiated in one of the lodges of the Scottish order in Egypt where he was consul and, therefore, they considered him "one of their own."[63]

In 1804, when Napoleon became Emperor, he appointed his brother Joseph as Grand Master of the *Grand Orient de France,* and, with help from Prince Cambarcè, he succeeded in appointing other members of his family to senior positions within the French Freemasonry. As the old Scottish rite—the rite of Saint John of Scotland—became recognized together with the *Grand Orient de France,* Napoleon's stepson Eugen Beauharnais was appointed Grand Master of the *Grand Orient of Italy* in Milan and *Sovereign Grand Commander* of the *Supreme Council* in Milan.[64]

Until the 1789 Revolution, the ranks of the French Freemasonry were mostly filled by aristocrats and civil servants. Changes in the spirit, status and role of the French Freemasonry came about in 1799, when Napoleon staged the coup d'état of 18 Brumaire (November 9) to come to power as first consul. He then made a decisive and strategic change of tack—he first decided to exploit the influence wielded by the Freemasonry immediately prior to the

---

[63] According to Giordano Gambierini, Napoleon was initiated into the Army Philadelphe lodge between 1795 and 1798, or in Malta between June 12 and 19, 1798. It appears that his first wife, Joséphine, was also "adopted" by the Freemasonry at the Le Francs Chevaliers lodge in Paris in 1804, together with her numerous ladies-in-waiting. This information is consistent with the information listed in one American publication. In fact, Joséphine was member of a quasi-Masonic female association, recognized by the *Grand Orient de France.* Napoleon, allegedly, established this order to consolidate his power. The *Saint Josephine* lodge of Paris and the Milan lodge bearing the same name were constituted on June 24, 1814. Both lodges were allegedly named after Joséphine Bonaparte. William R. Denslow, *10, 000 Famous Freemasons,* vol. II, p.361. According to the French author Valentin Erigène, Napoleon used a network of pre-revolutionary secret societies to establish a world-wide empire. See: Valentin Erigène, *Napoléon et les sociètes secrètes: le rêve d'un empire universel.* Paris, 1986.
[64] Andreì Combes, *Le Grand Orient de France au XIXe siecle,* Paris, 1960. p. 37.

French Revolution, and then assumed control over the existing network of lodges, and created a network of new lodges in the occupied lands. The lodges were now required to facilitate propaganda and became backdrops for the dissemination of Francophile propaganda.

Accordingly, the French started establishing lodges as soon as they would occupy a country. During Napoleon's Empire, Freemasonry had around three hundred lodges and was an organization espousing the ideological and military expansion of the new class. This "nationalization" of Freemasonry buoyed its membership twofold, even threefold. The highest officials of the Empire joined the lodges. Many of the lodges were named *Napoleone*. During the Napoleonic era, both the membership type and the very essence of the Masonic organization of the French lodges were changed. Instead of meeting to discuss ideas of brotherhood, equality and freedom, they organized parties to sing the praises of Emperor Napoleon.[65]

After the conquest of Dalmatia, and, particularly after the founding of the *Illyrian Provinces*, lodges were constituted in the French propaganda spirit.

Thus, the first lodge was constituted in Zadar on March 31, 1806, immediately after the French army entered the city (February 20, 1806). The lodge operated under the name of *Loge de Saint Jean de Jerusalem franco-dalmate,* under the distinctive title of *Eugène Napoleon à l'Orient* de Zara. The lodge in Split was also founded in 1806, followed by lodges in Koper 1807, Kotor (1807) and Dubrovnik (1808), and Šibenik, Rijeka and, again, in Trieste and Karlovac (1809).

Ljubljana became the administrative seat of the *Illyrian Provinces* in 1810, but its first lodge under the French administration was constituted in 1808 and named *La parfaite Amitie*. The lodge formed part of the 105th infantry regiment. Its members were drawn from the French and military personnel. The second lodge *Des Amis du Roi de Rome et de Napoléon* was founded between June 8 1811 and February 1, 1812.

---

[65] Andreì COMBES, ibid, p. 22.

With the establishment of the *Illyrian Provinces*, some lodges became directly dependent on the mother lodge in Paris. The *Eugène Napoleon Lodge* in Zadar, constituted on March 31, 1806 and on October 1, 1810, was placed directly dependent the Paris mother lodge. Also, the *L'*Ètoile *Illyrienne* Lodge in Dubrovnik, founded on March 30, 1810, was also put directly dependent on the *Grand Orient de France*.

In 1811, a lodge was constituted in Udine under the name of *"Napoleon,"* while it appears that in Rijeka two military lodges were established.[66]

At the time when the *Illyrian Provinces* were founded, France was a vast empire stretching from the Pyrenees and Amsterdam to Lübeck, Rome and Boka Kotorska in Montenegro. The territory was divided into one hundred and thirty departments where French institutions and ideology suppressed all other institutions and customs with help from the unifying French administration. In 1814, the year when the French Empire held its largest swath of territory, there were 1,219 active lodges, and numerous *Carbonari* societies that were considered emulated-Masonic organizations, since they were established by the French Freemasonry in the south of France.

However, even though a network of numerous lodges was formed in the *Illyrian Provinces*, there is no immediate information on the subject. The reason may lie in the French Empire's centralized administration, and the fact that the lodges were mostly active within or alongside the military units and thus information about the lodges would have constituted an integral part of confidential military information.

Giuseppe Stefani, a historian from Trieste who reviewed a large number of Trieste police records dated to the Austrian restoration era, believes that notwithstanding the wealth of information available, nothing is known about the organization of the French lodges, nor is anything known about their interplay on the level of the *Illyrian Provinces*.[67] Based on a report by a police confidant named Gi-

---

[66] France KIDRIC, *Framasonske lože hrvaških zemelj Napoleonove ilirije v poročilih dunajskega policij- skega arhiva*. Rad JAZU, book 206, Zagreb, 1915 pp. 35-60.

[67] [67] Giuseppe Stefani, "Trieste e l'Austria dopo la restaurazione (dai Carteggi riservati della Polizia Imperiale)," in *Archeografo Triestino*, ser. IV vol. III and IV. 1940 /1941.

acomo Mestrone, who was a Freemason himself under the French administration, the suggestion is that there was a lodge in Ljubljana with the status of a "mother lodge" for the *Illyrian Provinces*, but the relationship between that lodge and other lodges along the Adriatic coast remains unclear, as is its relationship with the lodge in Karlovac that was also part of the *Illyrian Provinces'* lodge system.

Giulio Gratton, another Freemasonry historian from Trieste, claims that the lodges in Gorica, Zadar, Split, Rijeka, Šibenik, Makarska, Dubrovnik, Kotor and Karlovac were subordinate to the French lodge in Ljubljana named *Loggia franco-illyrienne des amis du roi de Rome et de Napoléon* à *l'Orient de Laybach*, but it is uncertain whether a mother lodge existed at all. Luigi Troisi states that the *Grand Orient of Italy* was constituted in 1805 in Milan, then part of the Kingdom of Italy.[68]

In consonance with their writings, it is clear why there were no records of the Rijeka lodge (or lodges) during the period of the *Illyrian Provinces*, apart from the fact that it operated, as could be expected, under the guardianship of the *Grand Orient of Italy*.

As there were no military units deployed permanently in Rijeka, we believe that a civil lodge was housed within the new theater constructed by Adamić in 1805. The theater was colossal by the standards of the time. It had three opera boxes and a gallery, and could house an audience of 1,600. Inside the theater, there was a grand foyer and a billiards hall. The theater also had a tavern, and the same building also housed a maritime insurance company named *Gli Amici Assicuratori di Fiume*. The company's management included: Adamo Carlo Schramm, Adamić himself and Ivan Krstitelj. The theatre was thus the social hub for occupied Rijeka's high society, and the Freemasonry was public, so it was not hard to organize the lodge's work. Aside from that, Adamić also lived in the theater.

---

[68] Luigi Troisi, *La Massoneria. Profilo storico-cronologico.* 1990, p. 34, Giulio Gratton, *Trieste segreta*, Bologna, 1948. According to another Italian author, the *Grand Orient of Italy* was established with Napoleon's permission in 1805 in Milan, which at the time was part of the *Kingdom of Italy* (Regno d' Italia) and since Austria lost Venice and Dalmatia under the Peace of Pressburg (December 26, 1805), it is possible that the lodges along the Adriatic coast came under the jurisdiction of the *Grand Orient of Italy*.

A painting of the theater's interior reveals an indiscernible coat of arms on the stage curtain, which makes it a national institution, while everything else in the theatre was probably arranged according to the taste and style of the new (revolutionary) French citizenry.[69]

After the *Illyrian Provinces* were abolished, a return to the previous state of affairs would have proven fatal for all French collaborators, had they not been collaborating all along with the French and the British at the same time. Adamić in particular was adept at this. His "French connections" included the Intendant of Rijeka, De Chassenonon, and even the Governor of Dalmatia, Marshall A. F. Marmont. Namely, as a wholesaler who supplied the French army with wheat, Adamić did not find it difficult to posture as a French supporter.

However, through John Baptist Leard, the English consul in Rijeka, who had been exporting timber from Gorski Kotar to England since 1803, and with permission from the government in Vienna, Adamić made several trips to London starting in 1809. This is when his secret connections with the British were established.

During the continental blockade, Adamić liaised between the Viennese court and the English fleet in the Adriatic. However, Adamić was at his most enterprising between 1811 and 1813, when he replaced Leard, the English consul, while moonlighting for the French.[70]

Count Laval Nugent-Westmeath (1777-1862) was key to preserving the credibility that the Francophiles of Rijeka had with England and Austria once the *Illyrian Provinces* had been abolished. Adamić and Nugent had mutual interests stretching from 1823 until Adamić's death in 1828.

---

[69] *The Adamić Era 1780-1830.* p. 38

[70] Irvin Lukežić, "Biography of Andrija Ljudevit Adamić", The Age of Adamić 1780-1830 op. cit., pp. 15-76. The most important information on Adamić's secret actions to Britain's benefit can be found in the British archives. Using the documents from these archives, Hedwig Pavelka describes the activities of John Leard and his associate Adamić, including Malta's place in the supply chain of the British and Austrian ships on the Mediterranean during Napoleon's blockade. Hedwig Pavelka, *English-Österreichische Wirtschaftbeziehungen in den ersten Hälfte der 19. Jahrhunderts.* Graz, Wien, Köln, 1968.

An autobiography of Count Laval Nugent, sent on February 23, 1847 to Count Inzagha from Graz, the chief chancellor, secret advisor and guardian of the Treasury, provides accurate and authentic information from his tumultuous biography. The information is authentic because it was confirmed by his superiors. Laval Nugent addressed Count Inzagha asking to be awarded a diploma of an Austrian count, because his family did not possess (Austrian) one, and considering that he owned estates in Kranjska (**Carniola**) and Croatia—where his family would live—that he would like to expand through new purchases.

To prove that he deserved the title not only by his merits but also by virtue of his birth, Laval set forth the genealogy of both the Protestant and the Catholic members of the Nugent family branch to which he belonged. He then set forth their various military merits, his extended family's estates in Normandy, Italy and Britain, from which it was clear that they were all members of a mercenary army in the service of various kings. Laval also lists the battles in which he fought and the ranks assigned and medals awarded to him.

The first and the most important was his status as the Prince of Rome awarded to him by the Pope in appreciation for his help in making his return from exile to Rome possible. This is followed by his Austrian medals: First Class Iron Crown, Commander's Cross of Maria Theresa and Leopold's Cross.

The two unsigned confirmations attached to his application speak of the important stages and people in Laval Nugent's operations. Laval points out that it was at Prince von Metternich's request that he conducted the following important missions:

1. In 1809, he was appointed authorized delegate at the Hungarian Altenburg Congress.
2. During the strained relations between Austria and England, he was in charge of making the Austrian Emperor's viewpoint known without compromising him, and of seeking to provoke war with Spain at that time. While on this mission, he visited England on two occasions – in 1810 and 1812 and carried out the three missions successfully, to Prince Metternich's satisfaction.
3. When in 1813 war broke out, at Prince Metternich and Prince Schwarzenberg's request he conducted a mission based on a pre-agreed

plan for Croatia and the Adriatic Sea, and liberated these parts from the French without going into battle.

4. When in the spring of 1815 Napoleon escaped from Elba, it was decided that Laval Nugent should occupy the island. However, since hostilities broke out with the Kingdom of Naples, he made a stop in Tuscany, won over the local troops, broke off negotiations with the Kingdom of Naples and cut off the French troops at Florence, effectively ending the war.[71]

We gleaned further information, from the obituary of Field Marshal "Laval Nugent, Prince and Count," on his estate in Bosiljevo (Croatia).

Laval Nugent, a good Catholic and a military man, did not want to sign the decree annexing the Papal State to France on May 17, 1809 in Vienna and the decree removing Pope Pius VII from office in July of the same year. He resigned from his post in the Austrian Army and returned to England where he was awarded the same rank that he had obtained in the Austrian Army. From that point on Nugent had been on a secret British mission aimed at Berlin (Prussia) and Vienna (Austria), his goal being the formation of a broad coalition against Napoleon (it was a fifth coalition). He was awarded the title of "Lord Grand Prior of Ireland" for his merits, in 1860, shortly before his death in 1862.[72]

---

[71] Count Laval Nugent,, *Die Abstammung der Familie Nugent* (gothic letter), Stuttgart, 1904 p. 14, and 24-25.

[72] *The Universal News*, London, August 30,1862. Laval was also awarded the medal of the Grand Master S. M.I. and R.A. First Degree Knight from the Austrian Emperor Ferdinand I. *Scematismo del Litorale ungarico 1838,* Fiume, 1840. The fact that they both conspired together against Napoleon is not all that links Laval Nugent and Georgi Melissino, a merchant from Rijeka, and in our opinion, research there on would help understand the origins, sources and the ideology of European conservatism after the Napoleonic era. On Prince Laval Nugent's military activities, see Gaetano Morese, "Croatian Estates of Prince Laval Nugent in Documents of the State Archives in Naples," in *Gazette of the State Archive in Rijeka*, volume L-LII, 2010, pp. 61-85. On the features of the Masonic organizations in Ireland, see Robert Macoy, *A Dictionary of Freemasonry,* New York, 2000, reprint (undated!). Author (1815-1895). Alexander Buczynski, "Le Brasier latent du patriotisme de la Carniole et la siége de Zadar en 1813," in *Illyrian Provinces*, Zagreb, 2010, p. 303-352.

There is limited information on Freemasonry in Ireland. What is known is that in 1729, Lord Kingston was elected Grand Master of Ireland, that the Duke of Leinster was elected Grand Master in 1813 and that it was then that the Grand Lodge was joined by the Grand Conclave of Knights Templar, the Supreme Grand Council of the Ritual and the Grand Royal Arch. In short, this was the unification of all Masonic orders.

The "Grand Cross of the Sovereign Military Order of Malta", awarded to Laval Nugent for his merits as an officer in the Austrian Army, confirms that he belonged to an order of knights – Freemasons. This is to say that Laval Nugent fought against Napoleon and took part in the creation of the anti-Napoleon coalition not only as a professional soldier, but also as a staunch Catholic and a Freemason—a Crusader.[73]

Furthermore, his obituary states that as of 1811, Laval Nugent played an important, albeit strictly covert role in Napoleon's defeat. To achieve his goal, Nugent returned to Vienna from Ireland in 1811 and made suggestions on several occasions that an attack against the French should be launched precisely from the *Illyrian Provinces*.

After several attempts by Laval Nugent to convince the military authorities in Vienna to launch an attack against the French from the territory of the *Illyrian Provinces*, British Commander Haller finally accepted Nugent's suggestion. Nugent was tasked with crossing into Croatia from Italy and reaching Rijeka, where his troops would intercept the French troops that were retreating from Dalmatia and rendezvousing with Admiral Fremantle's ships.

This plan was successful and an allied Russia and Prussia defeated Napoleon at Schafhausen on December 9, 1813.

Negotiating the coalition and following through on the plan to defeat Napoleon required a great deal of mobility. Neustädter detailed information about this topic, which covers the years between 1810 and 1813.[74]

---

[73] Robert Macoy (1815-1895), op. cit., p. 371 and pp.202-206.

[74] Josip Neustädter, *Ban Jelačić i događaji u Hrvatskoj od 1848.(Ban Jelačić* and Events in Croatia of 1848), Zagreb, 1994. p. 73.

Neustädter states that, from 1809 onwards, Counts Ferdinand Winzingerode, Ludwig Walmolden and Laval Nugent had, with assistance from the
Hanoverian minister, Count Ernest Münster, worked on a secret alliance
against Napoleon.Neustädter further states that what is particularly strange
was Laval Nugent's behavior between 1810 and 1813, during which time he
hurried from Vienna to the Ionian isles and to Malta, Sicily, Spain, Portugal,
visited Wellington, and then London, Gothenburg, Kolberg and Berlin, to
return to Vienna and embark on the same journey again.

Given that Count Ferdinand Winzingerode was once again in Vienna at
that time (following his return to the Austrian Army in 1807 having served as
adjutant-general to the Russian Emperor Alexander I), that Count Münster
had been appointed minister for Hanoverian matters in London in 1805,
and that Walmolden was Cavalry General in the Austrian Army, it is evident
that it really was a secret coalition aimed at launching a two-pronged attack
against Napoleon: in Russia and Spain, and then in Portugal.

When Nugent occupied Rijeka on August 26, 1813, having cut off the
French Army that was retreating from Dalmatia, this spelt the end both for
the French Masonic lodge (or lodges) and for the French regime in Rijeka
that was, to a certain extent, embodied in those lodges. An interim military
government was installed, with the French laws remaining in force for a while
thereafter. All French lodges were outlawed and disbanded.

2. COUNTS GEORGI (1755 – 11/7/1833) AND MIHAJLO (1798 – 1858) MELISSINO AND A HYPOTHESIS ABOUT A MELISSINO MASONIC ORDER IN RIJEKA

There is a wealth of information about Georgi Melissino, a Greek from Rijeka, since he lived in the city, albeit sporadically, for some forty years. The first reliable piece of information about his time in Rijeka comes from the Register of Married Catholics: in 1794, he married a Tereza Tilak in Rijeka in a Catholic ceremony.

The next piece of information comes from the baptismal records of the Rijeka *Orthodox Municipality*. It is where Georgi Melissino had his daughter Ekaterina and his son Mihajlo baptized in 1797 and 1798 respectively. Georgi Melissino settled in Rijeka from the Greek island of Kefalonia. At the time of his arrival in Rijeka, the island was part of the *Venetian Republic*, as it had been since 1386. However, after Napoleon had abolished the *Venetian Republic* in 1797, its dominions belonged to France, including Kefalonia and other Ionian islands.

In 1799, Russian Emperor Paul I (who reigned from 1796-1801) managed to drive the French away from the Greek islands in an alliance with the Ottoman Empire, and thus that same year the seven Ionian islands formed the *Septinsular Republic*, which was, of course, recognized as a sovereign state by Russia and Turkey.

When in 1803, after the mysterious death of his father Paul I (March 23-24, 1801) Alexander I inherited the throne, he first recognized the *Septinsular Republic,* then the priority of the Orthodox church over the Catholic church in the new state and he expanded the Orthodox clergy's jurisdiction to include civil affairs. It was essentially these measures that heralded the Orthodox theocracy on the isles. In 1803, he appointed a Greek count, Ioannis Antonios Kapodistrias as secretary of state for foreign affairs of the *Septinsular Republic*.[75]

---

[75] Prior to taking office as secretary of state for foreign affairs of the *Septinsular Republic*, di Capodistria was member of the Greek *Hetaireia*, and was head of this Alliance between 1817 and 1820. In 1822, he parted ways with Alexander I over foreign affairs matters, handed in his resignation and

In 1802, the *Septinsular Republic* opened its consulate general in Trieste, then part of France, whereas in Rijeka its appointed vice-consul was a local Greek wholesaler named Teodor Manasteriotti. However, he soon quit office and was replaced in 1803, probably at his own request, by Georgi Melissino. Soon after his appointment as Russian vice-consul, Georgi Melissino disappeared from the list of Rijeka merchants. In 1805, he appeared for one last time. According to an authentic piece of information, on April 8, 1813, he was back in Rijeka as godfather to a daughter born to Nikola Kurtović, a merchant from Trieste. He was then registered as консул русский [Russian consul], residing in Rijeka.[76]

This is to say that during the *Illyrian Provinces*, that is the French reign, Georgi Melissino disappeared from Rijeka. He was also absent from the list of merchants in charge of contributions. It appears that at the time Melissino was in Malta, which had been British territory since 1800, a conclusion that can be drawn from the fact that on July 20, 1808 an agreement was made between Andrija Adamić and the *Giorgio Melissino e Comp.* company on a joint venture to ship wood and tobacco to Malta and Tunisia, wherefrom they would ship salt and other colonial goods. It appears that the business partners parted ways because, in 1810, Georgi Melissino was involved in court proceedings against Adamić.[77]

---

moved to Geneva. He was elected president of Greece and was murdered in an assassination plot by conspirators in 1831. The Russian Masonic encyclopedia lists Ioannis Antonios Kapodistrias as a Freemason, but without any information as to which lodge he belonged to and even less as to when and where he was initiated into the Masonic ranks. А. И. Серков, Русское масонство 1731-2000., энциклопедический словарь. Москва, 2001. p. 376.

[76] *Artefacts. Contributions to the history of the Serbs in Croatia,* No. 2/1996 p. 62 note No. 191.

[77] Ljubinka Toševa Karpowicz,"Jadran i Srdozemlje u doba Francuza", ("The Adriatic and the Mediterranean during French Rule,"),*The Era of Modernization* 1780-1830, Rijeka, 2006, p. 199 idem: *The Orthodox Municipality in Rijeka 1720–1868,* Rijeka, Belgrade, 2002 pp. 46-58.

There is later confirmation dating to 1826, given by Georgi Melissino to Lazar Ilić—a merchant from Rijeka (or just a ship companion), smuggler and a corsair during the *Illyrian Provinces*—confirming that Georgi Melissino had been receiving goods through the Orthodox corsairs from Rijeka while he was in Malta.[78]

During the continental blockade, Malta was the busiest place in the Mediterranean. It was a strategic port used by Austria and England, not only for the purposes of mutual assistance and trade, but also to reach agreements on their fight against Napoleon.

During the French (continental) blockade, Malta was already an important point used not only to supply England with food, but also for the transporting post to the Ottoman Empire. The Orthodox merchants from Rijeka had a certain advantage when it came to this, since they knew the language of the hinterland of the *Illyrian Provinces,* but also owing to the business carried out on the island by Georgi Melissino, who they were already acquainted with.

It cannot be ruled out that, apart from managing his business from Malta, Georgi Melissino may have resided temporarily on the Ionian islands that were also frequented by Count Nugent, on his secret mission against Napoleon.

That Georgi Melissino's position in the anti-Napoleon coalition was a well-known one is further confirmed in an official report by Maréchal Pavle Radivojević (1759–1829) about his visit to Rijeka together with Nugent, just before the end of the *Illyrian Provinces.* According to Attilio Tamaro, Radivojević had a "propaganda and intelligence mission" to undertake in Rijeka, but no information exists about the objective thereof. On September 22, he informed his superiors that: "I deemed it imperative to open the ball with the Russian consul's daughter".[79]

---

[78] There is extensive material in the archives of the Serbian Orthodox Church Municipality in Rijeka worthy of comprehensive research on the actions taken by Lazar Ilić as an Austrian corsair. Based on what has been published so far, it is obvious that Lazar Ilić was a person in the confidence of the Austrian authorities during the French blockade and that he smuggled goods for the English via Malta to England.

[79] Attilio Tamaro, op.cit.

The ball was organized by the Fund for Invalids. Ekaterina, Georgi Melissino's daughter, was sixteen at the time. After the ball had been opened, Radivojević escorted Count Melissino home.

The manner in which Mareshal Radivojević treated Georgi Melissino confirms that he was a person whose merits were known to the new regime, embodied in the Austrian army officers. It was probably owing to those very merits that Melissino not only resurfaced in Rijeka in 1813, but was also Russian consul to the Austrian Empire, although the official notice thereof was received by the Rijeka Captaincy only on August 5, 1815.

Georgi Melissino's further career development as a diplomat can be traced through the baptismal register of the Orthodox Municipality in Rijeka. He appears as "Russian Consul" in baptisms held in April 1813, in August 1814 (twice), and as "Agent of the **Russian consul in Trieste, nominated for Rijeka**" in 1817, 1820, 1821 1823 and 1828. He acquired these titles during the reigns of Emperors Alexander I (1801–1825) and Nicholas I (1825–1855).

Melissino father and son probably wanted to apply for knighthood on the grounds of their merits in the anti-Napoleon Coalition and at their request in 1820, they were conferred as Russian nobility. Thereafter, they placed a coat of arms on their house.[80]

Ever since the time of Peter the Great, the Melissino family had belonged to ancient Russian court nobility.[81]

---

[80] Gigante, Blasonario Fiumano, op.cit., pp. 100-169.

[81] The Melissinos were a well-known Greek family that in 1182 lived in Constantinople, and at Emperor Alexios' request they settled on the Island of Crete, together with another twenty families. Nikifor, a famous member of this family, was married to the sister of Emperor Alexios. Their descendant, Ricardo Melissino, moved in 1454 to the island of Kefalonia, wherefrom Ivan Ivanovich Melissino, a doctor, moved to the court of Peter the Great. The last "Russian Melissino" was Aleksey Petrovich Melissino, who died as a Major General in the Battle of Dresden in 1813. князь Лобанов-ростовский, Русская Родословная книга. Томь первый, 1895. pp. 378-379.

In 1831, Georgi was made Knight of the Order of Saint Anna, as was his son Mihajlo in 1834.[82]

To the uninformed, father and son were thus merely made knights, but to those au courant, they also became members of the Templar Freemasonry.

Georgi Melissino died alone in his house in 1832, and Iginio Scarpa, a Rijeka patrician and a Freemason was appointed executor of his last will and testament, as agreed with this absent son. After Georgi's death, an inventory of his possessions was made in their apartment by the City Commission of Rijeka.

After his will had been opened, point seven named (his excellence) Count Antal Mayláth de Székely (1801–1873), who was at the time counselor at the *Hungarian Regency Council* in Rijeka, guarantor of the execution of the remaining provisions of his will, Georgi Melissino left to him, as a "token of remembrance", a weighty pouch of diamonds that was to be handed over to him immediately. It can be assumed that Georgi Melissino and Antal Mayláth had previously reached an agreement on this matter.

Antonio (Antal) Mayláth was son of Josip Mayláth de Székely, the first Governor of Rijeka and the first Prefect of *Severin County*, and the family belonged to the "Szekler" minority that still inhabits the easternmost parts of today's Moldova, formerly Transylvania. Civil servants were recruited from their highest ranks, often belonging to the Seventh Province of Templar Free-

---

[82] The Orden of Saint Anna was established by Empress Elizabeth I, daughter of Peter the Great, in 1754. The Orden's significance was in the public display of a Grand Master's cross of a Templar province. This medal and the medal of imperial Russia were almost identical in form. In 1798 (after Napoleon had conquered Malta on June 9, 1798) the *Knights of Malta* elected Russian Emperor Paul I (reign 1796–1801) their Grand Master and he took them under his guardianship. Since then, the medal of Saint Anna held a specifically Masonic meaning and its purpose was to identify the person wearing it as member of the Templar Freemasonry. Napoleon offered Malta to Paul I in the Treaty of Lunéville (9 February 1801); however, the emperor was murdered on the night of March 23-24, 1801, and the following year Malta was returned (Treaty of Amiens, 25 March 1802) to the Knights of Malta with six major powers acting as guarantors (Great Britain, Russia, France, Portugal, Spain, Prussia, Austria). René Le Forestier, *La franc-maçonnerie templiere et occultiste aux XVIIe siecles,* Paris, Lovain, 1970. p. 155. Maria Arrigoni, *Come gl' Inglesi andarono a Malta e vi restarono,* Milano, 1940.

masonry of *Draškovic's Observance Order*, whose seat was in Jaszi.[83]

The jewels listed in the will include a very interesting ornament.

The list includes: a rose, made up of twenty four crimson diamonds worth a total of 144 forints; a chain with a cameo pendant trimmed with seven brilliants, worth 80 forints together with the cameo; a small rose made of diamonds with a sapphire in the middle, held together by high-quality gold, a 65 carat golden medal representing *S. G. M. ex S. Giuseppe* (probably Joseph II); a gold-plated chain decorated with two signet rings and a tiara, all weighing 279 carats; and a Greek relic or saintly power on a chain together with a cross, and various metal coins ("related to the coronation").

The jewels listed in Georgi Melissino's will, the silver candelabra that he donated to the Orthodox church in Trieste and Rijeka, the opening of a theater in Rijeka (in 1800) and his various medals suggest that Georgi Melissino's role was more significant than what was known to the public. Most intriguing among the described jewels and even more so if it belonged to a man, was a rose made up of twenty-four crimson diamonds.

According to the glossary of symbolic Freemasonry, a rose represents silence and secrecy, the blood shed by Christ on Golgotha, and it also symbolizes the Heart of Jesus. At the same time, it represents the Order of the Rosy Cross. The purple-red or crimson color of the precious stones represents fire, and in the middle ages it also represented Knights Templar and sacrifices made for the religion.[84]

The Masonic Order of the Rose, whose symbol is a red colored rose, originates from eighteenth century Germany and is part of the symbols of the German branch of the *Strict Observance* order or the military Freemasonry, whereas its Hungarian branch, i.e. *Draškovic's Strict Observance,* took the knightly armor as its symbol.

---

[83] Between the twelfth century and 1876, the Székely minority enjoyed considerable autonomy. First within the Kingdom of Hungary, then as the Principality of Transylvania and finally as a province under the Habsburgs. They enjoyed autonomy in the eighteenth century, for special merits, and then as the frontier guard corps. As of 1867, they were made part of the Hungarian political class. In 1876, their autonomy was abolished.

[84] Robert Vanlo, Philippe Klein, *Les Bijoux Rose Croix 1760-1890*. Paris, 2003 p. 67.

"A Greek relic or saintly powers with a cross" may represent, in terms of Templar Freemasonry symbolism, a symbol of mortality and happiness that comes after death. The coins that are mentioned were not intended for circulation, but represent the etched history of the Freemasonry, whereas number seven (7) in the description of the cameo piece of jewelry, according to the same glossary, is a sacred number and represents perfection, as does the number three. The candelabra donated to the Orthodox Municipalities of Trieste and Rijeka are a Masonic symbol for reason and knowledge.

Iginio (cavaliere) Scarpa

Given that members of the Mayláth family were members of the Templar Freemasonry from Transylvania, the question arises as to whether the diamonds, bequeathed to Antal Mayláth in Georgi Melissino's will, were in his possession for a reason unknown to us and actually belonged to a lodge. Did Georgi Melissino only have them for safekeeping or did he trade in diamonds?

That Georgi Melissino belonged to a Masonic brotherhood is obvious from the fact that all persons who were directly or indirectly involved with Melissino father and son were Freemasons: Iginio (cavaliere) Scarpa, Nikolai Bosichi de Trendafilo—a Greek from Trieste, appointed Russian consul after Georgi Melissino,—and Georgi Melissino's (secret) associates, Count Laval Nugent-Westmeath and Adamić.

The most intriguing of the whole series of questions is whether there was a secret lodge in Rijeka belonging to the forbidden *Melissino system*.

The *Melissino system* is listed in all Freemasonry encyclopedias. However, the description of the order's actions is not based on authentic documents, but on accounts. This is probably the reason why different authors describe the rituals in different ways. According to Von Lennings, Count Ivan Ivanovich Melissino (of Greek origin), as a great observer of the local provincial (Russian) lodge, established in 1765 specific high degrees in the existing lodge *K* šutljivosti – *Tišina (Zur Verschwiegenheit)* [*Being Silent - Silence*] Lodge in Petersburg.

His order was banned in 1782, and the lodge was shut down and ordered to completely distance itself from the Freemasonry.[85] According to Boris Bashilov, a Russian anti-Masonic author, Count Ivan Melissino lived during the reign of Catherine II, was a handsome polyglot, well educated (at the University of Moscow), a cadet in the military service, a member of the *Holy Synod*, traveled West, visited the French, Italian and English lodges, and was a student at the Egyptian Cagliostro order.[86]

In 1777, Ivan Melissino constituted a lodge with a special, mystical ritual, named *The Silence.* The first three degrees of the lodge were the same as in all Masonic orders. The following degrees, up to the seventh degree, were a kind of a mystical praxis that was mostly found within the Church.

Nikolai Pokrovsky states that Melissino, as head of the *St. Synod*, was a restless reformist proposing radical reforms of the nature, rituals and doctrines of the Orthodox Church.

Other data on the Melissino order can be found in work by the Russian Freemasonry historian Tatiana Bakounine. Her work is interesting because it raises some questions about the possible existence of a Melissino order within the Rijeka Orthodox Municipality.

According to her book, the Melissino order did not vanish from Russia when Freemasonry was banned in 1798. It appears that the order was active with Major General Aleksey Petrovich Melissino (1759–1813), son of Peter Ivanovich Melissino, who died in 1813 fighting against the French at Dresden.

What we find interesting is a quote that refers to Baron Johan August von Starck (1741–1816), who was initiated into the *Melissino order* between 1763 and 1765, and at the same time established a *Strict Observance order* (*Le*

---

[85] The oldest source about the Melissino order is *Altenburger Zeitschrift für Freimaurerei,* (1823., pp. 20-31), which Von Lennings used as a source for his work. Von Lennings, *Allgemeines Handbuch der Freimaurerei,* zweiter Band. Leipzig, 1900. p. 33.

[86] Борис Башилов, История русского Масонства, Москва, выпуски 1993/6-5. pp. 98-96.

A photograph of the floor section beneath the "Heaven" at the Saint Nikolai temple in Rijeka

Chapitre de la Stricte Observance) in Saint Petersburg named the *Phoenix*. A branch of this lodge was ecclesiastical, under the name of *Capitulum clerico-rum regularum,* whose higher degrees were known as *Capitulum Petropoli-tanum.*[87]

According to Eugen Lennhof, a German author, the Melissino system, as Templar and Occult Freemasonry of sorts, was active in churches. This order did not receive members, but their children were baptized into the Freema-sonry.[88]

---

[87] Tatiana Bakounine, *Répertoire biographique des Francs-maçons russes,* Paris, 1967

[88] Eugen Lennhoff, *Die Freimaure.,* Amantea Verlag, 1926, also mentions Melissino. Everything was forbidden in 1822. Emperor Nicholas I then reintroduced the ban in 1825, because members of the lodge were connected to the *Decembrists.* All members were exiled to Siberia in 1826 and it was then that the Russian Freemasonry died off, to be renewed only in 1906.

According to a contemporary Russian historian, Platonov, in 1774, a lodge named Mars No. 469 was opened in a Russian camp in Iasi in Moldova. The lodge was probably a military one, its Master being Major General, Engineer and Knight of the *Order of St. George*, Peter Ivanovich Melissino. The author claims that the "Elegin system" that was well-known in Russia, included the Melissino system that emerged for the first time in 1765.[89]

The latest description of the Melissino system, described as based on the existing literature by Arturo de Hoyos, lists all the degrees of the system. The Melissino system had seven degrees, of which the first three were common to all Masonic orders, while the fourth degree was named *The Dark Vault,* the fifth *The School Master,* the sixth *The Philosophical Degree* and the seventh *The Spiritual Knight (magnus sacerdo),* the high priest of the temple or the spiritual knighthood. Members of the seventh degree met exclusively in churches, or in chapels specifically intended to serve this purpose. The service began by consecrating the rose oil, whereas the "brethren" called themselves "brethren of the Rosy Cross and priests", but did not identify themselves with members of the German Knights of the Rosy Cross order.

It is interesting that over a period of thirty-five years, with an almost ten-year break, Georgi Melissino baptized thirteen children, mostly Greeks from Rijeka, and acted as witness to five marriages.

Apart from these facts, which in a manner suggest that the Temple of St. Nikolai of Rijeka may have housed the Melissino system, several questions remain unanswered:

1. Why would an affluent person whose last name places him within the ranks of the Greek Byzantine nobility of the Komnenos family, who moved to Russia during the reign of Peter the Great, continue to live in the small town of Rijeka?[90]

---

[89] Платонов, терновый венец росии. Тайная История Масонства. документы и материалы, том ii Москва, 2000. p. 350.

[90] The Melissino family originated from Greece, and they occupied high offices at the Byzantine court. After Byzantium fell, they lived in Russia. Nikolai Melissino moved to Crete in around 1462, and then to Corfu. His descendants returned to Russia. Ivan Atanasovich Melissino (who died in 1758) was physician to Peter the Great. He had two sons Ivan and Peter. Peter's son, Major General

2. Why does Georgi Melissino's will open with the words: "In the name of the St. Trinity" – a cult that the Orthodox church in Rijeka had in common with the Rosicrucians? Why does the Orthodox church in Rijeka have a mosaic representing the Holy Trinity beneath the *Heaven*, and at the same time the holy number seven (*Gadicke*)?[91]

3. Why, according to Georgi Melissino's will, did the afor ementioned church receive donations of "icons representing various officers" that were his personal mementos, if the Commission's description is accurate?

4. Why did he not keep the described jewels in the Russian consulate's treasury, and why were the diamonds handed over to a Hungarian official rather than to the Russian consul following the death of their probable owner?

Aleksey Petrovich, died at Dresden in 1813, and the Melissino family ceased to exist in Russia. The Melissino order was linked to Peter (1730–1797), who was an Artillery General. Peter was one of the finest artillerymen of his time. In 1783, he was appointed Director of the Artillery Engineer Corps. In 1796, he was head of all Artillery Corps in Russia, but he resigned in the following year. Енциклопедический словаръ, томъXIX, С. Петрбургъ,1896. p. 326.

The *Mackey's Revised Encyclopedia of Freemasonry,* vol. 2, 1929, states that the Melissino order was a mixture of the York, Swedish and Strict Observance orders. The order's characteristic feature was the belief in the Holy Trinity that was the last degree of the Rosy Cross. The twelve lodges that belonged to the York, Swedish and *Strict Observance* orders were united on September 3, 1776 and founded the National Grand Lodge. In 1794, Empress Catherine harbored fears that her enemies might be hiding among the ranks of the Masons, but she did not ban the lodges. It was Paul I who did so, under the influence of the Jesuits.

According to some suppositions, Russian Emperor, Alexander I Pavlovich (1777–1825), who triumphed over Napoleon, and became Emperor after 1801, was initiated in 1803 by I.V. Boeber at the *Alexandre à la Fidelité militaire* lodge and he secretly belonged to the *Grand Orient of Poland*. According to some suppositions, he presided over the lodge in 1814. In 1817 and 1818, he visited the *Trois Vertus* lodge, on December 11, 1820 he was present at a dinner held in his honor at Pont-Euxin. In 1822, he became suspicious of the lodges, considering them politically dangerous and on August 1,1822, he banned the Freemasonry. His successor, Nicholas I, ratified the edict on April 21, 1826. This meant the end of the Russian Freemasonry for a long period of time. William R. Denslow, *10,000 Famous Freemasons, vol. I.* p. 25.

[91] The triangle in Masonic symbolism represents the Trinity. A triangle with three circles represents the three divine persons - Father, Son and the Holy Ghost united in divine nature. The sky is a baldachin, symbolizing the protection of the Trinity - *trinitas, trinitates*. Gray is the color of the ashes, and represents sacrifice and humility, death of the body and immortality of the soul, white is the color representing the soul's innocence. The black combined with the white is a symbol of humility and purity of life. Red is the color of the blood, a symbol of love and hate. All this on a white background represents the universality. According to: Robert Macoy, op.cit. 688-689.

5. What is the meaning of Georgi Melissino's appointment as "Russian cavalier" (Russian knight) in 1831?[92]
6. What were the ties, both in form and doctrine, between the Templar Masonic Melissino order and the *Order of Strict Observance*? Why did Governor Szápáry open a *Strict Observance* lodge in Rijeka after the Freemasonry was banned from Hungary? Did the lodge simply move after his departure in 1798 to the newly built Orthodox temple, whose construction permit he helped secure?

All this is coupled with the solid evidence that Georgi Melissino was a citizen of Rijeka as of 1797, judging by the baptismal records kept by the Orthodox Municipality.

All the hypothetical answers to these questions suggest an equally hypothetical conclusion: Georgi Melissino and a *Rosicrucian system* were active on the premises of the Orthodox church. It was a Templar and military system named "Melissino". It is possible that this order may have been merely a version of the forbidden *Latomia Libertatis sub Corona Hungarie* order.

In any case, the intriguing data demand further research, this time in the Russian diplomatic and military archives.

---

[92] Georgi Melissino advanced in his career as follows:
• 1811–1823 Russian consul
• 1828 Agent of the Trieste Consulate
• 1830 Russian counselor,
• 1831 Russian cavalier.
Only before his death was his high Masonic title acknowledged. Namely the title of Ritter – Кавалеръ. Since 1908, Chevalier had been a monastic military brotherhood of the *Order of Saint John of Jerusalem* (white with a cross). The order was placed under state protection, and if they were secular individuals, they were governed by various statutory regulations. To become a member, one had to be a descendant of a courtier, and their distinguishing mark was a cross, the title of "Кавалеръ." Emperor Paul I reformed the "Cavalier Corps" in 1797. Two years later, in 1799, he made it the Guard of Paul I, the Grand Master of the *Order of Saint John of Jerusalem*. It contained 189 various ranks, made up of court members who held the Maltese Cross. энциклопедический словарь, op.cit. p. 33.

3

REINCORPORATION OF RIJEKA
UNTIL THE "COMPROMISE" OF 1867

---

1. THE MILITARY REGIME IN RIJEKA
(August 26, 1813 – November 1, 1822)

After Laval Nugent and Captain Lazarić drove the French troops out of Dalmatia across Rijeka, Nugent continued to harry them across Kastav and Veprinac, to resume fighting in Istria. A small garrison remained in Rijeka, together with a small number of volunteers, probably to secure the interim military regime, which sought to restore things to their previous state.

This was a very difficult time for Rijeka. Ravaged by the contributions imposed by the French, and with its economy devastated, it was now forced to support the remaining army and a hospital, and rejuvenate the port and sugar refinery, the city's main industries.

The September 1814 beginning of the Congress of Vienna (which ended in June 1815) was greeted with relief in Rijeka and the outcome thereof with anticipation.

On the basis of its decisions, Austria reorganized the recovered lands into four member territories:

1. Hereditary Lands (divided into ten provinces)
2. Lands of the Bohemian Crown (divided into three units)
3. The Kingdom of Galicia (and Lodomeria)
4. Lands of the Crown of Saint Stephen (Hungary, Croatia, Transylvania).

Rijeka, as a separate and independent entity, fell within the Lands of the *Crown of Saint Stephen*. The newly established old order of things lasted for thirty years, i.e. until the Revolution of 1848. This period is known as the *Age of Metternich* (1815-1848), i.e. an age of reactionary conservatismism and that of the Austrian chancellor's ascendency in the world of international politics as arbiter between Russia, which was committed to the *Holy Alliance* coalition, and England, a member of the *Quadruple Alliance*.

However, even though the social order that had existed prior to the Napoleonic conquest was partially preserved, given that the feudal class managed to retain its lands, liberal ideas—both in terms of philosophy, economy and politics—paved the way for political discontent.

The philosophical principles of liberalism in the first part of the nineteenth century were based on the principles of freedom and equal rights to all men, on the preservation of the natural and inalienable human rights (freedom, property, safety and the right to fight oppression), and also the right of association and freedom of thought, unconstrained by religious and all other external restraints.

On an economic front, liberalism advocated the concept of the economically free individual who, driven by his interest in his own wellbeing, furthers the general good, given that society is a collection of individuals.

As a political thought, liberalism advocated the idea that the nation is the source of sovereignty, that the law must be interpreted so as to reflect the common will, and also political freedoms, universal suffrage being the most important among those. Liberalism also advocated freedom of the press, equality before the law and the liberation of peoples from foreign domination. This was a basic political freedom, advocated by those political groups that opposed inherited status. The most important among them was the bourgeoisie.

The British bourgeoisie, as the bourgeoisie of a country that was one of the first, if not the first to take the road of capitalism driven by the ideology of liberalism, found Rijeka to be impoverished due to the contributions imposed by the French, economically devastated, and a fertile ground to expand the on-going exploitation of the hinterland of Rijeka, the forests of Gorski kotar.

Old contacts were renewed and new ones were made through Freemasonry, which was the well-established manner of British capital inflow into the market. While lodges in European countries were disbanded, as a reaction to French Freemasonry during the Napoleonic reign (of Bavaria partially in 1799 and completely in 1845, of Milan and Venice in 1814, of Portugal partially in 1816 and completely in 1824, of Prussia partially in 1820, and of Russia that same year), Britain kept opening new lodges. During the course of the nineteenth century, it first opened its overseas consulates. During that period, eighty-nine consulates were opened on all continents, including in Rijeka. Consulates were tasked with joining British industrialists together by trade into an overseas trading network, and strengthening these ties through private contacts, so that English industrialists no longer needed to make contacts through consulates. Having in mind the status and obligations of British consulates, it is understandable that British consuls had to develop wide trading networks, not only for trading purposes, but also to obtain useful information. This created the link between trading connections and Masonic connections that directly served the British imperialism.[93]

Since in Austria the fleet was under state control, British consuls, including those in Rijeka, had to communicate with the government in Vienna. Informing its Ministry for Trade about the current state of affairs, the British Consulate in Rijeka served British-Austrian trade and naval interests regarding Rijeka, which was at the time in the process of post-Napoleonic restoration.[94]

---

[93] See: Jessica Harland-Jacobs, *Builders of Empire: Freemasons and British Imperialism 1717- 1927*, University of North Carolina Press, 2007. Apart from listing certain countries and British Masonic lodges opened in them, the author describes the 1870 conflict between the British (Grand Lodge) and "The Latin Freemasonry," a term employed by the British to designate *the Grand Orient de France*, under the pretext that the latter included atheists in its ranks. In 1902, *Alpina*, the *Grand Lodge of Switzerland* established the *International Bureau for Masonic Affairs*, striving to unite Freemasonry and to annul the isolationist position of the British Freemasonry. Its efforts were, however, in vain. The idea of international Masonic unity after World War I drove the Freemasons to create the *International Masonic Association (MIA)* in 1919. Its first congress, held in October 1921 was attended by members of all lodges, including the *Grand Orient of Turkey* and the *Grand Lodge of New York*. The *Grand Lodge of Britain* (Imperial) and the USA did not send their representatives. Op.cit. pp. 288-289.

[94] Hedwig Pavelka, op.cit. Ivan Crkvenčić, "British consular service on our shores and British timber exports via Rijeka during the first half of XIX century," in *Jadranski zbornik*, III, 1958, pp. 359-370.

Ljubinka Toševa Karpowicz

A. MASONIC NEPOTISM OF THE BRITISH LODGE IN RIJEKA DURING THE MILITARY REGIME

During the military regime (1814-1822), the *Captaincy of Rijeka* or district office included, apart from Rijeka, other parts of the coast, and parts of the mainland: Čabar, Kastav, Pazin, and the islands of Krk, Cres and Lošinj.

In 1815, the *General Civil Code* was introduced, making all citizens equal and disregarding all differences between them, thereby establishing the legal category of citizenship.

On November 1, 1814, the *Chamber of Commerce* of Rijeka that was established by the French ceased its operation. At the same time, new customs regulations entered into force that were less favorable to Rijeka than to Trieste, which resulted in the further decline of exports via the Rijeka port.

The combination of adverse circumstances, the war above all, caused an Empire-wide economic depression. The situation in Rijeka was the same. In addition, there was the famine that started in 1814 and continued throughout the following years, culminating in the 1817 great famine. It was only in 1820 that the first signs of economic recovery were noticeable.[95]

The first step towards the reestablishment of Hungarian governance of Rijeka was made by **Francis (Franz)** I, on July 1, 1822, in **Laxenbourg.** To re-organize the state administration, he asked that a commission be established in the recovered lands, to submit economic data. József (Johann) Mayláth, the son of former Governor of Rijeka, was appointed to that position.

On November 15, 1822, Count József (Johann) Mayláth, the imperial commissioner, took over the city's administration. The state of the administration was reverted to that of 1809. The populace of Rijeka was thrilled to receive notice of their ruler's order, as was pointed out by a Hungarian author, probably hoping that it would bring prosperity, and great festivities were organized on November 7, 1822, the day Rijeka passed into Hungary's hands.

---

[95] Danilo Klen, *Privredno stanje Rijeke u doba Ilirije, (Rijeka's economic standing at the time of Illyria),* Zagreb, 1959. pp. 81-85.

98

On February 23, 1823, the first meeting of the municipal council was held, following the election of fifty new patrician counselors.[96]

Data about the return of Freemasonry coincide with the data about the legal and administrative changes. Nugent taking Rijeka, after having cut off the French Army that was retreating from Dalmatia, not only meant the end of the French regime, but also the end of the French Masonic lodge of Rijeka that included the top officials and collaborators with the French regime.

Since the French laws remained in force for a while longer, more precisely during the interim military administration, French lodges were forbidden and shut down, including the one in Rijeka. The interim administration remained until November 1, 1822, and members of the French Masonic lodge of Rijeka took their old posts in the town's administration and the commercial court.

John Baptist Leard, the former British consul (1753–1831), was the first one to return to Rijeka, having been replaced by Adamić as trade consul in his absence, during the 1811–1814 French occupation.

During the struggle with Napoleon's troops, Leard, a naval officer on a British vessel, took the island of Lošinj and other territories in the Adriatic, and in 1814, King George appointed him once again English consul to Rijeka. This is the reason why his deputy Adamić stepped down from this post.[97]

Upon his return, Leard continued the career he started in Rijeka in 1803. Given that he was a shipbuilder in the British Royal Fleet and his experience as a timber supplier for the Navy Board, he was familiar with the forests of the Military Frontier and Gorski kotar, and hand-picked the tree trunks and personally drafted projects to improve land to sea transport.

According to an imperial decree dated December 10, 1803, Leard was allowed to embark the trees from the following regiments: 1,070 from the regiment of Slunj, 200 from Varaždin-Karlovac, 100 from Varaždin-St. Jurij,

[96] István Soós,"Rijeka u središtu interesa mađarske politike"("Rijeka at the Center of Hungarian Political Interests,") in *Foundations of Contemporary Rijeka 1780-1830*, Rijeka, 2006. pp. 179-191. Giovanni Kobler, op.cit. vol. I. p. 220.

[97] Irvin Lukežić,, "Biography of Andrija Ljudevit Adamić," in *The Age of Adamić 1780-1830. ibid.* Rijeka, 2005, pp. 15-75

and as of 1805, another 200 from the Gradiška regiment were permitted.

According to a private contract signed in around 1803, 30,000 trunks were ready to be delivered, and, as of 1805, another 2332 trunks.

However, only partial export of the agreed contingent was achieved in 1805. The remaining part was requisitioned by the French. They used the timber to build bridges and other public constructions, or it simply disappeared during transport on the Kupa river.

In 1812, export was resumed. This time, Adamić was the main exporter, so that the French would not realize that it was a British business. At the same time, Leard was a naval officer on the Adriatic and his presence guaranteed support to the exports from the Adriatic.

Just before the *Illyrian Provinces* came to an end, on March 12, 1812, probably hoping for the breakdown of the regime and controls, Adamić arranged a shipment of timber stock to Malta worth 12,192 pounds based on a secret contract. However, the French discovered the transaction and he was taken to prison in Ljubljana, the then administrative center of the *Illyrian Provinces*, of which Adamić was a citizen. As a consequence of this episode, Adamić's plan for timber transports by the Danube to the Black Sea, and then to Malta, failed.

After Leard was once again appointed British consul, Adamić resumed working with him, as of 1814, but the price of timber plummeted, and transport costs through Rijeka port shot up, meaning that timber had to be exported via Trieste.

However, in parallel with the private Adamić-Leard-Nugent enterprise, Leard sold trunks from Gorski kotar together with the state of Austria. Nicolò de Susanni managed this business.[98]

---

[98] Nicolò de Susanni, founder of the aristocratic family, was elevated to the ranks of nobility by Maria Theresa in 1751, for his merits in the War of Succession (1741–1748). The de Susannis were a naval family that probably had lands on the Adriatic. All members of the de Susanni family belonged to the various Masonic lodges of Rijeka. Lajos Horvàth, "Representative of Rijeka at the Diet of Hungary 1848-49," in *Vjesnik Državnog arhiva,* (hereinafter DAR), Rijeka, volumes XLI-XLII, 2000, pp. 127-133.

Exports of timber to Britain, under de Susanni's care, were supposed to cover Austria's war debt to Britain in the amount of 23,500,000 pounds. In 1823, this debt was taken over by Rothschild bank, making Adamić-Leard-Nugent and de Susanni creditors of the Austrian government.

This deal was also top secret, since the timber came from Nugent's lands, and Adamić got his share from transport costs.[99] However, the price of timber kept plummeting, among other reasons because Leard started exporting timber from Albania, then part of the Ottoman Empire (1814), at even lower prices.

Timber exports from the Military Frontier were continued until 1819. The entire transport process was carried out through Adamić, but the profits were not significant until 1840.

However, apart from the Leard-Adamić trading connection, Adamić kept correspondence with Robert Steward Castlereagh, who was at the time British Foreign Secretary, sending him various reports that, among other reasons, explained how trade with Malta was conducted during Napoleon's continental blockade.[100]

Malta was the focal point of Mediterranean transport to many countries (Austria, Turkey, Greece, and the Italian states) that had obtained (limited) concessions from Great Britain to dock and supply their ships. Concessions were valid until 1835 and were granted from fear that some of those countries, Austria in particular, would develop closer ties with France.

When Leard moved to Rijeka in 1803, Adamić sold him *Villa Giuseppe*, which he had recently bought in 1802. This was a house opposite the former castle, and in 1809, Leard had it transformed into a summer house.

---

[99] Details about the Austrian debt payment to Britain through deliveries of timber from Gorski kotar and Adamić's interest in this, Gaetano Morese, "Croat Properties of Prince Laval Nugent in Documents of Naples State Archive," in *Vjesnik DAR,* 50-52/2011. pp. 61-85.

[100] Hedwig Pavelka, op.cit. Pavelka lists documents from British archives (Public Record Office, London, Foreign Office, 7 Austria). This correspondence is evidence of secret information sent by Adamić to the British Government and of the manner in which goods were smuggled from the port of Rijeka to Malta.

Leard bought his other house from Adamić as well, in 1813. This was a house outside the town, surrounded by vineyards. Today, this house is the seat of the National Archives in Rijeka, and as Attilio Tamaro wrote, the third lodge of Rijeka was opened with pomp and great publicity.

The list of "the enemies of Austria", which meant collaborators with the French regime, that was sent by   police commissioner Rijeka Agostino Dani to Austrian police on 8 April 1813 contains, almost without exception, the old Freemasons of the new lodge. It includes: Antonio de Verneda and Giuseppe de Zanchi, Austrian officials; Paul Scarpa and Vincenzo de Terzi, former mayors during the *Illyrian Provinces*; brothers Elia and Giovanni Bratich, originally from Dubrovnik (the latter was police commissioner under Marmont); Giovanni Musich, police commissioner; his sons Giuseppe and Antonio (the former was secretary of the French Government in Ljubljana), the latter police commissioner in Rijeka; Alfredo and Agostino Ladavese, French refugees; Marinich, police commissioner; Giovanni Vierendels, sugar refinery employee; Francesco Tranquilli, judge; and finally, Adamić, whose name was crossed out.

France Kidrič lists the same persons as Freemasons at the time of the *Illyrian Provinces*. However, a report written by Lederer, the Austrian consul to Rijeka, to Hager, his superior, dated February 12, 1813, lists other data partially substantiating the hypothesis that Georgio Melissino and Laval Nugent were Knights Templar Freemasons.

Lederer claims that a society was established in Paris, the so-called *Novotemplars* (*Chevaliers du l' Ordre du Temple*), that appeared in public in 1806, 1810 and 1811 and whose aim was to revive the order and that, to that purpose, emissaries were sent to various countries. Allegedly, on March 5, 1813, Emperor Francis I ordered Lederer to join the *Novotemplar* order, to spy on them.

When in October 1813, Mastwyk was appointed Police official in Rijeka, he immediately sent the list of Freemasons of Rijeka to Zagreb to General Gyrkovich, the vice governor (*Verzeichniss der in Fiume befindlichen Freimaureri*).

The list contains almost the same names as the list published by Attilio Tamaro, except that it was stated that Adamić was known to be a friend of Austria and that he used his secret English connections so that England would help Austria. The part about the "secret English connections" partially coincides with the data about the secret actions taken by Laval Nugent, who was the actual "secret connection" person in the period between 1809 and 1813.

The Mastwyck report mentions that the least known among the lists of Freemasons was that of the Lodge in Karlovac, military seat during French administration, but that it contained familiar names from the Rijeka Lodge (Ivan Vierendeels, brother of the Freemason from Rijeka bearing the same last name, Franjo Gerliczy, judge, probably related to de Gerlyczi of Rijeka, and Katić, an Orthodox merchant).[101]

A conclusion may be drawn from these data that Adamić was the pivotal figure of Masonic nepotism, having traded in real estate with Leard and Nugent, with the tacit support of Giuseppe de Susanni (? - 1880).

The author of Rijeka during the fascist era, Silvino Gigante judges Adamić's personality based on a report from Agostino Danni, in a note which justly reflects the actions of a person who intimately shares Masonic values:

> ... *"Seemingly a loyal patriot, essentially extremely dangerous to the state, because, obsessed with personal interest, he never ceases to take action aimed at destroying places of devout religious faith (holy places), having made little or no profit through their destruction, and directing the people towards luxury, resulting in liabilities for the state, and then, through certain, seemingly useful endeavors, compromises the state until eventually revealed, and finally, ever since these Illyrian Provinces ceased to exist, he maintained intensive relationships with the present government, even though it seems impossible to combine the profile of a good Frenchman with that of a good Austrian, and if he is the latter, then it is only for reasons of personal egoism."*

---

[101] Attilio Tamaro, "Origini della massoneria a Fiume", *Archeografo triestino*, serie IV. vol. XIV-XV, Trieste, 1948. pp. 355-369. Same author, "Episodi di storia fiumana", Fiume, 1933/34. Silvino Gigante states his opinion about Adamić's anti-Austrian activities according to a report from an Austrian commissioner (confidant) Agostino Danni, and also a list of Freemasons of Rijeka and collaborators with the French, sent by Danni, and returned by *Polizei Hofstelle* to the authorities of Rijeka, with Adamić's name crossed out. France Kidrič, "Masonic Lodges in Croatian Countries during Napoleonic Illyria", po.cit., Rad JAZU, Volume 206. /1915, pp. 25-60.

Scarpa family tomb in Kozala, a cemetery in Rijeka

Apart from Adamić, de Susanni, who was named by a police rapporteur from Trieste as Vice Governor of Rijeka, was also a key figure of Masonic nepotism. He belonged to a Masonic lodge during the *Illyrian Provinces,* which is to say that he was a French Freemason, until he was confirmed as a member of the Order of *St. John of Scotland* or *The Grand Lodge* at the time of the return of British Freemasonry.

Aside from that, he was not only a representative of a state institution, but was also related to Count Revedin from Venice, who had close links to the local Venetian police. He also had close links to the Bratić brothers, who were important smugglers during the *Illyrian Provinces,* turning a blind eye to their activities. The brothers lived in his house.

When in 1813, the government in Graz suggested that de Susanni should take action against smugglers in Rijeka, the suggestion referred to Adamić and Tommassini, the Mayor of Bakar, buthowever de Sussani, who, having to arriving in Rijeka on a work assignment duty due to a work obligation, he only visited his relatives and friends, and took no action against the suspects, even though the suspicions of smuggling were not unfounded.[102]

According to another report that was also mentioned by Tamaro, Adamić maintained relationships between Austrian and Italian Freemasons. This was probably the *Grand Orient of Italy*.

With Adamić and de Susanni subsequently crossed out, the Mastwyck report states that the Mayor of Rijeka, Paolo Scarpa, belonged to the lodge, as did the former mayor, Vincenzo de Terzi, police commissioner originally from Dubrovnik, Elio and Giovanni Bratich, police commissioner Giovanni Musich and his son Giuseppe Musich, secretary of the *Illyrian Provinces* in Ljubljana, Judge Giovanni de Marochino, attorney Bembo Barnalotto, Baron Baselli, deputy intendant of *the Illyrian Provinces* Francesco Tranquilli, public prosecutor Pietro Werendels, member of a deputation of the *Illyrian Provinces* that in 1810 undertook a trade mission to Napoleon, Giovanni Celebrini, senior clerk at the Maritime Court, Enrico Fritz, police confidant, concluding with Adamić, who was the most prominent figure of the French regime in Rijeka, as the twenty-fifth member.

H. Stefich was the speaker of the lodge, and Peter Bernessi its representative. The lodge included several younger individuals who were probably anonymous to the Freemasonry and the police, which is why their names were never mentioned.

Offices occupied by the lodge members go to show that membership in Freemasonry was merely a means to secure the existing positions, to maintain the "brotherhood." Aiming to preserve and deepen the community sense and feeling of belonging, Masonic lodges of Rijeka constantly organized festivities, balls and other forms of social communication. This was perhaps only a way to conceal the real objective of the Masonic organization from the public.

---

[102] According to Attilio Tamaro, Giuseppe de Susanni (a Hungarian nobleman), was brother to "the illustrious" counselor bearing the same last name, most probably the son of Niccolo de Susanni.. Giovanni de Susanni was a patrician in Rijeka, governorate counselor and in September 1815, royal emissary to several cities. He represented Rijeka at the Diet of Hungary during the 1848/49 Revolution. Lajos Horváth, "Representative of Rijeka at the Diet of Hungary 1848-49", *Vjesnik državnog arhiva u Rijeci*, volume XLI-XLII/2000., pp. 127-133. Attilio Depoli, "Fiume nel 1848 e negli anni seguenti.", *Fiume*, genn. 1954. pp. 36-78.

B. FOREIGNERS WHO PERMANENTLY SETTLED IN RIJEKA

On July 5, 1822, Rijeka and the Littoral were officially returned to Hungary.

The former governor   (1807/1819) and mason, Count József Klobusiczky, bearing now the title of *"reorganizer"* was not elected for new governor, contrary to rumors that were circulating, but rather Count János (Johann) Mayláth de Székhely, son of the first governor of Rijeka. The economically devastated Rijeka, once again part of Austria, within the *Lands of the Crown of Saint Stephen*, presented itself as a challenge to entrepreneurs who sought economic gain in this situation.

Adamić found the situation particularly favorable, since he cooperated with Great Britain, the most important ally of Austria that was at the same time the winner in the Napoleonic wars. He was therefore the pivotal figure through which contacts were made with that intent, given that he was acquainted with a wide circle of people in high places on an international scale, familiar with local circumstances and experienced in trading over a wide geographical area. The importance of Adamić as the pivotal figure of Masonic nepotism is vividly illustrated through his correspondence with Laval Nugent that took place between 1821 and 1828, which is to say during the military regime in Rijeka and the Metternich Era.[103]

It is unknown when and where Adamić and Nugent were introduced to each other. They could have met in Malta, where Adamić smuggled goods for the Britany and where he had a representative office that employed his son-in-law, while Laval Nugent used Malta to arrange coalitions against Napoleon. They could have met in Rijeka, at the time when it was occupied by Nugent on August 27, 1813.

On July 2, 1820, Laval Nugent permanently left the *Kingdom of the Two Sicilies* because of the military revolt in Nola and once again joined the Austrian Army, where he was promoted to the rank of field marshal. In February 1823, he was made a patrician of Rijeka.

---

[103] Riccardo Gigante, "Stralcio della corrispondenza di L. A. Adamić col tenente maresciallo Laval Nugent," *Fiume,* god. XV-XVI (1937 – 38), pp. 131-172.

If he had not met Adamić earlier, they certainly met at the time of their correspondence, which, due to mutual benefits, lasted until Adamić's death (1828).

An excerpt from the correspondence begins on August 5, 1821, when Adamić made suggestions to Laval Nugent regarding the purchase of property across Croatia, and continued with favors sought in return. Laval's replies are not included in the correspondence, if there were any that, according to our opinion, might further illustrate the hypothesis about (Masonic) nepotism.

The correspondence revolved around the purchase of Trsat Castle (above Rijeka) and timber exports from Gorski kotar. Both ventures were connected.

Count Ferenz Űrmény, Governor of Rijeka and the Hungarian Littoral, 1823–1836

However, the success of both ventures is credited to newly appointed governor Count Ferenz Űrmény in (1823), who was elected new Governor of Rijeka instead of János (Johann) Mayláth de Székhely, as was suggested by rumors. Ferenz Űrmény remained in office as Governor of Rijeka until 1836, longer than any of the previous governors.

A conclusion may be drawn from the Adamić-Nugent correspondence that, at the time when it took place, the Governor of Rijeka and Laval Nugent did never met on purpose, given that a public meeting between such public figures could not have been kept secret.

The formal and informal social network of individuals who were implicated between 1821 and 1828 is best illustrated by their names and positions.

The pivotal person through which arrangements were supposed to be, and probably were made, was the torchbearer of European conservativism, Prince Metternich (1773–1859), who owed Laval Nugent favors for services done to him starting from 1809, until the conquest of the *Illyrian Provinces*.[104]

Based on the stated merits, it is clear that Laval Nugent was able to contact Metternich to obtain the business of paying off a part of Austria's debt to England, which was primarily of interest to Adamić.

The interest that bound Adamić and Nugent together—and, through the Governor of Rijeka, Metternich as well—was in connection with the main Austrian foreign debt to the amount of 23,500,000 sterling, 3,000,000 of which were owed to Great Britain.[105]

Acting in his interest, as of January 1823, Adamić wanted to impose himself as one of the members who would handle the loan of three million sterling, extended by the *Bank of London* to Austria. In his letter dated January 22, 1823, Adamić asks Nugent to act as an intermediary, and in the next one he states the ways in which the amount will be paid.

According to one item of the proposal, Austria would pay Britain ten million sterling in timber exports, ten million in feudal fiscal goods and ten in money.

Adamić's letter ends in an implicit suggestion that the presence of Laval Nugent in Vienna at the time when the decision on this loan will be made as made would be the condition which would guarantee the success of the plan. Apart from this proposition, according to the correspondence, Adamić intended to "put into operation" his old proposal to revive the Society for Navigability of the river Kupa, chaired by Prince Dietrichstein.

We do not know if Adamić started negotiating the purchase of the castle with the (interim) Governor of Rijeka (János Mayláth de Székhely). However, in his letter dated November 22, 1823, he informs Laval Nugent that

---

[104] Laval Nugent, *Abstammung der Familie Nugent,* (Gothic alfabet), Stuttgart, 1904. pp. 24-32. Numerous data is listed in the previous chapter. When in1834, the Chapter General of the Order of Malta was transferred to Rome, the order's history was linked to the papal throne. Since Prince Metternich was a special patron of the *Maltese Order* and created the Lombardo-Venetian Priory, it is unclear whether Laval Nugent was awarded the title of the Roman prince thanks to Metternich, or if Metternich supported him on account of the title, but both championed the papal cause and Roman clericalism. Laval Nugent petitioned Emperor Ferdinand to acknowledge all his styles and to make his sons, Johann and Albert, counts of the Austrian Empire on June 12, 1848, when the Revolution was already underway, which is why the original diploma is today kept in Venice.

[105] Gaetano Morese, op.cit.

the new governor (Ferenc Űrmény) promised to take up the cause to buy Trsat Castle, and to bring the works of art into it.

Since the castle was part of the Bakar municipality, Adamić and the new governor went together to to the town of Bakar on January 14, 1824, where, with specific efforts made by the governor, they agreed that the castle should be sold to Adamić so as to avoid the mention of Laval Nugent's name, with Adamić making payments of one forint each year. In his letter, Adamić undertook to sign the castle over to Laval Nugent and his heirs. This is how Trsat Castle be-

Andrija Ljudevit Adamić

came one of the estates bought hurriedly by Nugent fath, consisting mostly of castles in Croatia (Bosiljevo in 1820, Stara Sušica in 1823, Trsat in 1824, Dubovac in 1827, Stelnik in 1834 and Januševac in 1855).

Some of the castles were bought because they were on the estates in the heavily forested area of Gorski kotar, and with help from the above mentioned British consul, Leard, with Adamić and an (unknown) Adam Smith acting as brokers, they started to export oak tree trunks from Nugent's estates. 20,000 loads—a volume of fifty feet—were in question, which were supposed to pay for one third of the debt to England. Adamić's share in this venture was paid from the costs of transport via the *Lujzijana* road (finished in 1809), that was adjacent to the forests owned by Nugent.

It appears that this monopoly met opposition from some Hungarian noblemen from nearby estates, which can be seen from a letter sent by Adamić to Laval Nugent on January 14, 1824. In this letter, in which he informs him that the castle had been bought, Adamić mentioned the objections made by Vincenzo Batthyany, whose estate was close to the Kupa river, and who also opposed Adamić's project to improve navigability on this river.

Since at that time Hungary seized Vincenzo Batthyany's estates of Grobnik, Brod and Ozalj, conditions were created for the unobstructed export of timber from government estates to England, which was hailed by Adamić as a victory of "our good governor".

Other machinations that were mentioned in the correspondence (an expensive silver sabre presented as a gift to Laval, acting as an intermediary with Metternich so that young Count József Maylath, son of the former governor of Rijeka, would be elected first counselor of the new Hungarian Government, and so on), point to the persistent use of informal, mostly Masonic connections, considering that the majority of those involved were Freemasons.

Thanks to the Governor of Rijeka, **Antun** Mihanović and Adamić were elected representatives of Rijeka to the House of Representatives at the 1825 Diet of Pressburg, even though Mihanović became an official of the governorate in Rijeka less than two years before that! Governor Ürmeni also represented Rijeka in the Diet, in the House of Magnates.

Adamić submitted to the Diet a written study in Latin, entitled "Remarks on the Conditions Necessary for Hungarian Trade to Flourish, in particular of that Directed towards the Adriatic Sea." However, according to the **Hungarian** police, he spoke only once at the Diet during the two years when it was in session and his command of Hungarian and Latin was poor.

Close cooperation between the representatives of Rijeka at the Diet of Pressburg extended to the issue of the *Hungarian Trade Company* in Rijeka, as learned from the secret reports made by confidants present at the diet.

However, contemporaries believed that the proposal to establish the company came from the governor himself.[106]

In 1837, Trsat **Castle** was finally redecorated and art works were brought in. The importance and glamour of the art collection and of the castle itself is obvious from the fact that it was visited by Frederick, King of Denmark,

---

[106] Imre Ress, "Adamić and Mihanović at the Diet of Pressburg," in The Age of Adamić 1780-1830, Rijeka, 2005, pp. 187-221.

during his travels through Montenegro, Dalmatia and Istria in 1838. This may be just a speculation because he may have had other reasons for his visit, of which, unfortunately, there are no data.[107]

Due to the fact that Trsat Castle, thanks to the military rank of its owner, was in a certain manner exempt from the administration of the *Hungarian-Croatian Littoral* (governed by a loyal friend, Governor Ürmeny until 1836), we know nothing about the events that took place in the castle, who visited it and if decisions were made there.

What supports this statement is the fact that "one night in 1850," Josip Neustädter and the old Count Nugent, as stated by Neustädter, spoke about Pan-Slavism. Neustädter claims that Laval Nugent had a positive attitude towards Pan-Slavism, but pointed out that it received support from Russia only to serve its cunning politics aimed at absorbing all northern and southern Slavic peoples. Neustädter points out that the old Laval said that, if it ever occurred to Austrian ministers to Germanize all the peoples of the Empire, that spurious policy could push the Slavs of Austria into Russia's arms and towards Pan-Slavism.[108]

Considering the year when the conversation took place, he definitely had in mind the failure of the revolution in Hungary (1848 /49) and help from the Russian Tsar Nicholas I extended to the Habsburgs, without which the Hungarian Revolution could never have been quelled.

The castle is **afterwards** longer linked to the name of Albert Nugent, Laval's eldest son, (1816–1896), known as an "ardent Illyrian."[109]

There is relatively little data available in the literature about the link between Illyrianism(Pan-slavism) and Freemasonry, and even less about their political agendas.

---

[107] Matteo Gardonio, *Giacomo Peronuzzi 1801-1839, Scultore Neoclassico,* Aviano, 2013.

[108] Josip Neustädter, *Ban Jelacic and Events in Croatia as of 1848,* Zagreb, 1994. (reprint). p. 73.

[109] It is interesting that the Governor of Rijeka, Pal Kiss, informed the Hungarian Palatine Stephen that the "Illyrians" wanted the secession of Rijeka and the littoral from Hungary, and that on May 8, 1848 the Hungarian ministerial adviser put the matter of Rijeka's defenses on the agenda for the first time. Ferdo Hauptmann, "Korespondencija grofa Alberta Nugenta iz god.1848",("Count Albert Nugent's Correspondence from 1848,") *Arhivist,* Belgrade, No 1/1951. pp. 21-56.

For example, Croatian historian Ivan Mužić points out that the "spirit of Freemasonry" that was created during the existence of the *Illyrian Provinces* was kept alive in Croatia, even though lodges ceased their operations in 1824. According to him, this spirit was evident from the feelings of linguistic and cultural unity that, under the name of Illyrian Movement, as a political movement, incorporated the Illyrian or Croatian national movement that was supported by the Freemasonry. Mužić therefore lists Juraj Šporer from Karlovac, son of a Freemason and a Freemason himself, Bishop Maksimilijan Vrhovac, Janko Drašković, relatives of Drašković, who was the leader of the movement, and Ljudevit Gaj as Illyrian Freemasons, but he also mentions, without stating their names, some representatives of the Croatian National Revival from Dalmatia.[110]

Josip Neustädter also mentions brothers Gilbert and Albert Nugent as participants in the military-political events in Croatia. According to him, Gilbert Laval Nugent (1822–1864) was a quartermaster of the 22nd Border Infantry Regiment in 1844 and 1845 and honorary knight of the *Sovereign Order of Malta*, just like his father. Neustädter states that, apart from that, Albert Patrick Nugent (1825-1897), under the name of "Lužan Kapetan", was the hero of a Montenegrin folk epic about Omer Pasha's attack on Montenegro (1857), based on which we can assume that he took part in that battle. After his retirement, Patrick lived in Kostel, near Karlovac, and in Zagreb.

Certainly isolated, albeit interesting information about Albert Nugent was published by Jaroslav Šidak. This information partially explains the unusual political and military engagement of Albert Nugent, before he moved to

---

[110] Ivan Mužić, *Masonstvo u Hrvata, (Croatian Freemasonry)*, VIII revised edition, Split 2005. pp. 28-29. Mužić states that Janko Drašković was a member of the Parisian lodge *Philanthropes Reunis (L'union philanthropique)*. p. 28. Josip Kolanović,"Jedana sporna epizoda iz života Maksimilijana Vrhovca",("A Controversial Episode from the Life of Maksimilijan Vrhovac"), *Croatia cristiana periodica*, 7/1981. pp. 1-28. In 1832, Janko Drašković (1770–1856) issued "Velika Ilirija",(*The Great Illyria)*, in the Shtokavian dialect, including therein Croatia-Slavonia, Rijeka, Military Frontier, Dalmatia and Slovenia, the so-called inner Austria. R. A. Kann, *Eastern Habsburg Landes 1526-1918*. vol. VI, 1984, p. 265.

Paris.[111] It appears that it concerned top-secret policies, about which data occasionally appear in various sources.

Šidak points out that what Prince Metternich, Laval Nugent's friend, found disconcerting was not so much Albert Nugent's interest in *Illyrian* matters, nor his secret visits to Belgrade and cooperation with Ljudevit Gaj, but his links to the *Propaganda* (1844), a secret society of Polish immigrants with headquarters in Paris. In 1833, the society was founded by the Polish Prince Adam Czartoryski, and it was headquartered in his Paris palace, the so-called *Lambert Hotel*.

Václav Žáček and Jaroslav Šidak also mention Albert Nugent. They write about the foreign policy of the non-existent Polish state led by Adam Czartoriyski from Paris, with financial help from the *Grand Orient of France*.[112]

Václav Žáček mentions the diplomatic mission of a Polish man, Janusz Woronicz, carried out according to Czartoriyski's instructions, drafted on June 27, 1845, according to which Janusz Woronicz was supposed to go to Hungary via Rijeka, and there to incite to rebellion those Slavic peoples who were included in Czartoriyski's project (Serbia, Romania, Bulgaria, Croatia, Bosnia, Montenegro). Czartoriyski's policy—probably aided by the *Grand Orient of France*—was aimed at creating a buffer zone around the Russian area of influence and building a network of agents who would collect important data for independent Polish state made up of parts of the Russian, Austrian and German empires.

---

[111] Jaroslav Šidak,"Hotel Lambert i Hrvati",("Lambert Hotel and the Croats,"), *Studije iz hrvatske povijesti XIX stoljeća*. (*Studies of Croatian XIX Century History*), Zagreb, 1973, pp. 167-177. Ljubiša Doklestić, Prilog istraživanju oslobodilačkkih akcija na Balkanu u 40-tim godinama XIX stoljeća" ("Contribution to the research of liberation operations in the 1840s Balkans"), *Historijski zbornik 37* (1), 1984, pp. 1-30

[112] Václav Žáček, "Tajni polšti agenti v Horvatsku před r. 1848. *Historijski zbornik*, XXIX-XXX, 1976-77. pp. 295-307. Jaroslav Šidak, "The Secret Policy" of Lj. Gaj and the creation of his "Memoranda" to Prince Metternich 1846-47 pp. 195- 220 and "Lambert Hotel and the Croats," pp. 167-177. In: *Studies of Croatian XIX Century History,* Zagreb. 1973. Adam Czartoryski is mentioned as a Russian (since at the time a part of Poland belonged to Russia) and a Freemason by Russian author V. I. Starcev,В. И. СТАРЦЕВ, *РУССКОЕ ПОЛИТИЧЕСКОЕ МАССОНСТВО II ВЕК. ТРЕТА РОССИЯ*, С. ПЕТЕРБУРГ, 1996. pp. 19-20.

The first on the list of collaborators with Janusz Woronicz in Croatia was Ljudevit Gaj, the "Great Illyrian". However, both he and his actions were discredited by other Illyrians—librarian Babukić and Count Janko Drašković. Janko Drašković, who belonged to the Parisian *Philanthropes Reunis Lodge, L'Union philanthropique,* painted Gaj as a charlatan.[113]

According to a report by the Governor of Rijeka, Pal Kiss (1837–1848), to the Hungarian Palatine Stephen, the goal of *Illyrian politics* was the secession of Rijeka and the littoral from Hungary and its unification with Croatia. Prince Metternich encouraged the conflict between "Illyrianism" and "Hungarianism," fearing the strengthening of Croatian national consciousness through the conflict with "Hungarianism". Under his influence, in 1843, the Croatian parliament forbade the use of the adjective "Illyrian," to avoid the articulation and organization of a political party bearing this name as a national party.

Metternich exercised his influence to qualify "Illyrianism" as a literary term and this is the reason why he supported Gaj financially. This was at the same time a policy of opposing Russia's influence on Slavic peoples.

The *Illyrian movement* received financial aid from Smith and Meynie, paper mill owners and Freemasons of the British *Grand Lodge* that operated within the grounds of the paper mill. This means that it did not operate publicly, and only one piece of information is known about it.

Danilo Klen, a Croatian historian from Rijeka, states that Count Janko Drašković, leader of the movement, praised the Rijeka paper mill in his "dissertation," as did Juraj Šporer in the *Illyrian Morning Star.* In his travelogue "The Littoral and Lika," Ljudevit Vukotinović praised both the mill and Rijeka, and *Neven* magazine, which published the travelogue, was said to have been printed on the paper manufactured by the Rijeka paper mill. It can be assumed that the printing paper was a given away as a gift.

A notice sent by the mill's steering board to Ljudevit Gaj's wife in 1853 when he was arrested in Prague on allegations of high treason speaks in favor of the mill's support of the *Illyrian movement.* The steering board notified

---

[113] Ivan Mužić, op.cit. p. 28.

Gaj's wife that they would not "protest" the three outstanding bills of exchange to the amount of 2,000 forints and that they would continue working with her as usual.[114]

The wave of revolutions that started with the revolution in Paris (February 22, 23, and 24, 1848), continued with the revolution in Milan (March 2), Vienna (March 13), Venice (March 17) and Berlin (March 18) and demanded swift and organized reaction from the reigning feudal class.

The recourse to the professional army in the Habsburg lands was all the more dramatic because the Hungarian Revolution, led by Lajos Kossuth, put up a fierce resistance, until August 1849, when Russian troops of Nicholas I came to the aid of Austria and defeated the Hungarian revolutionary government at Világos. The professional army that Ferdinand I needed to quell the revolution was a good opportunity for professional soldiers such as Laval and Albert Nugent. Both sided with the Croats and Ban Jelačić. The assignments carried out directly by Laval and Albert Nugent between March 1848 and November 1848 are described in 126 letters exchanged between Albert Nugent and various people who were engaged in combat against the Hungarians (Jelačić, Gaj, Mayerhofer, the Austrian consul in Belgrade and others).

What bears the most importance is his cooperation with the army of Ban Jelačić, until November 23, 1848, when he joined the viceroy's army near Vienna.

The most interesting letter is dated June 17, 1848, and was sent by General August Jochmus from Vienna to Albert Nugent, in which he predicts an important role that Croatia was to play in the forthcoming events that were to take place in Slavonia, Bosnia and Serbia. The general mentions "Illyria", foreseeing its splendid future, if it were to remain closely connected to Austria. This is to say that the letter confirms the role that Albert Nugent played in the secret policy, directed from Trsat Castle and the city of Karlovac towards Bosnia, which was at the time under Ottoman rule.[115]

---

[114] Danilo Klen, *Tvornica papira, (Rijeka Paper Mill)*, (year of publication unknown), p. 42.

[115] Ferdo Hauptmann, "Count Albert Nugent's Correspondence from 1848," in *Arhivist*, Belgrade, No 1/1951. pp. 21-56, Josip Neustädter, op.cit.

C. THE 1848/49 REVOLUTION IN RIJEKA

At the beginning of the Hungarian Revolution there were no more Freemasons left in Rijeka. Adamić had died in 1828, Leard in 1831, and Laval Nugent was still alive but no longer in Rijeka. Paul Scarpa and Josip de Susanni were what remained of the old Freemasons.

Until April 1848, the city was still run by the patrician council. However, town councilors were elected based on limited suffrage. These were Antonio Celebrini, Giovanni Kobler, Giovanni Martini, Fran-

The de Susanni family crest

cesco Kuktzkaj and Giuseppe Emili. Rijeka saw peaceful changes adopted by the Hungarian Revolution, abolishing the town patricians' privileges regarding the election of town councilors. The main goal of the remaining patricians was to preserve the town's autonomy.

On June 24, 1848, the General Assembly of Rijeka and the Littoral elected Josip de Susanni as representative in the Diet of Hungary in capacity as its first official national representative. De Susanni soon arrived in the capital city and handed in his credentials.[116] He strived to keep Rijeka within Hungary and in that capacity he collected data about the supporters of the Hungarian Revolution.

The elected representatives of Dalmatia that was represented in Vienna travelled to the Diet in Vienna, and de Susanni, in a confidential letter dated August 8, informed Lajos Batthyany, the revolutionary Prime Minister of Hungary, about his idea to promote Hungarian interests in Dalmatia.

---

[116] Lajos Horvàth, "Representative of Rijeka at the Diet of Hungary 1848-49," in *Gazette of the State Archive in Rijeka*, volume XLI-XLII. /2000, pp. 127-133, Lajos Horvàth, op.cit.

Rijeka was attacked by the Croatian army on August 31, 1848, marking the beginning of interventions against the Hungarian Revolution. That same day, not waiting for orders from Jelačić, Josip Bunjevac, banal commissioner for Rijeka entered Rijeka. Nevertheless, Josip Jelačić, the commander in chief, commended him.

Pál Kiss, the Governor of Rijeka, left the town in July 1848, and was replaced by János Nepomuk III Erdödy, a nobleman from Varaždin. However, on September 1, 1848, Erdödy too fled Rijeka, accompanied by the supporters of the Hungarian regime, following his unsuccessful attempt to keep Rijeka under the crown of Hungary and after having organized the *National Guard* as part of the *Honved*, the *Hungarian National Guard* that was the newly created army during the Revolution. The remaining Hungarian officials at the governor's office did not contact Zagreb; even the imperial appointment of Josip Jelačić (1801–1859) as the civil Governor of Rijeka (December 3, 1848) arrived with a month's delay.

The Croatian parliament enacted a decision to cut its connections with the Diet of Hungary.

The citizens of Rijeka tried to preserve the town's autonomy, on the basis of its historical right as *corpus separatum*. Pietro (Junior) Scarpa, son of Iginio Scarpa, was in command of the town guard, and Tosoni, the vice-captain, signed the conditions for the continuity of Rijeka's independence.[117]

Neustädter, who is often the only source about the events in Rijeka in 1848, writes in favor of Pietro Scarpa, the young head of the town guard and of his family as well-known supporters of the (Austrian) Emperor. He points out that it was exactly because of this loyalty to the Emperor that the Scarpa family fell into disfavor with the Hungarians. Even though he commanded a 200-men-strong national guard battalion, Pietro Scarpa Junior was acceptable to the newly appointed Croatian administration as a partner who helped organize the peaceful annexation of Rijeka to Croatia.

---

[117] Josip Neustädter, *Ban Jelačić and Events in Croatia from 1848,* op.cit.

Neustädter points out that he alone was to be credited for the peaceful transition from the Hungarian to Croatian administration. Neustädter did not know, or did not mention that the entire Scarpa family were Freemasons.[118]

The Hungarian (revolutionary) Diet of December 31, 1848 decided that it would be temporarily relocated to Debrecen, because Windischgrätz's troops were approaching. On the following day, the revolutionaries and parliamentary representatives left Pest.

Josip de Susanni did not go to Debrecen with the Hungarian revolutionaries, and was therefore not compromised. However, he retreated in 1849 to Kršan, his estate in Istria. He was promoted to a new office in 1857, but was relieved of his office in 1861 and retired in 1864. He died in 1880, as the last among the Freemasons from Rijeka in the first part of the nineteenth century.

According to Rudolf Horvat, who does not state the sources for his book, in 1851—which is to say at the time of the Croatian administration of the Rijeka county—the town of Rijeka and the Rijeka county had 12,598 inhabitants with the following national composition: Croats, 11,584, Italians, 691, Hungarians, 76, Germans, 52, Czechs, 48, English, 13, and French, 10.[119]

---

[118] The Scarpa family (three brothers) originated from Venice. Paolo settled in Rijeka in around 1778 and in 1787 started a venture with Carl Muschler. In 1798, he became a citizen of Rijeka, and obtained patrician councilor status in 1803. As of 1802, he was Vice Consul of the *Kingdom of Naples* and Mayor of Rijeka during the *Illyrian Provinces,* more precisely from March 7, 1812 to August 26, 1813. He is listed, together with Adamić, as a member of the lodge opened in Leard's vineyard in 1813. He had one son, Iginio, who became Vice Consul of Denmark in 1822, patrician councilor of Rijeka in 1823 and Knight of the Austrian Empire in 1823. Iginio Scarpa was a merchant with immaculate credentials and chairman of the Chamber of Commerce. He owned the *Angiolina* villa, constructed in Opatija, still standing today. He had two sons: Paolo (+1884), member of the *Rappresentanza*, Vice Consul of Denmark and Pietro, a captain in the Austrian Army. In the 1848 Revolution, he was in command of the Rijeka battalion of the National Guard. He was friends with Michele Melissino, a cadet in the Russian Army and the executor of his father's will in Michele's absence.
Antonio Scarpa, brother of the first Paolo, was a naturalized Austrian during the French regime in 1806. He married the daughter of de Emilio, an attorney. In 1823, he became a patrician councilor and then Consul of Toscana. He was a grain merchant, and during the 1852–1872 period he owned a workshop that produced gas. Vincenzo, Paolo's and Antonio's brother, was just a merchant. Giovanni Kobler, op.cit. vol. III, p. 180, Irvin Lukežić,*Povijest riječkih konzulata, (History of Consulates of Rijeka),* Rijeka, 2004. pp. 71-75. Attilio Depoli, op.cit.p. 59.

[119] Rudolf Horvat,*Politička povijest grada Rijeke,(Political History of the City of Rijeka.* Rijeka, 1907. p. 35.

Josip Bunjevac was appointed viceroy's commissioner in Rijeka, to replace Josip Jelačić during his absence. All other authorities were subordinated to the *Viceroy's Council* in Zagreb. The harshly imposed centralization, and the imposed "loan" of 50,000 forints for military purposes and 4,000 forints in silver for the replacement of banknotes, motivated the organization of the first autonomy movement of Rijeka and the appearance of Mazzini's supporters (1854). Riots became more frequent in Rijeka (1854), and on November 1, 1859 the Mayor of Rijeka wrote a report about the citizens' despondency because of the riots in Italy. He claimed that the riots in Italy halted maritime traffic in the port of Rijeka.

In 1861, armed conflicts began between citizens of Rijeka and the army. The populace demanded that the regiments be replaced immediately and issued a proclamation demanding independence.[120]

Ban Šokčević replaced the deceased Ban Jelačić, and remained in that office until June 27, 1867, i.e. until the Austro-Hungarian Compromise.

According to Naustädter, Count Albert Nugent, Jelačić's fellow fighter, secretly left Croatia in 1860. Ciotta, Martini, Randić and Verneda, representatives of Rijeka failed to make their appearance at the 1861 session of the Croatian Parliament. Allegedly they were absent because of a secret and complex operation.

The 1867 Austro-Hungarian Compromise came amidst this political turmoil in Rijeka. "The secret operation" was then repeated.

---

[120] Croatian State Archives, Croatian-Slavonian governorship fund (1854–1861), Presidential records.

4

FREEMASONRY AND RIJEKA DURING THE DUAL MONARCHY

1. HUNGARIAN POLITICAL EMIGRATION AND THE REBIRTH OF FREEMASONRY IN HUNGARY

There is no reliable data on whether Hungarian or foreign Freemasons took part in or gave impetus to the evolution that spread to some countries within Hungary, even though there are indications that there were some attempts at doing so. One of those attempts took place in 1848.

In 1845, August M. Thoma, a trader in musical instruments originally from Prussia–Silesia, operating in Pest, was admitted to the *Truth and Friendship (Zur Wahrheit und Freundschaft) Lodge*. In Pest, he gathered members of foreign lodges in an attempt to establish a lodge that would be under the protection of the German national lodge. Since during the *Metternich Era* it was impossible to obtain the permission to open a lodge, on June 26, 1848, a Hungarian lodge was founded in Frankfurt, under the name of *Ludwig Kossuth zur Morgenrote des höheren Licht*, but L. Kossuth's name was immediately omitted. Thoma became the master of the lodge, but the lodge was shut down in 1849.[121]

---

[121] Eugen Lennhoff/Oscar Posner, *Internationales Freimaurerlexikon*, Zürich, Leipzig, Wien, 1932. p. 1615.

Both pieces of data point to the potential Masonic involvement in the Hungarian Revolution.

Jaroslav Šidak states that on April 18, 1849, while the Hungarian Revolution was still in progress, an agreement was reached in Paris between Adam Czartoriyski, the Polish prince in exile, and the emissaries of the Hungarian revolutionary government to Paris and London, Count Lászlo Teleki and Ferenz Pulszki. According to this agreement, in the event that the Hungarian Revolution was successful, the autonomy of Croatia, Vojvodina and the Romanian Erdély would be completely guaranteed, and as autonomous units they would be in confederacy with the Hungarian crown. Jaroslav Šidak points out the informal character of this agreement, and that Ferenz Pulszki's position was not genuine, because the Hungarians were pursuing their own cause.[122]

After the unsuccessful completion of the Hungarian Revolution (August 1849), the Hungarian political emigration was welcomed by and found support in the countries where they settled temporarily, mostly because of the heroic role that they played in the collapse of the Habsburg dictatorship or because the other countries had further political plans to fight against Austria. In the beginning, Hungarian refugees got most of their funding from Napoleon III, who sent three million francs to Lajos Kossuth, at that time already an exile in London. The money was intended for Kossuth's relocation to Genova, together with his supporters, and for his return to Hungary, via Rijeka and the Danubian Principalities, where he would resume his fight against Austria.

According to the same author, Gyula Andrassy was the person through whom sums of money were disbursed to the Hungarian revolutionaries. He claims that in Istanbul, during the flight of the leadership of Kossuth's Government, Andrassy received 1800 ducats from a man named Brown and another 600 ducats for his trip to Turin.

After a short stay in London, Andrassy settled in Paris where he met György Klapka, Miklos Esterhazy and Kasimir Batthyany, the foreign affairs minister in Lajos Kossuth's government. Andrassy also appears to have visited the

---

[122] Jaroslav Šidak, Lambert Hotel and the Croats, op.cit. p. 173.

Saint-Cyr military academy of Paris.[123]

According to the deal made with Napoleon III, or regardless of it, a number of the refugees sought political exile in the Piedmont, more precisely in Turin. A large group of mostly military officers settled there and established a *Hungarian battalion*. This battalion later evolved into the *Hungarian National Directorate*, a sort of a government-in-exile that was headquartered in Turin, where Kossuth also lived.

The larger part of the Hungarian battalion was not under the command of Lajos Kossuth and the *Hungarian National Directorate*, but fought together with Giuseppe Garibaldi's Army. The Italian *War of Independence* (1859–1861) gave hope to Hungarian refugees that Napoleon III, together with the Piedmont, would expand his operations to Hungary as well, and on September 10-12, 1860, they secretly negotiated about joining forces to fight against Austria. An alliance was forged between Count Camillo Benso di Cavour, who was at the time Prime Minister of the *Kingdom of Piedmont-Sardinia* and the *Hungarian National Directorate* represented by Lajos Kossuth, General György Klapka and Laszlo Teleki.[124]

Unlike Klapka and Teleki, who were Freemasons, Lajos Kossuth was not a Freemason, but became one at his own request during his 1851/52 stay in the USA, at forty-nine years of age. On February 18, 1852, he petitioned the *Cincinnati Lodge No. 133* of Cincinnati, asking to be admitted to Freemasonry, stating that he could not list his permanent place of residence because, being committed to the fight for Hungarian independence, he was in exile. Another four of his fellow fighters joined his petition and all of them were admitted in an expedited procedure to American Freemasonry. Later on, when he remained in exile in Turin, Lajos Kossuth was admitted in 1860 to the local

---

[123] Eduard von Wertheimer, *Graf Julius Andrassy, sein Leben und seine Zeit.* Stuttgart, 1910. I. Band, p. 5, 51, 67.

[124] Lajos Lukacz, *Chapters on the Hungarian Political Emigration 1849–1867*, Budapest, 1997. Ljiljana Aleksić – Pejković, Politika Italije prema Srbiji do 1870., (*pItaly's policy towards Serbia to 1870)*, Belgrade, 1979. Attilio Depoli, "La Parentesi costituzionale a Fiume nel 1861," in *La crisi dell' Impero austriaco dopo Villafranca.* Atti del XXXV Congresso di storia del Risorgimento italiano, Roma, 1959, pp. 275–303.

Ausonia Lodge.[125] György Klapka was also admitted to the *Ausonia Lodge.*

Klapka was born in Timisoara (1820–1892). In the 1848/1849 Revolution he led the northern Hungarian army and distinguished himself in the battles of Kápolna and Komárom, which is why he was promoted to the rank of general. Between the collapse of the Revolution and the 1867 amnesty, he lived in exile in Italy, France and Switzerland. In 1862, he was admitted, together with Ferenz Pulszky, Stefan Tür and Ferenz Kossuth (who were until then members of the *Ausonia Lodge)* into the newly founded *Dante Alighieri* Lodge in Turin. The following year he became member of the Hungarian lodge in Genova, named *Ister.* After his return to Hungary, Klapka was member of the *Korvin Matias* Lodge. He worked together with Kossuth and Tür to establish the *Grand Orient of Hungary,* and the *High Council of Hungary,* which is to say an order of the Scottish ritual. The *Korvin Matias* Lodge made him an honorary member.[126]

Count Teleki von Szék (1791–1855) was the Governor of Erdély from 1840 to 1848. Together with Kossuth, he organized the *Hungarian National Directorate* in 1859. A bilateral agreement between Cavour and the Hungarian battalion provided for the financial help given from the Piedmont to the Hungarian battalion, so that they may return to Hungary via Serbia and Romania and fight against Austria.[127]

It appears that Count Teleki, on behalf of the *Hungarian National Directorate,* with the help from his "brothers" Lajos and Counts Theodor Károly, Theodor and Koloman Csáky, Johann Teleki, Stephan Esterhásy and Baron Adalbert Vay, contacted the *Grand Lodge of Germany* in Hamburg in 1861 and asked them for protection for the *Szent István* Lodge. The language of the lodge was supposed to be Hungarian. However, the lodge from Ham-

---

[125] William R. Denslow, *10,000 Famous Freemasons,* 2002. vol. III, pp. 43-44. Giordano Gamberini, *Mille volti di massoni.* Roma, 1975, p. 115.

[126] Von Lenning, *Algemeines Handbuch der Freimaurerei. Encyclopädie der Freimaurerei,* op.cit.p. 541, idem, p. 35. Aldo A. Mola, *Storia della massoneria italiana dalle origini ai nostri giorni.* 1994. pp. 66, 69.

[127] idem, vol IV. p. 92.

burg requested that it be German. Since the majority of the "brothers" agreed that the language of the lodge should be Hungarian, the lodge was never established.[128] The disbanding of Garibaldi's troops, the declaration of the *Kingdom of Italy* and Cavour's death (March 17, 1861), and, above all, differences between Lajos Kossuth and the other leaders of the Hungarian battalion changed the relationships and positions of various leaders of the battalion. Consequently, in 1863, a new body, *Pest Revolutionary Committee*, was formed by the political emigration, as a secret organization headed by some of the old and some new members—Klapka, Komáromý and Csaky.

Ferenz Pulszky

However, at the same time when the international political situation was changed, changes were made to the Hungarian Freemasonry in exile. A Hungarian lodge named *Ister* was established in Genova, in which General György Klapka was appointed "Master of the Throne" which naturally raises the question if the *Pest Revolutionary Committee* was simply a secular name used by the lodge.

Until the emigrant *Ister* Lodge was formed, Hungarian Freemasons who settled in the Piedmont were admitted to and operated from the Italian *Dante Alighieri* Lodge.

Ferenz Pulszky (1814–1889) was the political leader of the Hungarian Freemasons organized within this lodge. He was a politician, art historian and an attorney, and Lajos Kossuth's personal secretary.

---

[128] Eugen Lennhoff/Oscar Posner, op.cit., p. 1615.

Since he was internationally famous, and had developed friendships with the most prominent individuals and intellectuals in various western European countries, he was tasked with raising funds intended for the return to Hungary.[129]

When Otto von Bismarck (1815–1898), thanks to whom the reorganization of the Prussian Army was initiated, was appointed Chancellor of Prussia (1862), the leaders of the *Pest Revolutionary Committee* saw an opportunity that was not to be missed. Bit by bit, they started moving away to Prussia, where they played the decisive role in the *Austro–Prussian war* of 1866. On August 2, 1866, under the command of General Klapka, the well-organized, although decimated Hungarian battalion returned to Hungary in triumph.

Austria's defeat in the war with Prussia in 1867 forced Austria to abolish the German confederacy and to change the structure of the state as it was at the time. This division created the real union of the two countries: Austria *(Cisleithania)* and Hungary *(Transleithania)*. Each of them had its own administration, constitution and parliament. The issues of foreign policy, army and finances were decided upon jointly.

The militant group of political emigrants who remained in exile never acknowledged the Compromise achieved in 1867 and the Dual Monarchy that was created thereby. This group, headed by Lajos Kossuth, remained abroad and as such became the symbol of the incomplete revolution.

While those members of the political emigration who returned to Hungary thrusted themselves vehemently into political life, members of the political emigration who remained abroad were in a position of *splendid isolation*. The zest that swept through the ranks of the political emigration that returned to Hungary was shared by the Hungarian Freemasonry, since it was almost the matter of identity between the new ruling class and the leaders of Freemasons. The identity was visible everywhere, but the most obvious example was the moment when in January 1867, Emperor Franz Joseph appointed Count

---

[129] János György Szilágy, "A Forty–Eighter's. Vita Contemplativa. Ferenz Pulszky (1814–1889)," in *The Hungarian Quarterly*, vol. 39, spring, 1998. p. 3-17.

Gyula Andrassy as prime minister, who was a French Freemason and a political emigrant sentenced to die in exile.[130]

Given that the Rijeka question had not been resolved under the *Compromise 1867*, those Freemasons in the corridors of power launched a campaign to win over prominent citizens of Rijeka in order to argue for, and if possible, gain the support of the town's citizens for abolishment of the legal status that tied Rijeka to Croatia and a return to its pre 1848 Revolution status. Hungarian historian Aladar Fest has written about this campaign.[131]

Four secret letters were sent by Baron Jozsef Eötvös (1813–1871), who was at the time minister for public education, to a prominent navy captain of Rijeka, nobleman and consul of various states, Luigi Francovich (1832-1888), in the period between July 17, 1865 and February 8, 1867.

This is the period when Ferenz Deák, the acknowledged leader of the Hungarian liberals, published his program of compromise with Austria, after secret negotiations with an emissary of Franz Joseph on April 16, 1865. The matter of the status of Rijeka was at the time at the center of interest of the new political class, and Eötvös contacted Francovich on their behalf—it is unknown when and where—making secret suggestions on how to organize elections in Rijeka, and then obstruct the Rijeka delegates to the Croatian parliament, as it had already been done in 1861.

---

[130] Gyula Andrassy, a Hungarian political emigrant in Paris, where he joined the Mont Sinai Lodge of the Scottish order, made himself available to Hungarian political emigrants as of 1854. Eugen Lennhoff, *Die Freimaurer,* München, Amaltea Verlag, Zürich, Leipzig, Wien, 1926, p. 297. Von Lenning points out that, having returned to his homeland, Andrassy shied away from the Freemasons. This probably refers to the time in his career when he was in Vienna. However, thanks to him the lodges secured legal grounds on which to operate. Lenning, op.cit.p. 35.

[131] Aladar Fest, "Il barone Giuseppe Eötvös e la questione di Fiume," in *Bulletino della Deputazione fiumana di Storia patria*, vol. II. 1913, pp. 215–257. Baron József Eötvös (1813–1871.) was a Hungarian statesman and writer who entered civil service after having completed his legal studies. He travelled across Germany, France and England between 1835 and 1837 to learn about the institutions in these countries. He was acquainted with many prominent figures in these countries. He took part in the 1848/49 Revolution, but having disagreed with Kossuth, he chose Munich as his place of exile from 1848–1851. In the first post-Compromise Hungarian Government, he was minister for education. After 1866, he was chairman of the Hungarian Academy of Science. Josip Neustädter, Ban Jelačić, op.cit.p. 434.

To finalize this agreement, Francovich went to Pest, where he met not only with Eötvös, but with General Klapka as well, and then became an *intimus* to him and started a rich correspondence that, as pointed out by Aladar Fest, "fell into the hands of the foreigners".

Francovich visited Ferenz Deák as well, became a confidant of Menyhért Lónyay's, who later became minister for finance, while in Rijeka he later co-operated with Giovanni Ciotta and Luigi Peretti, and the *Unionist Party* of Croatia and the *Liberal Party* of Hungary.[132]

Following Andrassy's suggestion, on February 19, 1867, Gaspar Matcovich and those who shared his beliefs organized protests in Rijeka demanding the immediate unification of Rijeka and Hungary.[133]

These protests were "helpful" to—if they had not been previously arranged by—Francovich, who was in Pest at the time, where he was privately received on March 27, 1867 by the newly appointed Prime Minister Gyula Andrassy, to agree with him in which manner the memorandum about the future posi-

---

[132] Luigi Francovich de Bersez (1833–1888) spent his studies in Vienna and travelled almost the entire "civilized" world. He entered consular service in 1856 as Vice Consul of the Kingdom of Belgium, and in 1879 he became Consul of Portugal. He received several medals (Order of the Iron Crown Third Class, Knight of the Holy Sepulchre (San Sepolcro) and the Spanish Order of Isabella the Catholic). He was one of the founders of *Casino Patriotico* of Rijeka, shareholder and a director of the *Adria Maritime Association* in 1888. His father, Giovanni Francovich, was leader of the eighth squadron of the national guard in Rijeka at the time of the 1848 Revolution, which recommended Luigi Francovich as an "offspring of a well-known Hungarian patriotic family". The Francovich family owned houses in Rijeka, as can be seen from cadastral books in the 1785 land census, although we do not know how Giovanni and Luigi Francovich were related to Helena Francovich de Bersez, the owner of two dwellings. She was a member of Venetian nobility recognized in the sixteenth century. After his services for the return of Rijeka to the Hungarian crown, in 1879 the Francovich family was awarded the title of *Knights of the Austrian Empire*. Riccardo Gigante described the family coat of arms. In the secret action, agreed between Luigi Francovich and Eötvös, it was Gaspare Matcovich who acted as the second participant, being a member of the sixteenth squadron of the Rijeka national guard, commanded by Iginio Scarpa. Paolino Scarpa was also in its ranks, who asked Luigi Francovich for a recommendation to meet Andrassy. The name of Ürmeny Ladislao, who was leader of the fourth squadron in Rijeka is interesting, although we do not know who he was. He may have been a son or a relation of the Hungarian governor bearing the same last name. Silvino Gigante, "La guardia nazionale del XLVIII," in *Bulletino della Deputazione fiumana di storia patria*, vol. Fiume, 1913. pp. 177–214.

[133] Ljubinka Toševa Karpowicz, "Biografia politica di un personaggio controverso," in *Quaderni*, Rovigno, vol. XIII, 2001. p. 353–367.

tion of Rijeka was to be handed in to the
Emperor. Naturally, after his two hour
meeting with Andrassy, Francovich had
lunch with Eötvös, who was probably
the one who arranged this meeting.

At the same time, Paolino Scarpa,
son of Iginio Scarpa, the former commander of the Rijeka battalion of the
(revolutionary) national guard, was in
Pest, and he asked Francovich to intro-
duce him to Andrassy.

Andrassy's secret actions with representatives of the "pro-Hungarian Party"
in Rijeka were intensified in the period
between January 1868 and October of the

Luigi Francovich

same year, and resulted in the Croatian-Hungarian Compromise, the so-called
Riječka krpica (the Rijeka Patch)—a breach of the constitution and a specific
state and legal forgery. Supporters from Rijeka (Randić, Scarpa, Ciotta, probably
Francovich as well), chosen by Andrassy, played a significant role in this secret
policy. If the correspondence between Francovich and Eötvös and Klapka were
accessible to researchers, perhaps the question of how the Rijeka Patch came to
be attached to the original would have been answered in a different manner.

It is interesting that all persons mentioned in the Francovich – Eötvös correspondence were Hungarian Freemasons. This piece of data perhaps did not refer
to Francovich, but he, being a "man of the world" could have been a member of
a (Hungarian) lodge in exile before the Hungarian Freemasonry came back to
the country.

The "awakening" of the Hungarian lodges started immediately upon the return of some of the emigrants. The first lodge to be established was *Einigkeit im
Vaterlande* (Unity in Fatherland) on June 26, 1868, with a British lodge patent
recognizing its founding. The language of the lodge was German, and Ludwig
Lewis was Master of the lodge. After him, Ferenz Pulszky became master of the
lodge, having returned to Hungary and left Kossuth back in Turin.

Szent István was the next lodge to be "awakened" the following year, and its language was Hungarian. During the next two years, another five lodges were "awakened", reaching the necessary number to establish a national lodge. Owing to this fact, on January 30, 1870, the "awakened" and newly established lodges renewed the *Ungarische Symbolische Johaniss–Grossloge* (the Symbolic Grand Lodge of Hungary). Ferenz Pulszky was elected its Grand Master. The French Freemasonry of the *Grand Orient* order helped the Hungarian Freemasons who were members of lodges in Paris. *Corvin Mátyás az igazságos,* the first Hungarian lodge abroad in the *Grand Orient order,* was constituted on May 23 1861, by a statute approved by *the Grand Orient of France.* Its members were: Count Theodor Czaky, Generals György Klapka, István Tür, and others. General Tür was the first master of the throne. The *Humbolt Lodge* was opened that same year, with German as its official language.

The process of constituting new lodges was continued in various towns in Hungary, making it possible in 1871 to establish the *Grand Orient of Hungary* by way of a patent issued by France. The Grand Master of the *Grand Orient* was Georg von Joanovics, who until his death played an important part in Hungarian Freemasonry (in particular in that of the Scottish order) among the Slavs of the Dual Monarchy, and among those in the Balkans.[134]

From the moment he assumed office as Grand Master, Georg von Joanovics strove to unite both orders. They were further polarized during the Franco-Prussian war of 1870–71. The two rituals were only unified on March 21, 1886. At that time, the *Grand Lodge of the Scottish Order* consisted of thirty-seven lodges, and the *Grand Orient* of thirty.

The unification of both orders was not approved by all lodges in Hungary. It was accepted by twenty-six lodges of the Scottish ritual, and approved by only sixteen lodges of the *Grand Orient.* The unification created a Masonic

---

[134] Georg von Joanovics (1821–1909) was a well-known scientist and member of the Austrian parliament (*Reichstag*) 1847 /48. After the collapse of the Revolution, he went to exile. He was sentenced in absentia to twelve years' imprisonment. After the 1867 amnesty, he was once again a member of parliament and then state secretary at the Ministry of Education and Worship. He became the first Grand Master of unified rituals and remained in that office until his death. Lennhoff /Possner, *Internationales Freimaurerlexikon,* op.cit. p. 1616.

body of thirty-nine lodges with 1,831 members, creating the *Symbolic Grand Lodge of Hungary*. **Ferencz** Pulszky was its Grand Master over the next ten years, whereas Georg von Joanovics was its honorary Grand Master. Hungary was at that time a country with a very dense network of lodges.[135]

How dominant a role Pulszky, and through him the German and above all Prussian Freemasonry, played in Hungary can be concluded from the fact that Pulszky, even though he retired after having led the Hungarian Freemasonry for twenty years, remained the representative of the famous Berlin *Zu den drei Weltkugeln* Lodge at the *Symbolic Grand Lodge of Hungary*.[136]

Freemasonry was in a completely different situation in Austria. Given that lodges there were humanitarian organizations by definition, they had to work without employing the Masonic rituals. The most important among the lodges was the Humanitas organization, recognized by the *Grand Orient of Italy* as the *Grand Lodge of Austria*.[137]

The *Humanitas Lodge* had around thirty to fifty members who met eight times a month in regular meetings. They prepared the admission of new members and followers of the Grand Master, but the lodge's work was carried out in **Pozsony** (now Bratislava, **Slovakia**).

At the time the *Symbolic Grand Lodge of Hungary* was founded, the lodge and its Grand Masters were so highly motivated that they wanted to expand

---

[135] *Bericht der Symbolischen Grossloge von Ungarn über ihre Tätigkeit, Geschäfts– und Kassagebahrung im Jahre 1897*, Budapest, 1898.

[136] **Ferencz** Pulszky (1814–1889) was a world-known archaeologist and, above all, Egyptologist. During the emigration period, he lived and worked in Great Britain, the USA and Italy. Having returned to Pest, he became the first president of the *Association of Fine Arts*. In March 1867, he organized an exhibition of exquisite antiquities, of mainly Etruscan and Roman origin. The following year he put his personal collection on exhibition at the Hungarian Academy of Arts (with around 600 visits in two months). The year after that, as a member of Deák's party, he became a member of parliament, director of the *Hungarian National Museum* and the central figure in the field of museology in post-Settlement Hungary. His biography has its dark sides related to the sale of his personal art collection to the *British Museum*. During his life and work with Kossuth in Turin, he was master of the Hungarian Lodge that operated within the *Dante Alighieri* Lodge. János György, "A Forty–Eighter's Vita Contemplativa. **Ferencz** Pulszky (1814–1889)," in *The Hungarian Quarterly*, vol. 39 spring 1998. pp. 3–17.

[137] *Rivista della massoneria italiana*, Roma, 1. V. 1873.

their political actions to neighboring countries. This plan was spearheaded by Prime Minister Gyula (Julius) Andrássy and his collaborator General Klapka.

Hungarian Freemasons were also interested in Croatia.

In 1890, Ivan von Bojničić joined the *Corvin Matias* Lodge in Zagreb. It was Pulszky who pushed for the opening of this lodge.

Later on, Ivan von Bojničić wrote a book about the history of the *Ljubav bližnjega* (Love of the Neighbor) Lodge from Zagreb. Two years later, when Ivan Bojničić traveled to Budapest with a delegation of seven selected Masons from Croatia, the Freemasons from Zagreb not only got admitted to the *Demokratia* Lodge, but also to the temple of the *Symbolic Grand Lodge of Hungary*, where their "brother" Joanovics spoke to them in Croatian which was, according Bojničić, the first and last instance in which this happened in the history of Hungarian Freemasonry.[138]

In 1897, the *Symbolic Grand Lodge of Hungary* obtained the ownership of a large building. They had it decorated with their symbols, and this building accommodated all of their activities—political, philanthropic, scientific and administrative. A "national" report was made up from field reports and it contained data about the Hungarian Freemasonry numbers and their work. The reports reflected the strength, organization and the work of the Freemasonry in the Dual Monarchy.

Such was the strength of Freemasonry that after the unification of the two orders, the *Symbolic Grand Lodge of Hungary* had sixty-seven lodges.[139]

After a period of its intensive work, from 1886 to 1896, another twenty new lodges were opened, but not all of them were always active. There were only forty-one active lodges, with 2,805 "brethren" working in them. During the same year, another 105 "brethren" were admitted, and at the end of 1896, there were 2,910 active members.

As of 1873, twelve lodges were headquartered in Budapest, of which only three operated from private premises, meaning that they had no official head-

---

[138] Ivan von Bojničić, *Die Freimaurerloge "Ljubav bližnjega" in Zagreb*, Zagreb, 1917.

[139] *Bericht der Symbolischen Grossloge von Ungarn*, op.cit.

quarters. It is interesting that one of the oldest lodges, *Mathias Corvin*, headed by Michael Kugler, a railway inspector, operated from private premises. Other heads of lodges in Budapest were: three medical doctors, one industrialist, one architect, and one state administrator, while others were liberal professionals.

Freemasonry in Austria, especially in Vienna, worked exclusively from private premises, with the exception of the lodge in Bratislava, then Hungary (National Hotel).

The three largest lodges in the Habsburg monarchy were *Humanitas, Kömives Kálmán* and *Demokratia*. The largest, *Humanitas*, worked in Bratislava and as of December 31, 1896 had 244 members. The *Kömives Kálmán* Lodge in Budapest was the second largest, with a membership of 205 that in a year grew to 210 members, and the *Demokratia* Lodge in Budapest was the third largest with 164 members, increasing in the following year to 184 members.

The *Freundschaft* Lodge from Budapest had the best financial standing, with assets in the amount of 173,412 forints, liabilities in the amount of 108,389 forints, and a positive difference of 65,023 forints.

The second richest lodge was the *Galilei* from Budapest, with assets in the amount of 135,807 forints, 99,125 in liabilities and 36,682 forints remaining.

No other lodge could ever come close to those two.

Immediately after the headquarters of the *Symbolic Grand Lodge of Hungary* were opened on March 26, and 27, 1896, memories of the deceased "brethren" were published and above all highest honors were given to "brother" Ferencz Pulszky. Not only do the minutes of meetings of the lodge describe him as the central figure of the Freemasonry, but as a person with a wide social and business network that was neither entirely clear, nor involving persons with an immaculate past. This was the reason why, while alive, Pulszky was removed from top Masonic offices, but it does not mean that he distanced himself from Freemasonry.

According to a 1903 report, in comparison with 1896, the number of lodges increased to fifty-nine, and the number of "brethren" rose to 3,713.

When in 1901, the Rijeka lodge, *Sirius,* was established, it had twenty-eight members and was one of the smaller lodges. In 1903, the lodge had thirty-three members. However, the lodge had a large number of third degree Freemasons-twenty-one. The master of the lodge was Artur Steinecker, a

Swiss an who was banchier and director of Kreditbank in Rijeka. The address of the lodge was designated as "private".

By analyzing the minutes kept by the lodges, we can observe ideological differences that arose within the Masonic ranks. The most obvious was the tension between the Hungarian type of liberalism and the issues of Hungarian socialism: the struggle for universal suffrage, the struggle for laws regulating the right to work and the issue of social welfare for workers. Hungarian Freemasonry never accepted the social, nor the socialist program, given that the Hungarian Masons were mostly noblemen and liberal professionals, thus representing

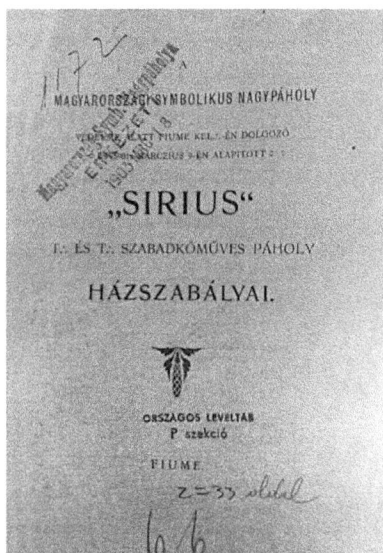

The Constitution of the Sirius Lodge

the national—Catholic or Protestant—liberal political stands. On the other hand, the constant and strong support offered by the German and above all Prussian Freemasonry to Hungarian Freemasons made them always in readiness to provide help, secretly if need be, to the German military Freemasonry in its expansion towards the Balkans.

In the first years after their repatriation, the Hungarian Freemasonry started its publishing activities aimed both at propagating Masonic ideas and disseminating information about what was happening in the lodges.

The following publications were printed:

1. *Hajnal* (Dawning, Sunrise), periodical of the *Grand Orient of Hungary* (1871–1888)
2. *Kelet* (Orient), periodical of the *Symbolic Grand Lodge of Hungary* (1889–1919), *Orient,* the German issue
3. 3. *Dél* (Noon), 1908-1909
4. *Galilei,* political journal published by the Eötvös Lodge (1899)
5. *Világ* (1910–1926), banned in 1926

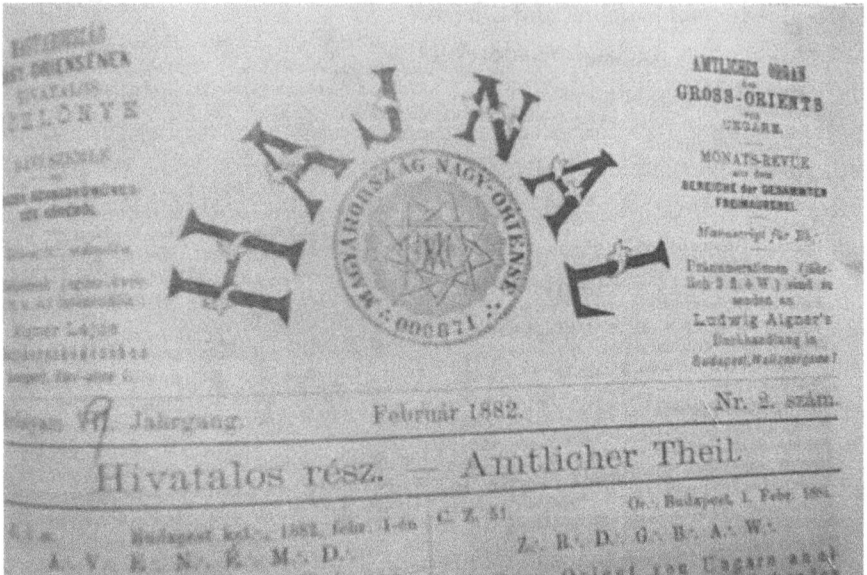

Hajnal (Dawning, Sunshine), periodical of the Grand Orient of Hungary (1871–1888)

Kelet (Orient), periodical of the Symbolic Grand Lodge of Hungary (1889–1919)

2. HUNGARIAN FREEMASONS—LIBERALS, GOVERNORS OF RIJEKA (1875–1905)

When in the second half of 1866, the Hungarian political emigration started returning to the Austrian Empire after twenty years of living and working in Western Europe, they were an ideologically, socially and politically peculiar and non-homogeneous group, even by European standards. Having returned to a country that was increasingly Germanized, the Hungarian Freemasons were not only required to clarify their views on the Habsburgs, but also to define from an ideological point of view the position of the Hungarians in that state. The latter question proved to be the key bone of contention between those Hungarians who remained in the country after the Revolution and those who came back afterwards.

The "left," militant wing of emigrants, represented by the Klapka Legion, opposed the *1867 Austro–Hungarian Compromise*, and this group occupied a marginal position after repatriation. However, the need for foreign capital, their knowledge of economics and their international, above all Masonic contacts, soon made this group the very hub of political life. Apart from that, their contacts with the Prussian Chancellor Otto von Bismarck, thanks to whom they were repatriated, made them even more desirable for cooperation.

Apart from that, the appointment of Count **Gyula** Andrássy (1823–1890) as prime minister (1867–1871), meant that Napoleon III's France would not find the new role of the former revolutionaries who returned to Hungary suspicious.

From the very beginning, Andrássy strove, in the spirit of European liberalism, to create an efficient Diet. The body of representatives consisted of the House of Magnates in which four hundred magnates, priests and lifelong advisors had seats, whereas the House of Representatives consisted of the representatives elected on the basis of a very rigorous election system. The Diet's basic task was to adopt liberal legislation through which constitutional reforms could be implemented.

However, as Andrássy went to Vienna in 1867 to be the first Prime Minister (1867-1871) and Foreign Minister of the Austro-Hungarian Empire

(1871-1879), and then the best representatives of liberalism started dying off or were removed from office for corruption (Lonyay, 1872 and Joseph Szlavy, 1872-74), the five largest banks that remained in Pest after the Settlement went bankrupt, which called Hungary's independence into question.

To avoid collapse, the government took out a one hundred and fifty million forint loan under unfavorable terms from Rothschild's bank.[140]

Due to a fall in popularity after the 1872 elections, Deák's liberals suggested unification with Kálmán Tisza's center-left party and in 1875 the Liberal Party was formed. Kálmán Tisza thus came to power,

Giovanni de Ciotta
in Hungarian magnate robes

where he would remain with his son - Ist遗ván, with a short interruption, until the dissolution of the Dual Monarchy.

Tisza father and son were not Freemasons. However, they did not hesitate to appoint Freemasons to decisive positions in the civil administration. The appointment of the young Sándor Wekerle, a German and a Freemason, as secretary of state in 1887, and two years later as minister for finance provides a good illustration.

It should be noted that Tisza father and son were representatives of the medium-rich landowner class. They protected that class during their rule, whilst leaving trade, banking and manufacturing to the Jews and to the middle class, i.e. the bourgeoisie.

---

[140] Gésa Andreas von Geyr, *Sándor Wekerle 1848–1921*. München, 1993, pp. 105f.,114

In 1872, Rijeka obtained its own statute, based on which it was entitled to choose one administrative body, the *Rappresentanza* (representative body), consisting of fifty-six members, from whose ranks the mayor of the city was chosen. During the *Rappresentanza* elections, Rijeka's representative to the *House of Representatives* of the Diet in Budapest was elected.[141]

At the same time, the parliament in Pest nominated the Governor of Rijeka and *Hungarian-Croatian littoral*. Both of them, the Governor and Mayor of Rijeka, then had to be confirmed by the king.

The first and the most influential Governor of Rijeka, immediately after the Dual Monarchy was established, was Giovanni de Ciotta, an engineer who held office for a total of twenty-four years, from 1872 to 1896. Ciotta was one of the grandchildren of the famous Freemason Andrija Ljudevit Adamić. He was himself a Freemason, admitted to the *Humbolt* Lodge of Budapest in 1871, which however he left in 1894.

Based on a notice contained in a Masonic periodical, and referring to his death (November 6, 1904), Ciotta was not very active as a Freemason, nor was he frequently present at the meetings in Budapest. However, he was active in the "Hungarian Party" of Rijeka and cooperated with the Governors of Rijeka. Within that "party" he worked to ensure the economic progress of Rijeka as a port, progress which is precisely a Masonic ideal. Somewhere around 1900, he withdrew from public life and lived in seclusion in his villa in Laurana (nowadays Lovran).[142]

---

[141] Ljubinka Toševa Karpowicz, "Lo Stato di Fiume nel periodo del liberalismo. Il sistema politico del *Corpus separatum* fiumano in conformita' dello Statuto del 1872," in *Quaderni*, Rovinj, VIII/1984–1985, pp, 19–29.

[142] "Johann Ciotta," A *Magyarszági Symbolikus Nagypaholy Jelentése az 1903.évi, müködésről, ügyvezetésről és pénzkelésről.* Budapest 1904. p. 21.

At the time when Ciotta was Mayor of Rijeka, Rijeka underwent the most comprehensive and most thorough period of modernization. This included the following projects:

- The completion of the construction of the Rijeka-Vukovar railway line, began in 1847, but abandoned during the 1848 Revolution.
- The construction of a modern port with warehouses for exports of agricultural products from Hungary (mostly wheat)
- The construction of a commercial fleet for maritime transport
- Urbanization with a view to constructing building to accommodate the new (Hungarian) administration.

While Ciotta was alive and running the town, the following governors were in office: Count Joseph Zichy (1870–1872), Count Géza Szapáry (1873–1883), Count Ágoston Zichi (1883–1892), Count Lajos Batthyány (1892–1896), Count Láslzó Szapáry (1898–1903), Baron Erwin Roszner (1904–1905) and then Pál Szapáry (1905). Prior to taking office as governors of Rijeka, all Hungarian magnates were among the most educated persons of their time and often came from the same families (Szapáry, Zichi).

The first governor of post-"Compromise" Rijeka, Joseph Zichi, for example, obtained his doctorate at the University of Vienna, was awarded the Iron Cross and traveled to Palestine, Russia, Germany, Turkey, Egypt and Asia Minor. During his governorship, the statute of Rijeka was enacted and the motto of his inaugural speech *"Nihil de nobis sine nobis"* has been repeated throughout Rijeka's history up to the present day. After he left Rijeka, he became minister for trade, and the Presidency (*Presidenza*) of Rijeka made him an honorary citizen.

Governor Géza Szapáry belonged to one of the oldest and the most respected noble families of Hungary. There are mentions of his ancestors dating back to 1560. Since they fought against the Turks, members of the Szapáry family occupied top positions in the state administration. Before Géza Szapáry came into office, János Peter Szapáry, who came from the same family, was governor from 1788–1791, and was known to be a Freemason of the *Drašković's Observance Order*. All members of the Szapáry family were well-known German Freemasons.[143]

Count Pál Szapáry was mentioned as a participant in the Wilhelmsbad Conventus in 1782 where, as a representative of Hungary, he was admitted to the *Order of the Templar Masters (Tempelherrenorder)*.

Géza Szapáry, Governor of Rijeka, was one of the closest associates of the emperor. He was styled Grande Majordomo and Grand Cross of the Lipot Order. Before he was appointed Governor of Rijeka, he was at the head of the State Council for Public Works.

During his time, the port of Rijeka was modernized, and his wife also took an active part in the public life of Rijeka. In 1881, she founded an orphanage for abandoned children, the Red Cross and other charitable organizations.

Count Ágoston Zichi who held the office of governor for the longest period of time, was cousin to the previous governor from the same family—Joseph Zichi. He was a student in Budapest and Vienna and obtained his doctorate degree in law. He was one of the most educated Hungarian magnates and was at the head of the Imperial Navy and traveled almost the entire world—America, East Asia, China and Japan. He was a writer and delivered lectures at the Budapest Geographical Society. In his office as governor he was focused on trade, and is credited with having the *Adria palace* constructed, with the idea that is would accommodate all trade institutions and trade representative offices.

The family of the next governor, Lajos Batthyány (1860–1951), was one of the most prestigious families in Hungary, quite possibly the most prestigious family, second only to Lajos Kossuth himself. Since they owned estates in Croatia, in Varaždin and Zagreb counties, they can be rightfully considered Croatian nobility.

In 1628, they were given the title of Barons, in 1630 Counts, and in 1764 Herzogs. Count Lajos Batthyáni (1806–1849) was the most prominent among them, having fought alongside Lajos Kossuth. He was prime minister in the independent Hungarian Government. After the failed attempt to reach an

[143] Ljubinka Toševa Karpowicz, "The influence of Hungarian Masonic Liberals on the Modernization of the *Corpus separatum* of Rijeka (1785-1906)," in *Power and influence in South –Eastern Europe, 16th-19th century*. Wien und Berlin, 2013. pp. 441-448.

agreement with the Austrian Imperial government, he stepped down from his office in December 1848, and was subsequently head of the peacekeeping delegation sent by the Hungarian parliament to negotiate with General Windisgrätz. However, Windisgrätz ordered Batthyány to be arrested, after which he was sentenced to death by the Austrian court martial. The verdict was carried out on October 6, 1849. Colonel Kasimir Batthyány (1807– 1854) was another reformer from the Batthyány family, and was an Austrian Freemason. After the Revolution had failed, he fled to England and was sentenced to death in absentia.[144]

Governor Lajos Batthyány (1860–1951) was the son of Géza Batthyány and grandson of Lajos Batthyány. He was a student in Budapest, Berlin and Paris, only to embark later on a diplomatic career. Before he became Governor of Rijeka, he married Gyula Andrássy's daughter, which made him Andrássy's son-in-law.[145] When in April 1892 he was ceremonially inaugurated as Governor of Rijeka and Head of the *Imperial Maritime Administration* (Governo Marittimo), Giovanni de Ciotta, being mayor and as custom dictated, organized a magnificent celebration in his honor. The governor replaced Theodor (Tivador) Batthyány (1859–1931) as head of the *Imperial Maritime Administration*, who was until then a member of the *Administrative Council* of the *Adria Maritime Society,* and at the same time Secretary at the *Hungarian Ministry for Trade*, and was then elected representative of Rijeka to the Diet of Hungary. He would remain in that post until 1901, when he was replaced by Laszlo Batthyány.

The personal presence of the prominent representatives of the magnate Batthyány family ensured that maritime trade via the port of Rijeka would thrive. The Batthyány family occupied an important position in the reformist efforts of the Hungarian nobility, whose aim was to reform the neo-traditional way of doing business, which was marked by state protection.

---

[144] Eva H. Balázs, "Freimaurer, Reformpolitiker, Girondisten," in *Beförderer der Aufklärung in Mittel– und Osteuropa, Freimaurer, Geselschaften, Clubs.* Berlin, 1979, pp. 127–140.

[145] Eduard von Wertheimer, op.cit. p. 326.

The next governor, Lászlo Szapáry, the eldest son of the former governor Géza Szapáry, who spent the better part of his childhood in Rijeka, obtained a degree in law from the University of Budapest as one of its best students, and then obtained his doctorate from the same university. He supplemented his education with diplomatic studies in Vienna and after his mandate as Governor of Rijeka was over he became Ambassador of Austria–Hungary in Britain.

Baron Erwin Roszner (1852–?), the last Governor of Rijeka and the Hungarian-Croatian Coast, but not the Head of the Maritime Administration like his predecessor had been, was the last governor of the era of the Hungarian liberals' rule (1904–1905). He was at the same time the first governor who was a German national. He studied at the *Theresianum* in Vienna and was an expert in political sciences. He became member of the Upper House of the Parliament in 1877.

3. THE MODERNIZATION OF RIJEKA DURING THE RULE OF THE *LIBERAL PARTY OF HUNGARY* (Hungarian Liberalism and Profitability)

A) THE PROJECT FOR THE COMPLETION OF RAILWAY CONSTRUCTION TO RIJEKA THROUGH THE HUNGARIAN PART OF THE DUAL MONARCHY

Ferenz Kossuth can be rightfully considered the initiator of modernization before the 1848–1849 Revolution. All plans to modernize maritime trade and economy proposed by him were in relation to Rijeka, where hi was frequent guest at local politician Gaspar Matcovich.[146]

The collapse of the 1848–1849 Revolution slowed down Rijeka's economic growth.

Before the Revolution started, Hungary had around 200 kilometers of railway lines. However, when in 1850 joint customs regulations were enacted, intensifying the export of Hungarian agricultural products to Austria, railway construction was also intensified, and in 1866, Hungary already had around 2,160 kilometers of modern railway lines.[147] The section leading to Rijeka took four years to build and was commissioned on October 23, 1873. At the same time, works started on the 1872 Rijeka port expansion. The works were continued in the second phase (1880–1888), but to obtain funding, Hungary had to push its agricultural sector into debt. Another measure was introduced: the duty-free zone status of the port of Rijeka was abolished and the state determined the customs fees. After 172 years of benefits enjoyed by the port of Rijeka, twelve hectares of land were taken away from its territory and turned into a *punto franco* that was connected, as a duty-free zone, with the

---

[146] Boulder Colo, *Southeast European maritime commerce and naval policies from the mid–eighteenth century to 1914*. N. York, 1988. p. 200–209. Ljubinka Toševa Karpowicz, "Gaspare Matcovich, biografia politica d'un personaggio controverso," in Quaderni, Rovigno, XIII, 2001. pp. 253–367.

[147] Helena Buljan, Važnost željeznice u razvoju riječke luke,("Significance of the Railway in the Development of the Port of Rijeka,") in *Riječka luka (Port of Rijeka)*, Rijeka, 2001. pp. 189–20.

punto franco of Trieste, under Act XVIII dated 1891, making both ports part of the free ports of Germany (ten in total).[148] This led to an increase in the total traffic through the port of Rijeka, but it mostly went through the *punto franco*, over which Rijeka had no jurisdiction. Through this process Germany started the economic conquest of Hungary and in the period 1905–1913, Germany had more securities in Hungary than in Austria.[149]

In parliament sessions held on February 13 and 14, 1900, the representative of Rijeka to the Hungarian parliament, Theodor Batthyány, kept pressing for Rijeka's right over the results of the traffic through Rijeka port's *punto franco*, which made him into the most agile autonomist of Rijeka. However, the German imperialism that conquered not so much Austria as it did Hungary, was the real cause for the formation and growth of the autonomy movement of Rijeka.[150]

B) THE CONSTRUCTION OF A MODERN PORT WITH WAREHOUSES FOR EXPORTS OF AGRICULTURAL PRODUCTS FROM HUNGARY (MOSTLY WHEAT)

The new Hungarian economic policy that improved the traffic through Rijeka port started in 1874 with the era of Ferenc Deák. Investments were made while Menyhért Lónyay was minister for trade. During that period,

---

[148] *"Punto franco"* is a name for a port's trading zone, whereas *"porto franco"* is synonymous with a free industrial port zone. *Maritime Encyclopedia No 4*, Zagreb, 1978. p. 376.

[149] Ljubinka Toševa Karpowicz, "Razvoj I promet robe kroz riječku luku 1905-1889 i njezine političke posledice " ("Development and Transport of Goods through the Port of Rijeka 1889–1905 and its Political Consequences,") in *Pomorstvo,* god. 17. vol. 17. Rijeka, 2003, pp. 153–165.

[150] *Discorso dell' on Theodoro Batthyáni pronunciato nelle sedute parlamentari 13 e 14 febbraio 1900. in merito ai diritti autonomi della libera città di Fiume e suo distretto,* Fiume, 1901. During the *Liberal Party* crisis of 1903, Theodor Batthyány left the party and joined the *Independence Party* in 1904. In 1909, he became Speaker of parliament, and after the party's collapse in 1910 he joined the Justh Party. In 1916, he was a member of Michály Károly's party, who was also a Freemason and worked in various Hungarian ministries until 1918. Ljubinka Toševa Karpowicz, "Rijeka u vrijeme vladavine Ma]đarske liberalne stranke" (" Rijeka during the Rule of the Hungarian Liberal Party"), *Vjesnik DAR,* 47–48/2006. pp. 173–192.

investments were made in port construction, in buildings and other ventures with a view to unloading goods of the value of 72,015.97 forints.[151]

The investments made in the port only made Deák's *Liberal Party* more prestigious, especially in Rijeka.

The previous representative of Rijeka to the parliament in Budapest undertook efforts to increase Rijeka's fleet, as of 1878 and during his four mandates. His name was Lájos Csernatony (1821–1901). Prior to his return to Hungary, he had been Lájos Kosutth's secretary in Turin and a member of the Hungarian Freemasonry in emigration. In parliamentary debates, he supported the export of Hungarian agricultural products to Western Europe, especially to England, where he had spent his long years of emigration.[152]

C) THE CONSTRUCTION OF A MERCHANT FLEET INTENDED FOR MARITIME TRANSPORT

During the parliamentary debates concerning the construction of the merchant fleet, Lájos Csernatony made an agreement with an influential entrepreneur and sea captain from Rijeka, Luigi Ossoinak. In 1881, with consent from the Hungarian government, he entered into an agreement with four British companies from Glasgow, Liverpool, London and Vienna and established the *Adria Maritime Company* with a capital of 2,500,000 forints. This company would soon become synonymous with Rijeka.

Already in the following year, the company had seven ships with a total capacity of 5,970 tons. In 1886, the Hungarian government became the company's sole proprietor, and in the following year the *Trieste Lloyd* signed an agreement with the Hungarian government through the Trieste office on the

---

[151] József Berkes, "izgradnja riječke luke od 1868 do 1918 godine"("Construction of the Port of Rijeka from 1868 to 1918,") in: *Riječka* luka, (*Port of Rijeka),* Rijeka, 2001. pp. 133–164.

[152] For a more detailed political biography of Lodovico (Lájosa) Csernatony (1821–1901) see: Ljubinka Toševa Karpowicz, "Rijeka u vrijeme vladavine Maļdarske liberalne stranke", ("Rijeka during the Hungarian Liberal Party Rule, op.cit. pp. 173–192.

division of maritime routes.

Exports through the port of Rijeka were on the increase even in 1891, but it was the last year of growth. This was caused by the so-called "agrarian crisis", the consequences of which would be visible later.

As of 1882, warehouses and other infrastructure were built, supervised by Theodor (Tivador) Batthyány (1859–1931), brother to the future Governor of Rijeka, the future representative of Rijeka to the parliament in Budapest and a Freemason through his family line. Since 1890, Theodor Batthyány completely left his office at the ministry and committed himself entirely to the company.

When Theodor Batthyány left the *Adria* Company during its last successful year, he left the son of Luigi Ossoinak, his old partner, in Rijeka. His son, Andrea Ossoinak (1876–1965) was a student in England at the time.

Andrea Ossoinak not only inherited his father's social position but also—due to historical circumstances—became the most prominent political figures of Rijeka at the time, next to Riccardo Zanella. He was the last liberal, the last representative of Rijeka to the parliament in Budapest and the last Master of the *Sirius* Lodge from Rijeka, during its Hungarian "history".

D) URBANIZATION (AND GERMANIZATION) WITH A VIEW TO CONSTRUCTING A BUILDING TO HOUSE THE NEW ADMINISTRATION

As agreed with Governor Ágoston Zichy, Ciotta, who was an engineer and the mayor, started in 1890 the construction of the governor's palace, which was supposed to be the governor's place of residence and to have a representative purpose. Construction was completed in 1896, just before Lájos Batthyány stepped into office as governor.

Before the construction began, three names were built into the foundations: that of Emperor Franz Joseph, Governor Lájos Batthyány and the representative of the incumbent Prime Minister of Hungary, Sandor Wekerle. Among the three of them, only the emperor was not a Freemason.

The governor's palace that dominates the city even today is material evidence of the overall effort of the Hungarian liberals to leave behind a visible reminder that for a long time Rijeka was an active part of central Europe, even though they were led by personal interest and linked together by Masonic nepotism and family ties.

Even though the dominant role in the field of foreign affairs fell within the jurisdiction of the monarchs, the rule of the Hungarian liberals during the period of liberalism of the Dual Monarchy (1867–1879) marked a new era in international politics as well. The secret Andrássy-Bismarck defensive alliance between Germany and Austria (October 7, 1879), aimed against Russia, would become the basis for Austro-Hungarian diplomacy over the next forty years. Franz Joseph's loyalty to Wilhelm II secured his place as the "splendid other."[153]

Since the secrecy of the Andrássy-Bismarck alliance had been maintained, Chancellor Bismarck managed to extend the duration of the *League of the Three Emperors* in 1884, and then his secret Reassurance Treaty with Russia in 1887. This created the preconditions for the beginning of German-(Austrian) imperial politics.

The first task was to construct and equip the navy, and Rijeka would play a prominent part in that, supplying the Austrian and German navies with torpedoes.

The key moment when the torpedo factory became the most important company supplying the German imperial fleet took place in 1877, when a purchase agreement was entered into between **Giovanni de** Ciotta and **British citizen Robert** Whitehead, who was an engineer at the time and the future co-owner. With help from Governor Géza Szápary, as of 1880 the number of torpedo orders was increasing.

---

[153] Ljubinka Toševa Karpowicz, " Development and Transport of Goods through the Port of Rijeka 1889–1905 and its Political Consequences", op.cit. On Artur Steinecker see: Irvin Lukežić, "I primi banchieri e agenti di cambiavalute fiumani," in *Fiume, Rivista di studi Adriatici*, Roma, 9/2004. pp. 84-92.

Fabrica torpedini di Roberto Whitehead (*Torpedo – Fabrik von Robert White- head*) was almost the exclusive supplier to the German and Austrian navies, and a tightly-knit group with complex and secret ties to a wide political network was formed around Whitehead's industrial venture, based on social stratification, kinship and friendship. The following were present at the torpedo factory employees' balls: the governor and personal friend of the Whitehead family, Joszef Zichy; his personal friend Georg Hoyos; director of the bank and Master of the *Sirius* Lodge, Artur Steinecker from Switzerland; Natalia, the late Paolo Scarpa's wife, who married into the Ciotta family in 1863; their daughter, who married Bernard Ürmeny, a governatorate official, Felix Meynie's wife; and others.

Apart from marital ties, German, Austrian, Croatian and Hungarian nobility were also bonded by common interest. Newly-settled and eminent Germans (Faber, Littrow) had links to the British, the Leards (**British Masons**) of Rijeka, who had links to Heinrich Krupp, Géza Andrássy and Giovanni Francovich (de Bersecz) son of Luigi Frankovich, and through Giovanni Francovich's (de Bersecz) daughter, who married a Leard, had links with Crown Prince Rudolf of Austria-Hungary.[154] This international elite, bound together by countless public and secret ties, which had the blessing of the Hungarian governors and the long-serving mayor, **Giovanni de** Ciotta, felt "at home" in Rijeka.

This society also included crown nobility: the Hungarian Prince Ferdinand (1887– 1908) and the Swedish King Oskar II. They were all bonded together by secret alliances that would soon lead to World War I and the ruin of the world in which they had lived.

---

[154] Irvin Lukežić,Robert Whitehead, engleski tvorničar iz Rijeke.(*Robert Whitehead, English Industrialist from Rijeka)*, Rijeka, 2010.

4. THE FOUNDING OF THE *SIRIUS* LODGE

Before *Sirius*—the first Masonic lodge in Rijeka—was opened, the citizens of Rijeka were members of lodges outside Rijeka. The opening of a lodge in Rijeka did not necessarily mean that all of them would become (nor did they all become) members of the Rijeka lodge. It can be assumed, but no evidence can be produced, that they remained members of their original lodges—whether on the basis of the lists of members made by the lodges or from the Masonic press.

The *Sirius Lodge* was established on March 9, 1901, at the time when Hungary was undergoing economic hardship, and Freemasonry numbers plunged. Apart from that, distinguished members of lodges from Budapest had already died (generals, famous scientists, members of the government, ministers), and the Masonic membership consisted mostly of middle class members (entrepreneurs, bank clerks, architects, doctors and the like). Since there were no conditions for top state officials to stay in Rijeka, except the governor, members of the lodge of Rijeka were, from its beginnings, liberal professionals, merchants and bankers, which is representative of the business and trade being conducted in Rijeka at the time .

This claim is confirmed by the list of the founding members of the *Sirius* Lodge, even though it dates back to 1910, in the atmosphere of public antisemitism. The list of members was published on the pages of an anti-Masonic, anti-Semitic, pro- Catholic issue of the *Giudaismo massonico* pamphlet.[155]

The list contains the names of sixteen members with the above mentioned religious affiliation, which means that nine of the founding members were Jewish, four Protestant and three Catholic. The founding members who were Jewish are listed as follows (names missing): G. Benvenisti, Ugo Eidlitz, A. Klein, A. Kirz., Dr. S. Mayländer, E. Neuberger, F. Rosenberg, G. Réti and G. Wertheimer. The Protestants are listed as follows: E. Cunradi, Fr. Csöke, Tibor Gaal and A. Steinecker. The Catholics are listed as Samarath Leitner,

---

[155] *Giudaismo massonico, numero unico, 16 marzo 1910.*

E. Rupnik and U. Hannapel.

In its 1901 issue dated April 30, year XIII (XXVI), *Orient,* the periodical of the *Symbolic Lodge of Hungary* intended exclusively for "brethren," informed the "brethren" about the opening of the lodge in Rijeka.

The notification states that on March 9, 1901, the Freemasons who lived in Rijeka founded a lodge that held meetings in improvised premises. A (private) address is listed as "Artur Steinecker, Kreditbank, Fiume, privatim – Lokal: Via della Ruota. Whitehead'schies Haus, I. Stock, Thür 1–2." Its work days were the first and the third Friday of the month.

The private address meant that the Master of the lodge was the

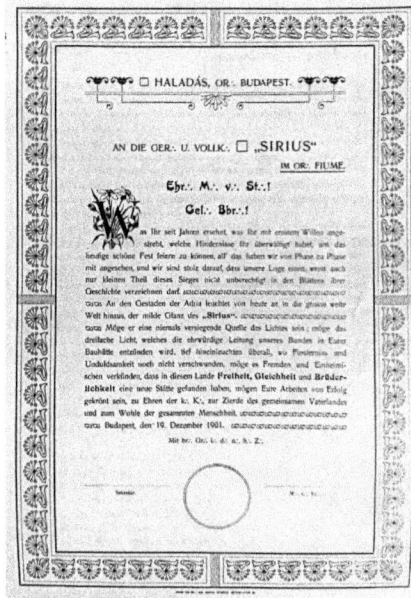

Internal notice to Hungarian Freemasons about the opening of the Sirius Lodge

director of the bank, Artur Steinecker from Switzerland, and that Robert Whitehead provided logistic support to the lodge, allowing it to operate from his private house.

The *Sirius* Lodge's motto was "Per aspera ad astra."

The article goes on to state the reason why the lodge was opened in Rijeka. The answer was that it was the only point of contact between Hungary and foreign countries, and that therefore undoubtedly this would make this lodge suitable for visits from those "brethren" who would come from abroad. "Its position is suitable to our needs and foreign visitors would be honored to be well received by our brethren," it states.

The article further states that the lodge's material resources are limited, given that its limited number of members means that the lodge cannot support the costs of independent operation. The article therefore asks the "brethren" to recommend the "brethren" from the new lodge to the relevant institutions, so that they may contribute to the economic independence of the lodge.[156]

It is interesting, although questionable, why it was only half a year later, more precisely on October 16, 1901, that the *Riječki novi list* commented on this event in an article titled: "A Masonic Lodge in Whitehead's House on Via Clotilde," considering that the Freemasonry and the work of the lodges in Hungary were public.[157]

The next year would prove that the opening of the *Sirius* Lodge in Rijeka justified the plans that the Hungarian Freemasonry had for it.

[156] "Neue Loge", Die *Symbolischen Grossloge von Ungarn* hat sub Zahl 1208/901 an die unter ihrem Schutze arbeitenden Logen folgendens Rundschreiben erlassen. *Orient,*1901. Manuskript für BNo. Freimaurer. p. 93. The cost of the membership fee was 100 forints. The lodge had five honorary members, which meant that they contributed to the lodge's treasury more than it was provided for in the regulations. An Italian copy of the regulations states: *Regolamento della Loggia giusta e perfetta Sirius, fondata 9. marzo 5901 nell' oriente di Fiume e posta sotto la protezione della Grande Loggia Simbolica dell' Ungheria,* Buda, 1912.

[157] *Novi list, "Slobodnoyidarska lo*ža u Whiteheadovoj kući*"(*"A Masonic Lodge in Whitehead's House on Via Clotilde,"16. X. 1901.

5. *SIRIUS,* ASSOCIATIONS AND POLICY

There were probably more than sixteen founding members, because a 1903 report on the lodge's membership and work states that in December 1902 the *Sirius* Lodge had twenty-eight members, and that twenty-one of them were third degree Freemasons, one was second degree and six were first degree, whereas two "brethren" were waiting to be admitted and one "brother" was affiliated, meaning that he came from another lodge, which at the end of the year meant a total of thirty-one members. During the same year, the lodge held eighteen meetings and fifteen conferences and organized one festivity.[158] The opening of the lodge in Rijeka seemed to have been justified. An article published in a 1904 issue of the magazine of the *Symbolic Lodge of Hungary,* states that the lodge receives visits by many "brethren" from Vienna, and "French, English and Swiss brethren," even "brethren" from other parts of the world, which is the reason why the lodge works in four languages and the "brethren" feel like they are part of a worldwide network.

The same article states that lectures were held on the following topics and by the following lecturers: "brother" Samuel Mayländer, one of the founders, who presented the working program of the *Medách* Lodge; "brother" Josip Janošič presented the program of the "League Against Duels;" Samuel Mayländer again about summer colonies; "brother" Theodor Huchthausen about the relationship between religion and Freemasonry; "brother" Siegfried Lászlo about contemporary progressive ideas; and a visiting "brother"—Icilio Baccich—about the Masonic work of "brother" Giovanni Bovio. "Brother" Franz Sirola delivered two lectures: one with a view to founding a home for abandoned children, and the other about the deceased "brother" Ciotta. "Brother" Sigmund Milch delivered a presentation of "an extraordinarily important issue—mandatory insurance for seamen."

---

[158] *"Bericht der Die Symbolischen Grossloge von Ungarn"* über *ihre Tätigkeit, Geschäfts– und Kassa– Gebährung im Jahre 1903.,* pp. 69–83.

The inaugural meeting held on March 16, 1904 was chaired by Samuel Mayländer in Italian and Ignatz Békey in Hungarian.[159]

The lodge seemed to have established contacts with other lodges and on November 18, 1904, it sent one of its representatives to the opening of the *Ljubav bližnjega* (Love of the Neighbor) Lodge in Zagreb.[160]

Thanks to its success, the lodge of Rijeka enjoyed great reputation among the Freemasons of Hungary, and its loyalty at the local level suited its members in the local authorities.

It is sufficient to state that in 1901 there were no known Freemasons in the municipal *Rappresentanza,* whereas in 1903, Dr. Samuele Mayländer, the most active member of the lodge, and Artur Steinecker, Master of the lodge, became members of the *Rappresentanza.* The local policy implemented discretely by the *Sirius* Lodge was to infiltrate associations or even to establish associations, without the obvious participation of Freemasons.[161]

One example is the relationship with the Rijeka *Giovane Fiume* association. At the beginning of August 1905, this association was established by a group of young people, whose political activity in the following years ranged from irredentism to fascism. The association was financed by *Dante Alighieri,* an emulated Masonic society from Italy, as was the case with other associations on the Adriatic coast.

Ninety-four members were present at the founding conference of the association. According to its statute, the association was supposed to provide quality entertainment to its members, organize field trips and make possible the reading of fine literature. The *Giovane Fiume* association was just one of several associations created by the Italian irredentist organization *Italia Irredenta.* Its very name suggests the political program of Italian irredentism.

---

[159] *Magyarországi Simbolikus Nagypaholy,* Budapest,1904. p. 51.

[160] Ivan Mužić, *Croatian Freemasonry,* VIII. supplemented edition, Split. 2005. p. 45. Artur Steinecker was the representative. Zoran Nenezić, *The Freemasons 1717–2010,* Belgrade, 2010. I. vol. p. 329.

[161] Ivan Jeličić, "Sulle tracce di una biografia perduta: Samuele Maylander (1866-1925)," in *Quaderni,* Rovigno, vol. XXVI/2015. pp. 227-270.

Its goal was to undermine the state system of Austria. Individuals and entire families were admitted as members of the *Giovane Fiume*, and membership could be obtained through recommendation by other members. The national headquarters *of Giovane Fiume* was in Ravenna.

On April 6, 1907, the first issue of *Giovane Fiume* periodical was published in Rijeka. It was the periodical of the association bearing the same name. The subsequent issues started a campaign to elect thirty-one members of the municipal *Rappresentanza*.

Together with the autonomists, four *Giovane Fiume* candidates made it into the *Rappresentanza* (Dr. Icilio Baccich, Silvino Gigante, Lionello Lenaz and Vittorio de Meichner). Two of them (Icilio Baccich and Vittorio de Meichner) were known to be members of the *Sirius* Lodge, while the same cannot be said about others with certainty.

A subsequent undated list of members of the *Sirius* Lodge states that the following Freemasons were the newly elected members of the *Rappresentanza* in 1907: Dr. Icilio Baccich, Mario Luppis, Giovanni Minach, Vittorio Meichner, Francesco Vio, engineer Giovanni Rubinich, Giovanni Ossoinack, Giovanni Prodam, and Enrico de Thierry. This means that there were nine representatives who were Freemasons or who would become Freemasons in the future as compared to two, which is how many there were in 1903, suggesting the tactic of quiet infiltration into the municipal authorities.

At the end of June that same year, the Mayor of Rijeka was elected from the ranks of the members of the *Rappresentanza*. A Freemason, Dr. Francesco Vio Jr., member of a family that would occupy an important position in the town's politics and in the membership of the lodge, prevailed by a majority of one over the other candidate, Riccardo Zanella – non mason.

Given that the opening of a lodge in Rijeka was justified by the visits made by "brethren" from other countries and other lodges, during a dinner that took place on May 11, 1906, Artur Steinecker, Master of the *Sirius* Lodge, suggested that a Masonic circle should be established in Opatija (then and nowdays famous tourist destination) to allow the "brethren" to meet "brethren" from other lodges, while on vacation. Since Opatija was under Austrian administration, the circle was supposed to be protected by the Grand Lodge

Young Turks delegation in Rijeka

Humanitas from Bratislava. The circle was only opened in December 1908, but by that time the international situation had significantly changed, which also reflected on Freemasonry in Hungary.

The Austrian annexation of Bosnia and Herzegovina on October 6, 1908, immediately after the unification of the *Kingdom of Bulgaria* with *East Rumelia* (September 22, 1908), that had been agreed, completely changed the international situation.

The *Sirius* Lodge carried out a "discrete" task to implicitly present the relationship between Austria–Hungary and the new Young Turks regime of the Ottoman Empire, even though it was on the city level only. A delegation of *Young Turks* visited Rijeka between November 10 and 12, 1909.[162]

---

[162] Ljubinka Toševa Karpowicz, "Mladoturci u Rijeci 1909".("Young Turks in Rijeka in 1909), *Sušačka revija,* Rijeka, No. 60.

The *Young Turks'* visit to Austria–Hungary was supposed to prove to the international public that the relationship between Austria–Hungary and the new regime in Istanbul was "patched up" after the annexation of Bosnia and Herzegovina. Apart from the governor and the town authorities, the *Sirius* Lodge played a role that was unknown to the public.

The degree of the secrecy of the visit is obvious from the fact that *Il Risveglio,* the Catholic periodical of Rijeka, only started writing about it about in 1911–1912, quoting articles from *Kelet,* a Masonic **periodical** from Budapest.

Since the association of *Young Turks* was established in Paris by the *Grand Orient of France,* it made sense that a group of Freemasons from the delegation should visit their "brethren" in Rijeka.

According to the *Il Risveglio* articles, Artur Steinecker, Master of the lodge of Rijeka was at the head of a committee that organized the stay of the Turks in Rijeka. The fourth group of the *Young Turks'* delegation consisted solely of Freemasons. They were supposed to have secret talks, and the magazine points out the close relationship between the Italian and Turkish Freemasonry.

Apart from these data, no other data refer to the meeting between the Turkish Freemasons and the Freemasons of Rijeka, though *Novi list* presented this visit as a sign of the increasing German influence in the Balkans.

The visit to the *Sirius* Lodge and Austria–Hungary took place after the annexation of Bosnia and Herzegovina. Having opposed that act, Serbian lodges left the protection of the *Symbolic Grand Lodge of Hungary.* This marked the beginning of the weakening of the Hungarian Freemasonry, and the expansion of the Serbian Freemasonry, even into the territory of the annexed Bosnia and Herzegovina, since it was considered a "Yugoslav territory."

The situation of the *Sirius* Lodge from Rijeka stood in contrast with the process that weakened Freemasonry in Hungary. In 1910, it had ninety members, 70 percent of whom were Jews, and in 1913, it had eighty-eight members. Apart from that, its revenue totaled around 50,000 forints.

The Jews were able to be Freemasons publicly, since during the 1911 international Masonic congress in Rome there was a rapprochement between the *Symbolic Great Lodge of Hungary* and the *Great Lodge of Germany.* This is why the *Symbolic Grand Lodge of Hungary* had the largest percentage of Jewish

Freemasons, who used their international connections to bind together the wide area of central Europe.

The lodge from Rijeka was able to get a 340,000 forint loan to construct a temple, thanks to its favorable material situation, in which Artur Steinecker, Master of the lodge and director of the bank, played an important part. On November 6, 1910, "brother" Lajos Brajjer, a member of the German Free-masonry, laid the cornerstone. This would become the future *Sirius House*. Its building permit was obtained in 1911 by engineer Giovanni Rubinich, a "brother" since 1906. It was to be constructed by the House Construction Consortium, represented by Giovanni Rubinich himself.

Numerous delegations were present at the foundation-laying ceremony. The largest delegation came from the *Ljubav bližnjega* Lodge from Zagreb.

It is understood that a conference was held after the ceremony, during which agreements were made about the further coordination of work in the divided Masonic bodies of both Hungary and Croatia. Some members of Croatian lodges within the *Symbolic Grand Lodge of Hungary*, having opposed the annexation of Bosnia and Herzegovina, left their lodges and joined the Serbian Freemasonry. These were mostly members of the *Croatian-Serbian coalition*, and Hinko Hinković and Adolf Mihalić were also mentioned.

Following the annexation crisis that continued into 1909, the Serbian Free-masonry tried to renew their broken ties to some of the lodges, and, with this in mind, an attempt was made by the oldest lodge from Belgrade, *Pobratim*, to reestablish its relationship with the *Sirius* Lodge through its member, Miroslav Pops Dragić, who was "undergoing medical treatment" in Opatija. Pops Dragić wrote two letters from Opatija, in March and May 1911 to describe the activities and the international membership of the *Sirius* Lodge and he established corre-spondence between the two lodges, so that they may cooperate directly without interference from their "national central offices".   The *Sirius* Lodge de-clined this, explaining that, unlike the *Pobratim* Lodge, it was not independent and therefore not allowed to have its own international cooperation activities, but it appointed a "brother" who would keep correspondence with them in Cro-atian. Once again it was one Susanni, but now "Franjo" A. Susanni, a member of the lodge since 1904, with an address at: F. A. Susanni, Fiume, Punto franco.

azon év deczember első munkáján a páholy elő terjeszteni tartozik akként, hogy a módosításokat még a tisztujitást megelőzőleg tárgyalni lehessen.

83. §. A 82. §. értelmében módosított házszabályok csak a tisztviselő-választások befejezését követő munkán a nagypáholy jóváhagyása után lépnek életbe.

84. §. Ha azonban a páholy a házszabályok megváltoztatására nézve a 82. §-ban előirt időben nem intézkednék, akkor a házszabályok kötelező ereje további egy évre érvényben marad.

A »Sirius« czimü »Per aspera ad astra« jeligéjü páholy 5901. évi nov. 15-én tartott munkájából:

Steinacker Artur
főmester.

Békei Ignácz
titkár.

Schwarz Mihály
szónok.

Gaál Tibor
I. felügyelő.

Eidlitz Hugó
II. felügyelő.

65/1902. sz.

Jóváhagyta a Magyarországi Symbolikus Nagypáholy Szövetségtanácsa 1902. évi január 13-án tartott ülésében.

Mártonfy Márton
hely·. Nagymester,

Dr. Bakonyi Kálmán
kancellár.

Registration of the Constitution of the Sirius Lodge

Even though they were not allowed to cooperate officially, personal relationships seem to have been functional. An "architect" from Rijeka (whose name was not stated)—who was not necessarily an architect by occupation, but an architect according to Masonic hierarchy—intended to spend a day in Belgrade on his way to Istanbul, and Pops Dragić arranged for him to spend his time in the company of his "brethren." There is no further information about this combination, but it is proof that Masonic connections, even though broken on the international level, were still functional on the personal level, which is the essence of the Masonic "brotherhood."

In the following year, the *Sirius* Lodge put together a delegation of three persons, to be present at the ceremonial opening of the premises of the *Pobratim* Lodge in Belgrade. Two persons were present at the ceremony: V. Vidmar and Dr. Lajos (Luigi) Brajjer (a member of the lodge since 1905). , Dr. Frederik Ružička (a member of the lodge since 1908), was absent for family reasons.

Ljubinka Toševa Karpowicz

The actions of the *Sirius* Lodge through *Giovane Fiume* were resumed and the association organized two field trips to Ravenna, its organizational headquarters, in 1911. After the second field trip, at the beginning of 1912, the society was banned under charges that its actions opposed the "idea of the state," which was of course the idea of the Hungarian state. Its assets were confiscated. Its members, however, kept working in secrecy, and the forthcoming political events only proved to be an incentive to them. Since the situation was such that the war was imminent, leaders of the association (the Baccich, Gigante, Prodam and Conighi families), whose members were at the same time members of the *Sirius* Lodge (except the Gigante family), were enlisted as volunteers at the very beginning even before Italy joined the war (May 24, 1915). This ensured their lasting "credibility" with Italian irredentism, and later fascism.

The preoccupation with the economic situation, and especially with the decrease of traffic through the port of Rijeka in 1912, which was a result of the annexation of Bosnia and Herzegovina, made the members of the Sirius Lodge appeal on April 16, 1913 to their mother lodge in Budapest. They asked it to advocate the beginning of the construction of another railway line on the Budapest-Rijeka section, and to oppose the construction of the railway network in Bosnia, which would result in a decrease in traffic through the port of Rijeka.

Since these demands were related to each other, *Sirius* sent a memorandum that was drafted and sent by the *Chamber of Commerce* of Rijeka to other *Chambers of Commerce* in Hungary asking two favors from their "brethren": that expert explanation be given regarding the necessity to construct a parallel line on the Rijeka–Budapest railway section to lodges, and to sway the public against the construction of a railway through Bosnia and Herzegovina..

The results of both processes were supposed to be reported to the *Sirius* Lodge by the end of May of the same year, so that "brethren" from Rijeka would know what to do next. Artur Steinecker continued to sign those documents as the Master.[163]

---

[163] Magyar nemzeti levéltar, M.E. 1919. Tetel XXIV, Alapszám 471.

The other task, to sway the public against the construction of a railway to Bosnia and Herzegovina, required media intervention.

It is unknown until when Steinecker was Master of the lodge, and when it was that Andrea Ossoinack took over. However, after World War I, Andrea Ossoinack was the Master of the *Sirius* Lodge of Rijeka, at the time when it was transitioning from Hungarian to Italian Freemasonry.

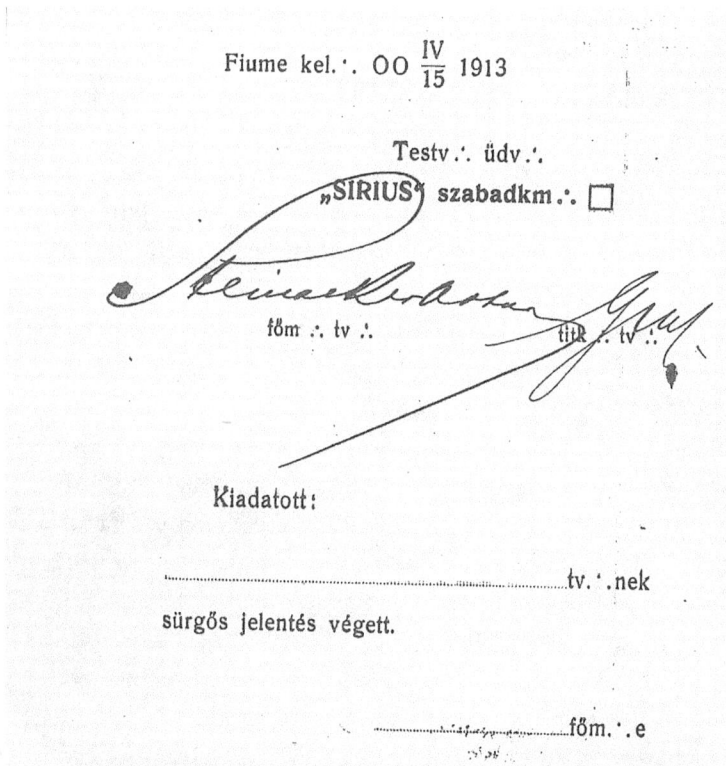

Fiume kel.∴ OO $\frac{IV}{15}$ 1913

Testv∴ üdv∴
"SIRIUS" szabadkm∴ ☐

főm∴ tv∴   tit∴ tv∴

Kiadatott:

....tv.∴.nek

sürgős jelentés végett.

........................főm.∴.e

Artur Steinecker's letter to the central lodge in Budapest, dated April 16, 1913

6. *THE RIJEKA RESOLUTION* AND THE *CROATIAN-SERBIAN COALITION*

Italian irredentism used the *Giovane Fiume* society and, to a lesser extent, the *Sirius* Lodge as its "modus operandi." The fact that both organizations had no Croatian members, or those who felt that they were Croats, was therefore not unusual. The Croats, including those from Rijeka, opted for Croatian lodges and their anti-Habsburg, sometimes pro-Yugoslavian programs. This program became prominent when the *Croatian-Serbian coalition* made its public appearance. However, the prehistory of this movement and its program date back to 1903, more precisely to the time of the shift of royal power in Serbia that introduced new politics in the Kingdom of Serbia, and also in the Balkans.

Even before the dynastic changes, the Serbian politicians cooperated with Dalmatian politicians coastal Croats and Serbs—particularly in the period when the members of (Serbian) Radical party were in exile, but there is little data available about their cooperation.

After the *May Coup* (May 29) and the shift of royal power in Serbia, the Kingdom of Serbia found itself in international isolation, and its diplomacy was looking for new allies. At the same time, its relationship with Austria–Hungary was changing because Serbia, its new dynasty (the Karađorđević dynasty), now wanted to be free from its tutelage. The new Serbian regime turned to the Kingdom of Italy (whose king was married to a princess from Montenegro, daughter of King Nikola and the sister of King Peter's wife) as the possible ally, and a secret action began to find collaborators. Political allies could not be sought publicly, but through associations and individuals who operated secretly and not in an official capacity. Immediately after Peter succeeded to the Serbian throne, radical party leader Nikola Pašić, as the secretary of state for foreign affairs, sent a memorandum in March 1904 to the king in which he presented a Serbian program, directed against Austria–Hungary. The memorandum was based on the thesis that the Croats and the Serbs had a mutual enemy: Austria–Hungary, and that in Hungary it was in fact Istvan Tisza's regime. Therefore, item four of this memorandum stressed the necessity to provide support and cooperation to the idea of a Croatian-Serbian coalition in Croatia.[164]

Croatian politicians Ante Trumbić and Frano Supilo, as representatives of the *New Course policy*, first turned to cooperating with the Italians, and then to the Hungarian opposition to Istvan Tisza's regime.

In Italy, Supilo contacted the Ferrero–Lombrozos, a married couple, and they introduced him to Ernest Nathan, Grand Master of the *Grand Orient of Italy*.

In Croatia, Trumbić and Supilo started cooperating with the (Hungarian) coalition.

The coalition between various parties opposing Tisza's *Liberal Party* was created on November 19, 1904, under the nominal leadership of Ferenc Kossuth, Lajos Kossuth's son. In the elections held in January 1905, the coalition won the majority in the Hungarian parliament, while in Rijeka, Riccardo Zanella, the candidate of the autonomy supporters, beat the liberal Andrea Ossoinack .

Frano Supilo's acquaintance with the leading Hungarian politicians made Rijeka and Supilo the hub of the new Serbian diplomacy's ambitions and, as of 1905, Serbian politicians were visiting Rijeka secretly or semi-secretly to hold discussion on cooperation. They established correspondence, and the cooperation got more concrete when Ljubomir Stojanović, a member of the *Ujedinjenje* Lodge from Belgrade, became prime minister in 1905.

According to the memoirs of Ivan Ribar Sr., in April 1905, when he was on military service in Rijeka, he became acquainted with Supilo, and he also met with Dalmatian politician Josip Smodlaka there, their acquaintance dating back to 1903.

They furthered their acquaintance during the September 16–19 Opatija conference, after which the *Rijeka Resolution* was signed on October 3. The

---

[164] Dimitrije Đorđević, "Pokušaj srpsko-š ugarske susaradnje 1906.godine" ("A Serbian-Hungarian Cooperation Attempt in 1906,") in *Istorija XX veka,ybornik radova, ("XX Century History, collection of papers")*, vol. II, Belgrade 1961 pp. 353–382. Nikola Pašić is considered to have been a Freemason, but there is no reliable evidence to support this thesis.

signatories of the *Rijeka Resolution* and members of the *Croatian-Serbian coalition* cooperated in the course of 1906 with members of the *Pobratim* Lodge from Belgrade (Adolf Mihalić, Slavoljub Bulvan and Demetrović), and in the following years their contact became more intensive.[165]

The 1906 May elections were won by Frano Supilo and Svetozar Pribićević (*Serbian Independent Party*), a member of the *Ljubav bližnjega Lodge* from Zagreb, after which Supilo became the key figure of the coalition. Through Riccardo Zanella, the newly elected representative of Rijeka to the parliament in Budapest, in a short period of time (only eight days), Supilo became a citizen of Rijeka (March 27, 1907). He then intensified his secret policy, failing to notify other members of the coalition about it, which was another argument in favor of the suspicion that he was a Freemason in the service of the Hungarian, Serbian and Italian Freemasonry.[166]

Regardless of whether the money he had at his disposal had been used for his electoral campaign, to pay for a costly fee for the publication of *Novi list* newspaper (21,000 forints), these were truly high amounts of money, even if we put aside the fact that Supilo was the owner of *Novi list*.[167]

The conflict between the members of the coalition and Supilo began in connection with the issue of the annexation of Bosnia and Herzegovina. After Russia (March 1909) and Serbia were forced to approve the annexation, the attack on Serbia began, and the attack on the *Croatian-Serbian coalition* was part of that. Only Supilo was singled out.[168]

---

[165] Ivan Mužić, *Croatian Freemasonry*, op.cit. p. 45. Ivan Ribar, *Iz moje političke suradnje*, (*From My Political Cooperation)*, Zagreb, 1965. idem, *Politički spisi*, (*Political Records)*, Belgrade, 1948.

[166] Mirjana Gross, *Vladavina hrvatsko-srpska kolaicije 1906-1907.(Rule of the Croatian-Serbian Coalition 1906–1907)*, Belgrade, 1960 p. 109.

[167] J. Szekeres, "Regesta spisa Kr. Riječkog gubernija o Franu Supilu u riječkom Novom listu 1916-1900." (Abstract of Files on Roy. Governorate of Rijeka on Frano Supilo" in *Riječki Novi* list (1900–1916). *Vjesnik historijskih arhiva u Rijeci I Pazinu, (Gazette of the Historical Archives in Rijeka and Pazin)*, Rijeka, 1970. pp. 385–409.

[168] Dimitrije Đorđević, "Pokušaj srpsko-ugarska saradnje 1906.godine",(A Serbian-Hungarian Cooperation Attempt in 1906), op.cit. [168] Ivo Petrinović, *Ante Trumbić*, Split, 1997.

The fact that Supilo retreated from the coalition during the *Friedjung process*, under the pretext that he did not want the Coalition to be accused because of the accusations made against him, did not mean at the same time that Supilo was no longer interested in it, which is proved by the confidential information he was providing to Carlo Caccia Dominioni, the Italian consul in Rijeka.[169] Supilo's motivation to give away important secret information about the Coalition is unknown, but the conclusion can be derived from the accompanying letters—sent by Consul Caccia Dominioni to the Italian ambassador in Vienna—that Italy was interested in the "pan-Serbian movement" (*movimento panserbo*) that, as can be seen from the report, referred to the secret cooperation between Serbia and Serbs in Bosnia and Croatia. Their interest probably had something to do with the Italian imperialist plans for the Balkans.

According to the names mentioned in the report and to other sources, we can see that the persons who were implicated in the secret politics network belonged to Masonic lodges, above all those French and Italian, i.e. the *Grand Orient of Italy* and France, mostly around 1906 but perhaps earlier.

The following persons of *Serbo-Croatian colition* were Freemasons: Franko Potočnjak, an independent representative of the Coalition; Milan Marjanović, initiator of the *New Course* in Dalmatia; Josip Smodlaka, leader of the *Dalmatian Progressive party*; and Milan Pribičević. The Hungarian politicians Ferenz Kossuth, Sandor Wekerle and Géza Polony were also Freemasons.

---

[169] Carlo Caccia Dominioni di Sillavengo was appointed Consul of the Kingdom of Italy to Rijeka on November 29, 1906, and became first class consul that same year. He remained in Rijeka until March 12, 1914. He was again Consul to the State of Rijeka from November 2, 1921 to March 4, 1922, when he was recalled by the Italian Ministry for Foreign Affairs. Dailo I. Massagrande, *Italia e Fiume 1921–1924*. Milano 1922. p. 23. note 26.

On the Serbian side, Jaša Prodanović and Ljuba Davidović were Freemasons, and it is considered that Nikola Pašić was also a Freemason.[170]

However, none of them could be compared to the "Masonic share," meaning the secret share of Freemasonry in the biography of Peter I, King of Serbia.

In 1870, during the Franco-Prussian war, he met General Paul Pegné, who during World War I would become the Grand Master of the *Grand Orient of France*, a circumstance that was to have a dominant influence on the history of Serbia and the Kingdom of Yugoslavia.[171]

---

[170] Pašić's biography provides little data about the period before 1903, i.e. until the time when Petar Karađorđević came to power through a coup d'état in 1903., when the time of his emigration was finally over. There are indications that Pašić was admitted to an Italian lodge during the 1875 Herzegovina uprising that was aided by the Italian Freemasonry. Petar Karađorđević, the future King of Serbia and Yugoslavia, who was then a young prince, took part in that uprising and it was then that he and Pašić became acquainted. The archives of the Serbian Academy of Science contain two letters written by Miroslav Hubmajer to Nikola Pašić from Sarajevo in 1898 that are littered with Masonic linguistic symbolism, and in which he suggested political action. Archives of the *Serbian Academy of Science*, private papers of N. Pašić (Arhiv San, fond Hartije N. Pašića). Furthermore, Giordano Gamberini, author of the book titled *Mille volti dei massoni*, states that the controversies of Pašić's life lead to the conclusion that he was a Freemason, but that it was unknown to which lodge he belonged, and to which country. op.cit. p. 167.

[171] Dragoljub R. Živojinović, *Kralj Petar I Karađorđević, (King Peter I Karađorđević)*, Belgrade, 2003.

7. ISTVAN TISZA'S RETURN TO POLITICS AND THE FORMATION OF THE *AUTONOMOUS LEAGUE*

When, after the four years' rule of the coalition, the reformed *Liberal Party* returned to power in January 1910, Tisza only gave it a new, pompous and even more inadequate name: the *National Party of Work*.

The party's membership was composed of the tired fighters for the *1867 Compromise* with Austria, landowners and the big bourgeoisie. In other words, it was a coalition of those who were in power, and above all who were economic magnates. In the elections held on June 8, 1910, the *National Party of Work* won 255 seats (62 percent of the votes), the coalition of pro-independence parties won ninety-five seats, the *People's Party* and the *Christian Socialist Party* won thirteen seats, while the various national minority parties won only eight seats.

This was the last parliament of the Dual Monarchy and the last period of rule of the *National Party of Work*.

The fact that the *Liberal Party* returned to power, albeit under a different name, reflected on the political situation in Rijeka, but once again in a specific way, according to the relation between the town's political forces.

The pro-autonomy movement was still the ruling political force even though it was on the decline, partially because its membership had dwindled. Since it had a significant number of supporters on the national level, not only did it stop being an opposition movement, but it also stopped being elite. Therefore the new Hungarian government—independently or in agreement with some lack of control processes—started working on its decomposition.

On June 8, 1910, the election day in Hungary, elections were also held in Rijeka. It was already known that the government would nominate the former Governor of Rijeka, the founder of the autonomous movement Michele Mayländer—nephew to Samuel Mayländer, who was a "brother"—and that the voting would be public, according to the law.

In the elections held a month earlier, the government's candidate won with a majority of 970 votes over the candidate of the Autonomy Party, Riccardo

Zanella, who got 566 votes out of a total of 2,337.

How and why Dr. Mayländer, after almost ten years of absence, made his return to politics, is completely unclear! A statement made by Francesco

Gilberto Corossacz, Chairman of the Election Commission (with Icilio Baccich as vice-chairman) resulted in an incident, when he declared that the choice of Mayländer was easy, since he was the government's candidate (and 40 percent of Rijeka's electoral body was made up of government officials). Michele Mayländer himself opposed his statement, with support from some Hungarians, af-

Michele Mayländer

ter which an open conflict broke out between Michele Mayländer and Riccardo Zanella, and Mayländer left the municipal building accompanied by security.

The incident clearly demonstrated that the autonomy supporters were divided, which logically meant that new administration needed to be elected. In the June 14, 1910 elections, Riccardo Zanella was elected president of the

Association, and its other members were Francesco Gilberto Corossacz, Icilio Baccich (Chairman and Vice-Chairman of the Electoral Commission), Giuseppe de Emili, Zanella's future long-term collaborator Dr. Mario Blasich, Giuseppe Host, Dr. Lionello Lenaz, Vittorio de Meichsner, Giovanni Schittar, and Iginio Sucich. All elected individuals, except Icilio Baccich, had up until then been politically anonymous.

The question is raised as to how it came to pass that Icilio Baccich ended up on the autonomists' list. Apart from the fact that he was a member of the irredentist society *Giovane Fiume* and opposed to the Croats and any kind of politics in which they partook, he was also a Freemason. Regardless of whether his membership was common knowledge or not, he was a politician that harbored anti-Hungarian views, and his ideas were completely at odds with those of the autonomists. The question therefore arises as to whether he had managed to infiltrate the presidency of the weakened *Autonomous Association* only to spy on it.

The newly elected Michele Mayländer was criticized by everyone, both in Rijeka and in Budapest, and he defended himself publicly by stating that he was in favor of Rijeka's independence.

Soon after that, he succumbed to a heart attack during a parliamentary session, and died in Budapest in February 1911.

However, the death of the "government candidate" meant that the victory of the pro-Hungarian option in Rijeka was not secure enough and at the beginning of 1911, the government in Budapest, with help from some autonomists, founded a new rival association opposing the *Autonomous Association,* under the name of the *Autonomous League.* Its name was "wisely" chosen, to make it look like a reformed *Autonomous Association.*

The elections held on May 4, 1911 to find a replacement for the deceased Mayländer were won by the candidate of the *Autonomous League* and (Istvan Tisa's) *National Party of Work*, attorney Antonio Vio Jr., against Riccardo Zanella, candidate of the *Autonomous Association.* This was despite the fact that during the elections it was publicly stated that Vio belonged to the *Sirius* Lodge.

Immediately after its foundation, members of the *Autonomous League* started attacking the *Autonomous Association.* Zanella's autonomists were referred to as "the minority," given that their representatives were the minority, unlike the "leaguists," who were the majority, and they made open attacks on the "leaguists," accusing them of foul play and cooperation with Khuen Héderváry and his representative in Rijeka, Count Wickenburg. However, Zanella did not know that the majority of members of *Autonomous League's* steering committee belonged to the leadership of the *Sirius* Lodge. Moreover, Antonio Vio, the league's No. 1, was at the same time one of the leaders of the *Sirius* Lodge.

According to a list made in 1934 that is not necessarily exhaustive, four out of nine elected members of the *Autonomous League's* steering committee became members of the *Sirius* Lodge between 1906 and 1913 (Rubinich in 1906, Antonio Vio Jr. in 1909, Ossoinack in 1909 and Descovich in 1913). Mini Ariosto, the representative of the *Rijeka Youth* became a member in 1913, followed in the same year by Giovanni Prodam, the member who declared open the *Autonomous League's* founding assembly, and Attilio Prodam, who later became the leading figure of fascism in Rijeka and abandoned Freemasonry at Mussolini's explicit request.

In 1911, the largest number of Freemasons (eight) joined the lodge, and this coincided with the time when the *Autonomous League* was founded, so the question is raised as to whether perhaps the *Autonomous League* was a secular name for the most active part of the *Sirius* Lodge's membership.

It is interesting that neither in 1914 nor in 1919 did Riccardo Zanella know that the "leaguists" were also Freemasons.

In a pamphlet titled Pitanja riječke politike, (Issues of Rijeka Politics), he attacked Andrea Ossoinack, Antonio Vio, and Luigi Nicolich for foul play in the warehouses of Rijeka that belonged to the state of Hungary, not knowing how they found themselves in the position to get away with foul play with state property, even if the country was at war (1914–1918).[172]

The very core of the "leaguists" was made up of a group that later, up until the annexation of Rijeka by Italy in 1924, continued in terms of ideas and finances the Italian irredentism that began with *Giovane Fiume.* The "leaguists" were the so-called "caste of Fiume," as it was dubbed by the fascism era Italian police, when it made records of the political behavior of the old citizens of Rijeka during the new regime. This group managed to infiltrate the town's institutions, and was therefore always at the center of political events, often creating or modifying them according to their own needs.

Up until the founding of the *Autonomous League*, this group did not exist as an organization. Thanks to its actions, the political events in Rijeka until

---

[172] Riccardo Zanella, *Questioni di politica fiumana,* Fiume, 1919.

1924 kept their local colors, something that was particular to *Fiume*, and that separated it politically from the wider and narrower political surroundings.

This is why "the irredentism of Fiume" often corresponds with that of the politicized Freemasonry in terms of organization and personalities, who were organized into various "cliques" during the Hungarian reign over Rijeka and finally, into the organizational form known as the *Autonomous League*.

The personal continuity of the "caste of Fiume," that remained uninterrupted over various state, legal and political eras of Rijeka, demonstrated that this political game was played by those people whose political habitus was unquestionable, regardless of how important the events taking place in Rijeka were, including the World War.

This interconnectedness of the "caste of Fiume," aimed at the formal and informal maintenance and strengthening of the political influence in various circumstances, can be considered Rijeka's political variable.

The connections between these individuals, their cooperation, mutual recognition, dependence and loyalty, were merely values in the service of a greater cause, while the instruments they employed to achieve such a cause and to galvanize and steer the masses of various ideologies included nationalism, irredentism, fueling hatred of political groups that were founded on different values, common symbols, and oaths and proclamations.

The ideologies that came to life in Rijeka were derived from the ideologies that came from abroad, such as autonomism, anarcho-syndicalism, socialism, irredentism, exulted nationalism, and mixtures thereof, even including fascism. However, all this could not diminish the strength of the "caste of Fiume," whose basis was not found in politics—and even less so in ideology—but in the social order.

The political culture of the citizens of Rijeka until the beginning of World War I, and during the period of D'Annunzio's occupation, was the historical inheritance of the Hungarian political culture and its way of doing politics.

The Hungarian way of doing politics, that found its new historical and political life and continuation through the politics of Rijeka, even though formally and in a somewhat changed form, is the most interesting cultural and political heritage of Hungary's long period of reign over

Rijeka. An important place in this politics is occupied by the Freemasonry as a class and a political organization.

When Rijeka was annexed to Italy in 1924, the most successful members of the "caste of Fiume" stepped into the center of the political power of the Italian state. The autonomists were excluded from this transfer as an anachronous but modernized movement of Rijeka's middle class who, with a view to protecting the historical—in this particular case the "Fiumian"—community, opposed the multinational non-democratic - estate state - Hungary.

5

ITALIAN FREEMASONRY AND THE *RIJEKA* QUESTION BETWEEN THE ARMISTICE (11/3/1918) AND THE *TREATY OF RAPALLO* (11/12/1920)

Austria and Hungary, the two states comprising Austria–Hungary, signed the Armistice together on November 3, 1918. The peace agreements were, however, signed separately by Austria on September 10, 1919, and Hungary on June 4, 1920. Accordingly, Austria became a sovereign state in international affairs as of September 10, 1919, whereas Hungary had to wait a year and a half. Until that moment it had been a country without internationally agreed upon and recognized borders, and as such it was subject to public diplomacy—above all to the Paris Peace Conference—and the object of interest for informal groups, including Freemasonry.

Furthermore, Hungary's international legal position was complicated, because some of its former territories were still under examination as they had been occupied by the newly-formed states (Romania, the Kingdom of Serbs, Croats and Slovenes, and Czechoslovakia), and remained so until ratification of the peace treaty, and for a year thereafter. This allowed Hungary more breathing space to find allies, even if only of the temporary kind.

The long-term solution for Hungary's borders came as a consequence of a string of circumstances, aside from those already stated.

Above all, the reorganization of Eastern and Central Europe based on the principle of a nation's self-determination, imposed by President Wilson as a requirement to determine borders, meant that state borders were no longer determined on a historical basis, which further compounded the issue of state borders for the former multinational *Transleithania (Lands of the Crown of St. Stephen)*

The other problem that interfered with the determination of Hungarian state borders after the collapse of the bourgeois revolution in 1918 was the communist republic, proclaimed in the spring of 1919 under the leadership of Bela Kun.

The third reason why the peace treaty with Hungary took a long time to settle, was the plan of the Allies to isolate Germany by creating new states on its eastern border, often from parts of the Hungarian state, in order to prevent its future expansion to the east, and at the same time so that those states might act as a buffer preventing the Bolshevik revolution from spreading to Europe.[173]

The solution to Hungarian state borders were, therefore, tied to the reorganization of the former Central Europe, and the Allies themselves often had conflicting concepts about this, depending on their own areas of influence.

The question of Rijeka offered a lot of room for manipulation, considering the fact that it had been an integral part of the Lands of the Crown of Saint Stephen, and the fact that the Italian delegation was adamant when it came to the implementation of the requirements of the 1915 Treaty of London, especially so because Rijeka was not included in the treaty. The prominent citizens of Rijeka were its potential allies in this matter, and among them there were those who certainly enjoyed its confidence. These were, above all, the prominent members of *Giovane Fiume* association, followed by those "recommended" by them.

---

[173] Zsuzsa L. Nagy, Peacemaking after World War I: The Western Democracies and the Hungarian Question, p. 32/52, in Stephen Borsody, ed. *The Hungarians: a divided nation,* New Haven, 1988. Margaret Macmilan, *Paris 1919.* New York, 2002, p. 257–270.

1. ITALIAN FREEMASONRY AND THE ANNEXATION OF RIJEKA

Even before Italy joined the war by declaring war on Austria–Hungary on June 24, 1915, some of the members of the banned *Giovane Fiume* association had already volunteered, waiting in Italy for the war to begin, siding with the interventionists. Twelve members of *Giovane Fiume* died fighting for Italy in this war, twenty were interned as political enemies, and forty-two survived the war as combatants.[174]

When on the ground in Hungary before the end of the war national councils began to be established as interim governing authorities, the first *National Council of Slovenes, Croats, and Serbs* was established in Rijeka on October 29, 1918. It was then, on the basis of a statement, given by Andrea Ossoinack (18.X.1918) in the Budapest parliament, that the *Consiglio Nazionale Italiano (Italian National Council)* was established on 29.X.1918. Thanks to the fact that the Italian army, as an Allied army, was present in Rijeka, the *Italian National Council* worked without obstacles as a legitimate authority aimed to bring about the annexation of Rijeka to Italy as soon as possible. With the plebiscite, that took place on December 30. 1918., the *Italian National Council* declared the annexation of Rijeka to Italy.

However, the armistice between Italy and Austria (November 3, 1918) could not pacify the chaotic situation which particularly characterized *Venezia Giulia* and Trieste as Austrian territories. And according to Article 6 of the armistice treaty, an interim administration was introduced in the form of the military command of the Italian army. The situation on the ground was frozen, and irredentist organizations in this area had to await the outcome of the peace agreements. However, the activism, whether it was pre-war or during the war, did not suit them now. Along with that, the decisions that were to be made at the conference were uncertain, so a new organization was established, renewed or just put on standby.

---

[174] Armando Odenigo–Gian Proda, *La Giovane Fiume, rievocata nel cinquantesimo anniversario della sua fondazione.* Roma, 1955.

Remembering the unsuccessful participation in the Masonic congress in Paris in 1917,[175] when the holding of referendums on disputed borders with a multi-ethnic population was agreed upon, the *Grand Orient of Italy* established the *Oberdan* Lodge in Trieste as the operating point for Italian irredentism connected to the question of *Venezia Giulia* and Rijeka.

The lodge was established by Giacomo Treves, a member of the *Grand Orient*, who, at the end of the war, moved to Trieste from Turin, with the aim of operating in Rijeka. On December 15, 1918 (which is to say some forty days after the treaty with Austria was signed and before the beginning of Peace Conference in Paris), Treves and another eight "brethren," former members of other lodges, founded the *Guglielmo Oberdan Lodge* in Trieste.

Ernesto Nathan who was still the Grand Master of the *Grand Orient*, advised Treves to establish the lodge under strict secrecy. The reasons why the Trieste lodge had to be established secretly are still unknown, and even less is known about how the lodge became obedient to the *Grand Lodge of Italy*, and not to the *Grand Orient*, within which it was founded. "Brother" Treves was soon informed by Carlo de Andreis, the Grand Secretary of the *Grand Lodge of Italy* that the *Grand Lodge of Italy* had already accepted its obedience and let them now that a bull had already been sent.This legalize the lodge's work five days after its founding, more precisely on December 20, 1918.

The *Guglielmo Oberdan* Lodge immediately started gathering supporters to open a new lodge in Rijeka. It can therefore be concluded that one or both Masonic orders intended to cover the disputed territory by a network of lodges, allowing the irredentist lodges to act as a reliable mechanism for implementing or simply passing on suggestions of both formal and informal state bodies of the Kingdom of Italy to the territories included in the *Treaty of London*, with the addition of Rijeka.

The *Sirius* Lodge of Rijeka was no longer suitable for this operation for various reasons. First, its status was questionable, given that it belonged to the system of the *Symbolic Grand Lodge of Hungary*, a mixed system of both Masonic orders, and the question of to which system in Italy this lodge would adhere could probably be settled later on. Its social composition was also questionable, since it included the rich middle class of Rijeka, often members of Rijeka municipal authorities and Hungarian state officials.

Its membership numbers and order were also problematic, given that the Rijeka municipality territory was **disintegrating** and could potentially be divided between two states.

On the other hand, irredentist **warriors** were young people, marginalized or torn away from the milieu to which they had belonged before the war, which called into question the cooperation between the Freemasons of the two lodges (*Sirius* and *Oberdan*).

In the first days after the war, the Rijeka's volunteers, irredentists and political activists of all persuasions were ready to continue their operations,which is to say that they were ready for a new kind of war. In this direction the former group of *Giovane Fiume* association also began operating.

We know about these activities carried out immediately after the armistice (treaty), from a comprehensive document which is in fact the autobiography of Attilio Prodam, who was one of the most active, if not the most active and the most prominent fascist of Rijeka. Since his data on the action in the Admiralty of Venice are devoid of the subsequent mythical dimensions (Argonauti del Carnaro), we can rely on his autobiography even though, as is the case with every autobiography, he made claims that could be called into question. Still, this document is interesting as an intimate portrait of an authentic irredentist and fascist, including his attempts to justify some actions, and at the same time regretting that he took part in them.[176]

---

[176] [176] Memoriale/Difesa. Curriculum vitae di A. Prodam. State Archives of Rijeka, further (DAR), JU–6, box 393.

Antonio Vio, the mayor, and Antonio Grossich, chairman of the National Council

The data in the autobiography is supplemented by the data from a letter addressed to Mario Petris on August 29, 1935, who was one of the founders of *Giovane Fiume* and a participant in the meeting with Admiral Thaon di Revel.

In his letter, Prodam asks Petris to confirm the chronology of events in which they took part together in the period between October 29 and November 4, 1918, when five irredentists from Rijeka went to Venice to be received by the Italian naval chief of staff, Admiral Thaon di Revel, on November 4, 1918.[177] Since he asked questions about an event in which both of them participated, these statements are very likely to be accurate. The chronology makes it clear that Mario Petris, Attilio Prodam, John Stiglich, Vittorio Meichsner and Giovanni Matcovich went to Trieste on October 29 to take part on the following day in the "procession of the citizens of Trieste," after which

[177] DAR, fond Narodni odbor grada Opatije, (The National Committee of Opatija) fund, box R–83.

they were invited to cooperate with the *Fascio Nazionale pro Fiume*. On the same day, they returned to Rijeka, had talks with the *Consiglio Nazionale* and went back to Trieste. They arrived in Venice from Trieste on the following day (November 4) and were received by Thaon di Revel at the Admiralty, where the five men asked him to "protect the Italian identity of Rijeka." Thaon di Revel agreed to send out the torpedo boat *Stocco* towards Rijeka, and that during that time three participants— Matcovich, Meichsner and Stiglich— would remain in Venice at the disposal of the Supreme Command, while Petris and Prodam would enter Rijeka on the torpedo boat *Stocco* on November 4, 1918. After that, other Italian navy ships entered the port of Rijeka. Thanks to this action, according to Prodam, the "Italian identity" of Rijeka was preserved and on

December 7, 1918, the *Italian National Council* was recognized as a legitimate authority. The entire action and meeting with the admiral were probably arranged by someone from the *Fascio Nazionale pro Fiume* from Trieste or someone from the *Oberdan* Lodge, presuming that it was not one person hiding behind the two organizations.

In his pro memoria, Prodam initially claims, that if his fellow-citizens (read "a group of masons of *Sirius* Lodge") had known before the action of departure to Venice, they would have accused him of treason.

The Grand Orient of Italy whose operations were, according to the Freemasons from the *Grand Lodge of Italy*, "obscure," also organized an irredentist action, but in their way and using their own people.

The *Grand Orient of Italy* established cooperation with the *Sirius* Lodge after *the Grand Lodge of Hungary* broke Masonic ties with the *Italian Grand Orient* six days after the Kingdom of Italy declared war on Austria-Hungary on May 29, 1915.

On January 7, 1919, immediately after the beginning of the Peace Conference, the reputable Italian in Rome *Rienzi* Lodge was visited by Dr. Antonio Vio, a member of the former *Lega Autonoma* (1910), and the present Mayor of Rijeka. His visit had been prearranged, even though according to the writings, it would seem that it was spontaneous.

In his speech held at the Roman lodge, he stressed that—according to a statement by the Consiglio Nazionale of Rijeka dated October 30, 1918—Rijeka was entitled to be united with Italy, and that this decision could not be contested. At the same time, he noted that the claim that Rijeka was a natural gateway to the sea for the Kingdom of Serbs, Croats and Slovenes was a manifest falsehood. It was an implicit answer to President Wilson's memorandum directed against Italy. This is the manner in which it was agreed that the Sirius Lodge would be placed under the guardianship of the Grand Orient of Italy. On March 18, 1919, Sirius informed The Grand Orient of Italy by telegraph of its members' consent to switch their obedience.[178]

---

[178] Since Antonio Vio arranged the transition of the *Sirius Lodge* to the *Grand Orient of Italy,* during his visit to the *Rienzi* Lodge in Rome (January 7, 1919). "Onoranze al F. ... A. Vio, podesta di Fiume," in *Rivista massonica,* Jan - Feb No. 1–2/1919. pp. 20–22 "La L. . •. passa al *Grande Oriente d'Italia*"in *Rivista massonica,* March, 3/1919. p. 68. Aldo Mola, *Storia della massoneria italiana,* Milano, 1992, pp. 453–454.

2. THE MASTER OF THE *SIRIUS* LODGE AT THE PARIS PEACE CONFERENCE

E ven though the *Adriatic question* raised in Wilson's memorandum was dated February 7, it was addressed only after the treaty with Germany had been signed on June 28, 1919. Since the Yugoslav delegation was not entitled to attend the meetings of the Supreme Council, they asked President Wilson to act as its arbiter in the negotiations, especially when it came to the question of borders between the Kingdom of Italy and the Kingdom of Serbs, Croats and Slovenes.

After Italy had refused to agree to Wilson's arbitration, Ante Trumbić, as minister for foreign affairs of the Kingdom of Serbs, Croats and Slovenes, explained in a keynote the requests of the Kingdom of Serbs, Croats and Slovenes regarding the *Adriatic question*, after which the *Supreme Council* decided that debate on this issue would remain under its jurisdiction. The Yugoslav delegation after that delivered a memorandum about the city of Rijeka to the Peace Conference Territorial Commission on March 3, 1919.[179]

After that, the *Council of Four* started their debate on the *Adriatic question* without a single member of the Yugoslav delegation present, given that their request had previously been declined.

The Italian delegation stated its opinion about the *Adriatic question* on April 3, but its proposal was met with strong opposition from President Wilson, who then presented a plan that became the subject of a long debate, both at the conference and later on: that Rijeka should become a state. The Rijeka question thus obtained a new dimension, the political interest was multiplied, especially because the autonomists of Rijeka came into play.

---

[179] Archivio MAE, Affari politici, Fiume 1919, busta 1045. Dragoljub Živojinović deduces, in a solitary sentence dedicated to the event, that nothing was achieved by the meeting between Wilson and Ossoinack. Dragoljub R. Živojinović, *Amerika, Italija I postanak Jugoslavija, (1917-1919), (America, Italy and the Rise of Yugoslavia,1917–1919)* Belgrade, 1970 p. 264.

Probably attempting to give strength to the argument against the concept of the State of Rijeka and the autonomists of Rijeka, the Italian prime minister and leader of the Italian delegation, Vittorio Emanuele Orlando, asked for a private meeting with Wilson. At the time when this suggestion was made, it had probably already been arranged that a witness should come forward in favor of the annexationist solution.

The suggestion that Andrea Ossoinack should speak about the "desire of the people of Rijeka" to have the city annexed by Italy, could have come from two sides.

Orlando was a member of the Propaganda (Fatica) Lodge that belonged to the Order of the Grand Orient so it may be assumed that someone from its headquarters in Rome suggested a candidate from Rijeka to put his argument to Wilson.[180]

Apart from that, in a memorandum of the *Italian National Council* published at the end of 1918 in French, English and Italian, Andrea Ossoinack had already been listed as the last representative of Rijeka to the parliament in Budapest, who, in its last session, publicly made a "historical statement" that Rijeka wanted to belong to Italy on the basis of its right to self-determination. Moreover, both Orlando and Ossoinack held the memorandum during their meeting with Wilson.[181]

---

[180] Giordano Gamberini, *Mille volti di massoni,* Roma, 1975. p. 188.

[181] *Memorial of the president of the national council, the sindaco and deputy of Fiume.* Archives of the Ministry for Foreign Affairs (hereinafter MAE), Rome, Affari politici fund, busta 1043/1919.
It is worth noting that when first trying to justify the annexation in a memorandum dated the end of 1918, the annexationists of Rijeka had to promote the Rijeka *corpus separatum* as a state, to be able to employ the principle of self-determination and thus they used the autonomist thesis. The relationship between the annexationists and the autonomists was not exclusive at that moment. Riccardo Zanella, having returned from Russian captivity through an intervention made by the Italian state, lived and operated in Italy with an Italian diplomatic passport, and was remunerated by the Italian government to take part in various annexationist and economic missions. Further reading: Ljubinka Toševa Karpowicz, "Riccardo Zanella dall' armistizio (3. X. 1918.), al Trattato di Rapallo (12. XI. 1920), Appunti per una biografia".in, *L'autonomia fiumana (1896–1947) e la figura di Riccardo Zanella. Atti del convegno 3. novembre 1996.* Trieste, 1997, pp. 81–95

Apart from being regarded as a "historical individual," Ossoinack spoke English perfectly since he completed his studies of commerce in London. He had his own vision of Rijeka's further economic development, was the co-owner and director of the *Adria Sea Trade Company*, Master of the *Sirius* Lodge and a man with rich international ties, especially among the British and Hungarians.

Since economic arguments were frequently used at the conference to justify political programs, Ossoinack made them his priority at the meeting, all the more because he was "professionally familiar" with the topic.

Andrea Ossoinack

The meeting between Wilson, Orlando and Ossoinack took place on the afternoon of April 14. There is a document about it at the Italian Ministry for Foreign Affairs, thanks to which we were able to reconstruct the dialogue.[182] The document states that Ossoinack presented the data from the *Italian National Council* memorandum and stated that the conference did not need to discuss the Rijeka question, only to recognize the annexation of **the State of Rijeka** (emphasized by Lj. T. K.) by Italy on the basis of the plebiscite dated December 30, 1918.

Ossoinack then stated that the fact that Rijeka was contiguous with Italy would make the **annexation** easier. According to the report, Wilson then interrupted Ossoinack and said that the borders had not yet been determined, which meant that it was not contiguous.

---

[182] Archivio MAE, Affari politici, Fiume 1919, busta 1045.

Ossoinack then stated that the entire Dalmatian and Liburnian coast was inhabited by ethnic Italians, since the process of denationalization of the Italians was unsuccessful. Furthermore, according to the report, Ossoinack stated that Yugoslavia was rich in timber and that it had no difficulty exporting the timber via Dalmatian ports and that therefore it did not need the Rijeka port, to which Wilson retorted that Yugoslavia did so only through great efforts.

Ossoinack stated that it was correct that the railway in Serbia was undeveloped, but that its lines could be linked to the Rijeka–Budapest line, whereas Rijeka was at the time separated from the Yugoslav lines, which caused losses to its traffic and that that was the reason why Croatia is not its natural hinterland. According to the report, Wilson then took a look at the map and said that it was not only Yugoslavia that needed Rijeka, but the entire hinterland. Ossoinack said that he was glad to hear that, because if Rijeka were to belong to Italy, Italy would only be partly interested in using it, whereas Yugoslavia and Hungary would be interested, as would be the entire hinterland.

"Rijeka should be a free city," were the words spoken by Wilson as quoted in the report, "because it is the only way for it to be an open port for its hinterland," to which Ossoinack replied that to fulfil that purpose it was not necessary for Rijeka to become a state, merely a *porto franco*, but that it was a pity that the city could not make itself into one.

If Rijeka were to become a free city, the question is who would want to invest in it? To which Wilson replied that those interested would make the investments, and then Ossoinack said that in that case it would not be a free city. Aside from that, it would become the "apple of discord" between the Kingdom of Serbs, Croats and Slovenes and Italy, and that the city's inhabitants would suffer further deprivation.

Wilson interrupted him by saying: "But the inhabitants themselves want Rijeka to be a free city," to which Ossoinack replied that maybe some Yugoslavs interpreted "porto franco" as a "free city." "This means," Wilson concluded, "that you want Rijeka to be politically dependent on Italy as a *punto franco,* but in that event the Yugoslavs would not be welcome in Rijeka!"

According to the report, this is where Orlando intervened, having stood by the whole time, and stated that all rights would be guaranteed to all non-Italian inhabitants of the city, after which the meeting was ended, with Ossoin-ack thanking President Wilson for receiving him.

Rumors quickly spread that Wilson was fighting for Rijeka to have the status of an international port-state, and the American media announced that the conference would be terminated, which happened quickly when the Italian negotiators left the conference on April 26. However, they returned shortly thereafter, on May 6.

A month later, more precisely on May 15, 1919, Andrea Ossoinack held a conference in the hall of the House of Commons Commission at the British Parliament, presenting the Rijeka question.

Since no confirmation can be found of this conference in the literature, we may suspect that the "report" was a forgery.

It states that the economic reasons for the annexation of Rijeka were met with approval by the British Parliament and that the Parliament found Wilson's behavior to be inappropriate when he dared interrupt a "statesman" (*statement*) while he advanced arguments that were contrary to his views. Apart from that, Wilson did not accept that at that moment, Rijeka was a de facto state and that, as such, it was unable to resolve its issues, which was the reason why it was asking for annexation.

Ossoinack's testimony before Wilson did not result in the resolution of the Rijeka question. The project of Rijeka as a state was binding to the future negotiators at the conference even after Wilson had left.

At the beginning of June 1919, Sem Benelli, a lieutenant in the Italian army and a poet, arrived in Rijeka from city Pula (Pola, in Italian). His arrival was probably arranged by the *Consiglio Nazionale di Fiume* to help pass the law on establishing an army to defend Rijeka. The law was passed on June 13, 1919, and Nino Host-Venturi, an annexationist from Rijeka, was appointed head of the "steering committee."

Soon enough, the "Rijeka Legion" began to clash with the members of the Allied occupation army in Rijeka, ending in serous clashes with a fatal outcome. Since the Allied Council in Paris had decided that the English or American police should be tasked with maintaining law and order in Rijeka and that the *Consiglio Nazionale* should be disbanded, its president, Antonio Grossich, and the newly-appointed commander of the Rijeka Legion, Host-Venturi, immediately went to Italy to find a "savior" for the "Rijeka cause."[183]

The *Oberdan* Lodge from Trieste took part in that operation.

On behalf of the Italian irredentist association *Figli d' Italia,* operating in the USA and the *Dante Allighieri* society from Boston, Andrea Ossoinack held a conference in the American Senate at the beginning of July 1919 against the policy of President Wilson, and pointed out, that Rijeka will be annexed to Italy.[184]

[183] ibid.

[184] Ferdo Čulinović, *Riječka država, (State of Fiume)*, Zagreb, 1953. pp. 74–82. From: Dragoljub R. Živojinović, *U potrazi za zaštitnikom. Studija o srpsko-američkim vezama 1878-1920.(The search for a protector. A study about Serbo-American Connections 1878-1920)*, Beoograd 2010. pp. 424- 425. The book was written using 66th Congress,1st session, 1121; Woodhouse and Woodhouse.n.m.269/271.

On September 6, 1919, the *Oberdan* Lodge received the visiting "brethren": Antonio Vio, Mayor of Rijeka, Dardi, an attorney and "secretary general" of the city and Guido Lado, an engineer representing the *Sirius* Lodge. The "brethren" came to ask their "brethren" from the Trieste lodge for help, given that, under the decision rendered by the Paris Conference, the Italian battalion had to leave Rijeka.

That same evening, a **mixed secret committee** was established by the *Oberdan* Lodge composed of both Freemasons and laymen, and on the next day this committee went to Venice to have talks with D'Annunzio. The mixed secret committee was probably made up of representatives from both Trieste and Rijeka. Judging by the data stated by Attilio Prodam in his autobiography, he too was one of the committee members from Rijeka.

After they had secured support from their "confrères" at the railroad and telegraph, the newly founded secret committees became open for military personnel.

Continuing his arguments in favor of the role played by the *Oberdan* Lodge in organizing D'Annunzio's appointment as the occupier of Rijeka, Aldo Mola, an Italian masonic writer, states the names of those "brethren" who sat together with him in the car in which he entered Rijeka. He then states that as of September 22, 1919, the *Grand Lodges of the USA*, Great Britain and France started sending their greetings to D'Annunzio.

The *Grand Orient of Italy* opened a two million lira credit line, earmarked for supplying the populace of Rijeka with coal and foodstuffs via the Italian Red Cross that was headed by Giovanni Ciraolo, a former "president" of the *Symbolic Grand Lodge.*

Aldo Mola then states that the occupation of Rijeka was supported by other "brethren," and among them "brother" Luigi Rizzo, who had sunk the Austrian battleship *Saint Stephen (Istvan),* for which he was promoted to 30th degree of the *Symbolic Grand Lodge.*

Apart from the politics of support to D'Annunzio's action, these data show that both orders were competing not only to help, but to contribute to the political and ideological goals of those in favor of D'Annunzio's occupation.

This competition left the "brethren" from Rijeka confused. They were not able to grasp that the two orders were competing with one another, which is obvious from a quoted letter dated August 16, 1919. The letter was sent to the Grand Commander of the *Grand Lodge of Italy* through Major Gabrielli. In it the anonymous author begs Raul Palermi, "the Grand Master of Italian Freemasonry of Scottish Rite," to make both orders act jointly so as to achieve "their patriotic duty"—Rijeka's unification with Italy—and not to be torn apart by rivalry.[185]

---

[185] The rivalry between the two Masonic orders did not only concern Rijeka, but the orders themselves arose from rivalry. The primary national lodge of Italy belonged to the order of the *Grand Orient of Italy* (abbreviated G. O. I.), that was named after its headquarters as the Freemasonry of Palazzo Giustiniani. After the 1908 splinter, a group numbering around 100 Freemasons rented a building on the Piazza del Gesù as its headquarters, which they took as their name. Its real name *was* the *Ancient and Accepted Scottish Rite or the Grand Lodge*. It was headed by the Sovereign Grand Inspector General, whereas the Grand Orient was headed by the Grand Master. The reason why they split is subject to numerous, however unfinished analyses. Apart from that, the relationship between Freemasonry and Fascism further complicated the issue. Anna Maria Isastia lists enough data about that in "Massoneria e fascismo: la grande repressione," in *La Massoneria, nella storia, gli uomini, le idee*, Milano, 2004. pp. 179–237. The 1908 split actually happened because of the Freemasons' attitude to accepting new members, i.e. the question as to whether Freemasonry was an association of laymen or believers. The *Freemasonry from Piazza del Gesù* remained adamant that it was an association of believers. Major Gabrielli, as a "brother" and activist of the Grand Lodge, is also mentioned by Amleto Ballarini. He quotes a pro memoria by Attilio Prodam, in which he stated that he became member of the Scottish rite Freemasonry in November 1919, persuaded by Major Gabrielli, who as an emissary of the order got close to Prodam, urging him to join. As Prodam did not state the name of the lodge, Ballarini concluded that it was *Italia Nuova*. 13/Amleto Ballarini, op.cit. p. 165, n. 45.

3. ATTILIO PRODAM AND THE ITALIAN FREEMASONRY OF THE GRAND LODGE ORDER (UNTIL THE *TREATY OF RAPALLO*)

Even though Attilio Prodam was a member of *Giovane Fiume* and took part in its "historical actions"—above all in the field trip to Ravenna in 1908 when the association was banned —he was unknown to the residents of Rijeka, until the dissolution of the Dual Monarchy. It was the "Argonauts of Rijeka" expedition, i.e. his trip to Venice aboard the Istria steamer to meet with Admiral Thaon di Revel, that thrust his "burning readiness to sacrifice himself tor Rijeka" into the limelight. After he had sailed into the Rijeka port on November 4, 1918 together with Petris aboard the torpedo boat *Stocco*, there was no more information about Attilio Prodam until August 1919. He resurfaced when the Italian troops, as Allied troops, had to leave Rijeka, and Prodam, as one of the members of the secret committee whose names and actions are not mentioned, once again went to Venice, where on September 6 D'Annunzio handed him his "famous message" announcing his now famous "March from Ronchi."

The *Grand Orient's* initial support to D'Annunzio's occupation began waning as of October 1919. Mostly it was due to the fact that on June 23, 1919, Francesco Saverio Nitti, Mason, member of *Grande Oriente*, who was a liberal,and opposed to D'Annunzio's actions became the Italian prime minister.

Aldo Mola points out that the new Grand Master of the Grand Orient, Domizio Torrigiani, got the impression that the citizens of Rijeka were more willing to negotiate the future of Rijeka, and at the end of October 1919, he made a short visit to Rijeka, probably to look into the situation himself. After that, in a letter dated October 25, he informed D'Annunzio that "he and the Italian Freemasonry do not intend to follow unconditionally the paths that are unknown to him and the Italian Freemasonry..."[186]

---

[186] A. Mola, op.cit. p. 457.

This was a sign that there was a turn in the attitude of the *Grand Orient of Italy* regarding D'Annunzio's occupation. However, it remains unclear whether they parted ways only because the prime minister had changed or because they had found out that the *Grand Lodge* also took part in D'Annunzio's occupation of Rijeka, a conclusion that can be drawn from Torrigiani's letter in which he points out that he was not familiar with all of D'Annunzio's "ways".

Yet again, Torrigiani made his way to Trieste on October 27, 1919, to be present at a top secret meeting. In this meeting, a heated argument took place about how to proceed with the *Grand Orient's* participation, considering the rumors that 3,000 volunteers from Rijeka were ready to disembark in Trieste, and then march to Rome. On the same day, Torrigiani met with Francesco Giunta, the organizer of the first fascist congress and D'Annunzio's commissioner, who was in favor of a republican revolution, but not in the form of a military coup to avoid triggering an armed reaction from the working class and peasants, which could cause the birth of a Bolshevik regime and the dictatorship of the proletariat. On the following day, the "brethren" from the *Grand Orient* of Trieste put together the *Committee of Public Safety* that was tasked with contacting D'Annunzio and informing him about the *Grand Orient's* decisions.[187]

A clear conclusion can be drawn that the D'Annunzio-Torrigiani link ceased to exist.

Attilio Prodam, of course, had a completely personal view of these events. However, what is important to us is the manner in which the *Grand Lodge* took over the leading role in D'Annunzio's occupation from the *Grand Orient*. Attilio Prodam's testimony is all the more important, because nothing has been published from the archives of the *Grand Lodge*, apart from a book by Santina Quagliani that is not very comprehensive.

Attilio Prodam claims that immediately after the Italian ships had sailed into Rijeka (on November 14, 1919, when they were supposed to follow D'Annunzio on his way to Dalmatia for negotiations with Admiral Millo), a

---

[187] idem, p. 461.

group made up of military personnel, among which he only remembered his "friend" major Gabrielli, came to him personally and started urging him to join the Freemasonry. Prodam points out that he refused, given that he was opposed to the membership and actions of the *Sirius* Lodge, but after he had been shown an issue of a Masonic magazine dedicated to Rijeka (*Rivista massonica*), he was delighted to become member of the Masonic order from Piazza del Gesù, i.e. of the *Grand Lodge*. While they were persuading Prodam, they explained to him the misunderstandings that existed between the two orders and once again pointed out that the work of the *Sirius* Lodge was "obscure."[188]

After he had agreed not only to join but also to establish a lodge, Prodam gathered his "friends, legionaries and fascists from Rijeka," founded a lodge and then became its Master. Since in his writings, Prodam does not state the name of the lodge, Amleto Ballarini concludes that it was *Italia Nuova* (all' Oriente di Fiume).[189]

However, Santina Quagliani, whose book was published by the *Grand Lodge of Italy*'s publishing house and who probably used their documents, claims that Attilio Prodam was Master of the *XXX Ottobre* Lodge from Rijeka.[190]

Even though it is questionable whether these were two lodges (*Italia Nuova and XXX Otto*bre), or one that changed its name or was a temporary lodge, the cooperation with Attilio Prodam is what is important, i.e. the fact that he was won over by the *Grand Lodge of Italy (Piazza del Gesù)*, and that all his subsequent actions as a fascist were imposed by the Freemasonry belonging to this order. Prodam would above all confirm himself as a loyal fascist, and his Masonic membership and status as Master of a lodge would be merely a focal

---

[188] Attilio Prodam, *Memoriale/Difesa* (typescripts), DAR, JU–6, box 393, pp. 4–5.

[189] Amleto Ballarini, *Antidannunziano a Fiume. Riccardo Zanella.* Trieste, 1995. p. 197. n. 45. The DAR Archives documents that refer to Freemasonry do confirm Amleto Ballarini's thesis, because no document mentions the name of the XXX Ottobre Lodge.

[190] Santina Quagliani, *La pulsione verso il trascendente,* Roma, 1995. An article written by a prominent Italian historian, Renzo de Felice, claims that the lodge was constituted in 1919 under the name Guglielmo Oberdan: "Una lettera di D'Annunzio al Grande Oriente da Fiume nel 1919." *Fiume,* Roma, anno XII, No. 3–4/1965.

point through which he received tasks "from the headquarters," whether it was the Freemason or the fascist headquarters.

His conviction that he was "on the right side," both as a Freemason and a patriot, was also confirmed by the fact that D'Annunzio received a confirmation on admittance to 33rd degree Freemasonry of the *Grand Lodge,* handed in to him personally by the nephew of Saverio Ferra, the Grand Master of the order.[191]

Having been warned of the "obscure actions" of the members of the *Sirius* Lodge, Prodam saw secret anti-D'Annuzian actions of the *Grand Orient* Freemasonry carried out by the leaders of the *Sirius* Lodge, in all events related to D'Annunzio's actions in Rijeka and to the official Italian politics. This is why he reacted when at the end 1919, a *modus vivendi* request was made to D'Annunzio when the *Opatija Pact* was signed, and he concluded that the *Sirius Lodge* had won.

Convinced that he needed to find sympathizers and fighters in Italy to help the annexation of Rijeka, Prodam points out that at the beginning of 1920 and at his own expense, he traveled to Milan, Rome and Venice, accompanied by his wife, looking for collaborators and in September 1920, in the editorial offices of the journal *Popolo d' Italia* he met Benito Mussolini, "an ardent supporter of the holy cause (*causa*) of Rijeka." It is probable that the "sympathizers" and "fighters" that Prodam was looking for in Italy for the "holy cause of Rijeka" were fascists and members of the *squadri d'azione.*

As of August 1920, Francesco Giunta, who was D'Annunzio's assignee, among other things, started visiting Rijeka often with a view to establishing the *Combat Fascio of Rijeka* (*Fascio Fiumano di Combattimento*). Its first meetings were held at the headquarters of the former *Giovane Fiume* association, and Giunta explained the causal link between Fascism and the occupation of Rijeka. The *Combat Fascio of Rijeka* was finally established on August 12, 1920. Carlo Conighi, a member of the *Sirius* Lodge was proposed as its first chairman, but he excused himself stating that he was not able to accept the

[191] Aldo Alessando Mola, *Storia della massoneria italiana,* op.cit. p. 454.

office due to his advanced age, and this is how Professor Edoardo Susmel, who was also included in a single list of Freemasons of the *Sirius Lodge,* was elected chairman.

According to an author named Antonella Ercolani, the *Fascio* of Rijeka was later joined by Attilio Prodam and Armando Hodnig, former members of *Giovane Fiume,* with links to the Rijeka headquarters of the *Trento–Trieste association* that spear-headed the action.[192]

This claim made by A. Ercolani is contrary to the data from a 1924 document. De Clementi, the quaestor of Rijeka was the author of the draft document, in which, on August 30, 1924, he suggested to the prefect of Rijeka that Attilio Prodam should be knighted, and attached the candidate's biography to the document. The biography states that Prodam was one of the founders of the *Combat Fascio of Rijeka,* and this piece of data is consistent with all the data from other documents.[193]

At the first meeting of the Rijeka *Fascio,* the conclusion was made about the strengthening of the fight against the autonomists, socialists and all those forces who objected and who are opposed to annexation.[194]

However, the newly founded *Fascio* of Rijeka had many internal problems due to its lack of determination in fighting the opposition forces, and so the first elected chairman, Professor Edoardo Susmel, was replaced by the more resolute Giovanni Mrach, a volunteer and a member of the *Rijeka legion* since May 18, 1919, one of the organizers (together with Host-Venturi) of D'Annunzio's march on Rijeka.

The Rijeka's *Fascio Fiumano di Combattimento* was established during the second phase of D'Annunzio's occupation of Rijeka as a means of fighting against the autonomists, Italian anarcho-syndicalists, who had arrived with Alceste De Ambris, who was at the time D'Annunzio's secretary and was working with him on the statute of Rijeka, the famous *Carta del Carnaro,*

---

[192] Antonella Ercolani, *La fondazione del Fascio del combattimento a Fiume tra Mussolini e D'Annunzio,* Roma, 1996. pp. 106–107.

[193] DAR, Ju–6, box 133.

[194] Antonella Ercolani, op.cit. p. 108.

and who was also a socialist. This complex political situation, in which anarcho-syndicalists and socialists prevailed, was the result of the economic crisis both in Italy, and in Rijeka.

The shift in ideology and the generally more modest attitude D'Annunzio was taking presented themselves as an opportunity to the members of the still active *Sirius* Lodge, above all to Samuel Mayländer and Doctor Brajjer, to reinterpret his enterprise.[195]

"Brother" Samuel Mayländer, one of the founders of the *Sirius* Lodge and Secretary of the *Communist Party of Rijeka*, suggested that a delegation of Rijeka communists should go to Italy and connect with the Italian socialists, and at the same time he suggested that the representatives of parties from Rijeka should go to D'Annunzio to inform him about the social problems of the workers. [196]

According to a 1931 document, Dr. Luigi Brajjer, ex-member of the *Sirius* Lodge, now a member of the *German Grand Lodge*, interviewed D'Annunzio on April 11, 1920 for *Neue freie Presse* and presented him as a humanist who, through his act, resisted the political and social injustice that came in the wake of the First World War.[197]

However, the completion of Italian-Yugoslav negotiations that ended in the signing of the *Treaty of Rapallo* and creation of the State of Rijeka, provided further motivation to the *Combat Fascio of Rijeka*, and also to Italian fascists, to employ even more elaborate and more secret methods to work against the autonomists, against the State of Rijeka and its consolidation.

---

[195] "Loggia Sirius sciolta 26 settembre 1924. con circolare." DAR, Interim Government fund, boxes 14 and 15.

[196] On D'Annunzio's relationship with the Freemasonry during the occupation of Rijeka see: Ljubinka Toševa Karpowicz, *D' Annunzio u Rijeci, op.cit. (D'Annunzio in Rijeka. Myths, Politics and Freemasonry's Role)*, Rijeka, 2007, the second part of the book in particular; The Italian and Yugoslav Freemasonry in the First World War and D'Annunzio's march on Rijeka, pp. 149–200.

[197] For a more comprehensive interpretation of the interview see: Lj. T. Karpowicz, op.cit. pp. 109–110.

6

ITALIAN FREEMASONRY AND THE *STATE OF RIJEKA*

1. ATTILIO PRODAM AND THE FASCIST COUP D'ÉTAT AGAINST RICCARDO ZANELLA

The internal problems that made the *Combat Fascio of Rijeka* more tolerant than it had been anticipated by its founders, and due to which the more "resolute" Giovanni Mrach was appointed, came as a consequence of the disposition of its members. Apart from the *Arditi,* legionaries, the unemployed, the young, and those disoriented by the war, middle class citizens joined the *Fascio of Rijeka*, which necessarily influenced the political views of Rijeka fascists.

The scheduling of elections for the Constituent Assembly of the State of Rijeka for April 24, 1921 was an opportunity to organize new political groups as new parties, to renew the old ones and create new coalitions. Apart from the sections of the Italian parties (the *Italian Republican Party* and *the Italian People's Party*), new local parties were created (the Yugoslav *Party of Rijeka* and the *National-Democratic Party*). The latter was established as support to the *National Bloc.*

Its eight-point program, published in the pro-fascist newspaper *La Vedetta d'Italia* on January 23, 1921, presents it as a political group which seeks to overcome the conflict between the fascists and the autonomists, stands for the economic prosperity of Rijeka, and advocates that the port of *Baroš* should belong to Yugoslavia. It did not oppose the State of Rijeka, and the party's main goal was that Rijeka should be declared a free port, that the use of common warehouses should be reviewed and that rail traffic should be diverted to Rijeka, as the main export port of central Europe.

This was actually the joint program of the "Masonic Bloc" of the united *Sirius* and *Italia Nuova* lodges that were united immediately before the elections and took part in the elections as the *National-Democratic Party*. A privately owned document dated to the end of 1922, which is to say after the coup against President Riccardo Zanella, states that party members were the well-known Freemasons of the *Sirius* Lodge (Vio, Bellasich, Mini, Ossoinack, Rubinic and Conighi).[198] In the elections for the *Constituent Assembly* held on April 24, 1921, 2,000 of the total of 13,000 voters abstained, and the autonomist bloc won 8,000 votes, whereas the pro-annexation bloc won 2,800 votes.

After the *Italian Legation* announced the election results, the legionaries and fascists led by Riccardo Gigante attacked the court and burned the electoral urns. At the same time, they set fire to Zanella's apartment, while he and a large number of citizens, around 4,000 of them, fled to the Yugoslav territory.

The Rijeka annexationists, Host-Venturi and Salvatore Bellasich then called the Trieste fascists for help and on April 27 they occupied the Rijeka municipality seat, headed by Francesco Giunta, and helped the provisional government of Antonio Grossich, constituted ad hoc, hand over the power to them. Forced by circumstances, the consul at the *Italian Legation*, Carlo Caccia Dominioni, met with Zanella in Sušak. Zanella asked that the Italian government send in the regular army and clean the city of fascists, and that if they did not do so, he would go to the Allies for help.

With the mutual efforts of Caccia Dominioni and Carlo Sforza, minister for foreign affairs of the Kingdom of Italy and a signatory of the *Treaty of Rapallo* and representative of the Kingdom of Serbs, Croats and Slovenes, the

---

[198] The document is probably a confidant's report, sent to Riccardo Zanella in Kraljevica after the fascist coup d'état of March 3, 1922. In our opinion, Ruggiero Gotthardi is the author of the document.

Attilio Prodam's fascist identity card

Rijeka (autonomist) refugees returned from Bakar and on October 5, 1921 the *Constituent Assembly* started its session. On the same day, there was a vote for the prime minister and Zanella won fifty-seven out of sixty-eight votes, and was thus promoted to prime minister, after which he appointed members of the government, i.e. the ministers.[199]

All these events felt like defeat to Attilio Prodam, and probably to other fascist originations that he was leading (*Fascio Fiumano di Combattimento, Legionari i Guardia Nazionale*). They did not, however, hesitate to further undermine the autonomist government.

The failure of the elections and ideological stratification within the *Rijeka Combat Fascio* became the subject of discussions, which resulted in further disintegration. Attilio Prodam blamed the members of the *Sirius* Lodge for his failure and certain fascists who joined them, but he also accused his associates in the Italian state institutions. His criticism paints the *Sirius* Lodge of Rijeka and her members as an omnipotent, international, rich and nepotistic group, closely related both to their "brethren" in Rome, and other centers of power in Europe. After these unsuccessful attempts to bury the autonomists of Rijeka

---

[199] Danilo I Massagrande, *Italia e Fiume 1921–1924*. Milano,1982. pp. 67–68.

politically, the crucial moment for the organization of the resistance arrived, promoting Attilio Prodam from local to national level fascist: on September 21, 1921, in the small hours of the night, Major Perata, Military Attaché at the *Italian Legation*, summoned Prodam to make haste to Opatija that very night, to the *Mahler Villa*, for talks with the Legation's envoy, Michele Castelli. Prodam replied that he would not be able to find public transport at those hours of the night and asked that the meeting be rescheduled for tomorrow.[200]

Prodam describes in detail the historic conversation with Castelli, and to unmask his secret and informal role we use the data provided by him, even though he kept silent about the important information about his cooperation with Castelli up to that moment. Later on, it became evident from the notes written on Castelli's visit cards that they had cooperated as of September 1919, and the next dates written on the visit cards were October 9, and December 6, 1919.[201]

According to the text written by Prodam, Castelli presented himself as an envoy of the Italian government and said that he wanted to talk to him, given that he was respected among the fascists, legionnaires and the *Arditi*. Castelli stated that his task was to remove Zanella from power and that to do so he needed Attilio Prodam's help.

Prodam, allegedly refused to cooperate and stated numerous reasons.

Castelli allegedly said that the *Constituent Assembly* would not stay in power for a long time, since the political views of the citizens of Rijeka were greatly divided, but that the difficult economic conditions would prove to be decisive in its downfall. According to Castelli, the Italian government, under

---

[200] Alfredo Perata played an important role in the overthrow of Riccardo Zanella's government. See: Ljubinka Toševa Karpowicz, *Tajne Opatije. Tajna diplomacija I obavje*štajne službe u Opatiji 1945-1890., *(Opatija's Secrets. Secret Diplomacy in Opatija 1890–1945.)* Rijeka, 2012 pp. 148–151. Perata also appeared on the list of the fascists whose biographies were reexamined in 1930. After the attempt on Zanella's life, he lived in Opatija. Riccardo Zanella made well supported accusations against him claiming that he did not send any of his letters (dated January 15, 1922) to the Italian minister for foreign affairs, in which Zanella informed him about the potential coup d'état against his government. The last-known information about Alfred Perata is from March 26, 1943 when he was conscripted and sent to the military operations zone. He was sixty at the time.

[201] DAR: Riječka prefektura, box 394/I-27.

Allied pressure, had to help the government of the State of Rijeka to start operating, but it was in the Italian government's interest that the Constituent Assembly should be short-lived.

After having thought about it, Prodam dictated to Castelli his terms of cooperation, to which he had no objections. The terms were:

1. that the Italian government, and not Zanella, should convene the Constituent Assembly session, and that Castelli, as a representative of the Italian government, should give Prodam precise and certain assurances that Zanella's government would remain in power no longer than a month, and that the Italian government would then abolish it;

2. that through its representative, the Italian government should give guarantees to Prodam that neither Zanella, nor any of the members of the Constituent Assembly, would receive "a cent" in any form either from the Italian government, or from a bank or a private enterprise, whether it came from Rijeka or Italy; and

3. the most important condition was that through its representative, the Italian government should declare that it would remain adamant that the <u>port complex and the part of the railway in Rijeka territory had to remain under Italian administration</u> (underlined in the original), all of which was to be accompanied by guarantees of huge subsidies already given by the Italian government to the state of Rijeka (Prodam attached the Italian government's statement to this condition).

In a note about his third condition, Prodam wrote that Castelli had misinterpreted that Prodam had implicitly asked for money in return for cooperation, because Castelli then started reassuring him that he should not trouble himself with the question of the prize, because it would be paid out of the "political fund," from which many citizens of Rijeka had already received "prizes" for their services. In this conversation, the name of a person who had received an enormous prize for favoring the Italian government with regard to the railway and the port of Rijeka was mentioned but not stated. This allegedly surprised Prodam, and the suggestion that he would be rewarded offended him. The conversation ended by both Prodam's hands being shaken which meant the end of this, according to his opinion, historic conversation, with which we are forced to agree!

On the same day, on the night of September 22, 1921, the Directorate of the *Fascio* of Rijeka was hastily summoned to a meeting, attended by all members and Prodam asked them for strict secrecy. He recounted his meeting with Castelli in detail and stated that the fascists should be against the "tiny State of Rijeka" and against President Zanella, who sold a part of its territory to *Standard Oil Company* from New York, and warned them that if they failed to prevent him, he would sell the rest of "our coast" to his French, British, American and Yugoslav friends. At the same time, he notified them that France already intended to establish its "naval base for the east" in Rijeka.

Almost all members of the directorate, with the exception of two members, agreed with the propositions of the agreement made with Castelli. The two who opposed them stated that Prodam was not authorized to carry out such negotiations and that they did not believe in Castelli's sincerity.

In reply to their remarks, Prodam undertook to take responsibility both for the action and for its consequences.

After the elections for the *Constituent Assembly*, the Italian government, under pressure from its war "allies," had to help the introduction of the government. General Amantea, Commander of Royal Troops in Rijeka, convened the session of the *Constituent Assembly* held on October 5, 1921. At the same time, he pointed out that the railway and port facilities would remain under the administration of the Italian government (documents attached), which was interpreted by Prodam as the beginning of the fulfilment of the arrangement he had made.

However, Prodam soon came to the bitter realization that, contrary to his agreement with Castelli, Zanella's government had already been in power for five months. His disappointment was even greater when he found out that on December 31, 1921, Zanella received two million lire, and a subsequent four million lire from the Italian government.

In a repeat meeting with Castelli at the end of October 1921, when he asked when the attack on the Constituent Assembly and Zanella should start, Castelli

answered that the Italian government was still unable to get rid of
Zanella and that they should wait
for the "fruit to ripen." Castelli suggested that Prodam consult other
members of organizations in which
he was active, and that during that
time he would go to Rome and
make arrangements about the further actions to overthrow Zanella.

The last agreement between
Castelli and Prodam took place
on February 28, 1922. It was the
last time Prodam and Castelli met.
Prodam started his action alone, in
cooperation with the fascists from
Trieste. He started working with
them in October 1921, probably

Attilio Prodam in fascist uniform

after his conversation with Castelli, attempting to coordinate the action to
overthrow Zanella.

The arranged murder of Alfredo Fontana, a young fascist, was the reason
for the founding of the *National Defense Committee*, and in its meeting, attended by Giovanni Giuriati and De Stefani, who were fascist members of
Rome parliament, Attilio Prodam was elected chairman of the *Committee*.
Apart from him, the *Committee* included another four fascists and three republicans. "With God's help and help from our friend Giunta," as written by
Prodam, they carried out the attack on the governor's palace. After the attack
on the governor's palace, Zanella was forced to sign the historically famous
statement in the fascist headquarters that he renounced politics forever. He
was placed in prison with his **collaborator** Dr. Blasich, until he was embarked
aboard a military vessel.

However, Prodam pointed out that only after the coup had been carried out,
did his old enemies from the *Sirius* Lodge, launch their actions against him.

Prodam accused them as the "camarillia massonica locale." He pointed out that, as of March 14, 1922, they started spreading rumors that Prodam intended to dissolve the *National Defense Committee* and replace it with a coalition government. It was supposed to contain only people from Rijeka. It would be headed by Prodam, while other members would be Armando Hodnig, a nationalist and Mario Jechel, an autonomist.

To defend himself from these "insinuations," Prodam went to the *Hotel Europa* with Giovanni Abramovich, a fascist, to room 59, where he was surprised to see Lieutenant Ernesto Cabruna with members of the military committee. The meeting was attended by the members of the "proposed" coalition government that Prodam had thought was just a rumor: Armando Hodnig, Mario Sanni, and others.

Only then did Attilio Prodam realize that he had merely been used as a temporary means to an end, that a shift had taken place in his employment and that he was being replaced by the old, experienced Lieutenant Legionnaire Ernesto Cabruna. Cabruna himself was even more surprised by Prodam's arrival than him and declared that the meeting had been adjourned to abolish the *National Defense Committee* which was to be replaced by a *Triumvirate* government (with people already selected, and Prodam as one of them). Prodam did not agree with this appointment, because it would be inconsistent with his coup, and, according to the fascist Giovanni Abramovich, he left the meeting. The following event involving the above persons was aimed at denying Ernesto Cabruna's role in the coup, and placing responsibility solely with Prodam.

Prodam points out that Cabruna, maybe even unwittingly, carried out Commander Michele Castelli's orders, who was "carrying out orders of the Freemasons from Palazzo Giustiniani". Soon, on October 31, 1922 in Rome, the fascists attacked the headquarters of the Grand Orient, and this made it all the more necessary to hide the "Masonic connection" with the coup against Zanella, if there really was any.[202]

---

[202] Attilio Prodam, *Memoriale/Difesa,* op.cit. p. 29.

Riccardo Zanella's identity card

According to the instructions of the Italian government, on March 6, 1922, Michele Castelli returned to Rijeka as the officially appointed government minister with the Italian Legation, tasked with pacifying the situation in Rijeka.[203] This means that the state before the fascist coup was meant to be "conserved".

According to instructions received, Ernesto Cabruna was supposed to persuade the remaining members of the *Constituent Assembly* in Rijeka to convene a session and elect a new government. Since they declined to do so, they were persecuted together with other members of the *Autonomous Party,* who took the roundabout way and great risks to reach Yugoslav soil.[204] Prodam

---

[203] The *Italian Legation* to the State of Rijeka was established on March 13, 1921. It replaced the Italian Consulate in Austria-Hungary. Count Carlo Caccia Dominioni di Sillavengo, who was a consul in Rijeka from 1906 to 1914, was appointed head of the legation. He was immediately removed from office in December 1922. Ministero degli Affari esteri, Segretaria Generale, *Storia e diplomazia,* Roma, 2008. The same information is cited by Danilo I. Massagrande, op.cit. p. 104, n. 24.

[204] Description of the situation according to: Danilo I. Massagrande, op.cit. p. 198, attachment, "Letter from the Prime Minister of Rijeka in exile, Zanella, to the Council of Nations" (in French).

---

withdrew from public life from the moment when Ernesto Cabruna started working on creating a coalition government, according to Michele Castelli's instructions. He was making a living from selling electrical goods in his shop.[205]

Since he was in disfavor, and the fascist party of Rijeka was declared an accomplice in the military coup, in October 1922, Prodam went to Milan to give his testimony to the "Duce" about the events. Soon thereafter Mussolini would form a government (October 28, 1922), and on November 22, 1925, the parliament enacted the decision on the banning of all secret and Masonic associations. This gave Prodam satisfaction because of the assumed or real role played by the *Sirius* Lodge in the political events and, specifically, its action against him.

However, the economic situation continued to worsen, and Prodam was isolated so he decided to write a letter to Mussolini and ask for help. In his letter, sent on January 29, 1935, Prodam asked to be received by Mussolini and employed by the *Servizi Pubblici* or appointed president of the Public Warehouses, to be able to solve the difficult economic situation in which his family found itself. To once again underline his merits, he reminded Mussolini about the delicate mission entrusted to him by Teruzzi and Balbo. Based on Mussolini's order, a conclusion can be drawn that Prodam's final mission in favor of Mussolini's rise to power (October 28, 1922) was a meeting with D'Annunzio, probably trying to find out whether he could be won over to take part in the march on Rome.

The data stated in Prodam's autobiography can shed some light on the data insufficiently known to the public.

Firstly, it is obvious that the *Italian Legation in Rijeka* was an unofficial operating point for taking actions and making connections with the unknown persons from the Italian government, the Italian ministry for foreign affairs and other institutions, including the informal groups of the Italian political system.

---

[205] Michele Castelli (1883–1939). For his part in the fascist coup d'état in Rijeka, on December 23, 1923, he was appointed state councilor and minister plenipotentiary. He is usually mentioned in documents alongside Carlo Caccia Dominioni. Castelli's family donated his personal documents in 1998 to the Central State Archives in Rome. The documents were deposited in thirteen boxes. *Rassegna degli Archivi di Stato,* Roma, genn. /aprile 1989. p. 205.

Even though Carlo Caccia Dominioni was the first diplomatic representative to the *State of Rijeka* and stepped into that office after a career in diplomacy spent also in Rijeka, on February 5, 1921, Attilio Prodam did not mention his name at all, even though it is impossible that Caccia Dominioni knew nothing about the agreement between Castelli and Prodam.[206] The question is raised as to whether the assignment of blame to the *Sirius* Lodge for the general failure of fascists from Rijeka and Prodam himself was the result of his unwillingness to admit the reasons for his failure, obsession or exaggeration. Was his attitude to a former Hungarian lodge, now acknowledged by the *Grand Orient of Italy*, just intended to exacerbate the conflict between the two Italian orders that tried to interfere with politics in Rijeka?

A document from his collection of documents supports Attilio Prodam's claim that the conflict between the two orders of the Italian Freemasonry spilt over to Rijeka.

In a letter (No. 23345), the *Grand Orient of Italy* addressed the Master of the *Sirius* Lodge on November 17, 1921 notifying him that the defector from "Ferra's lodges," "brother" Edoardo Frosini, brought an official letter from "Ferra's Red Cross," in which they were asking for funds to build a new (Masonic) temple. According to the same source, this letter was signed by a "brother," Attilio "Brodan," instead of Prodam (the mistake was corrected further on in the letter) and, later on in the text, the wording of the letter was adopted, ending in "brother" Prodam's request to the Freemasons of the Scottish Rite ("the ancient and accepted Orient, to vigorously oppose the irregular

---

[206] Count Carlo Caccia Dominioni di Sillavengo (1863–1936), consul in Rijeka as of November 29, 1906, became consul general in January 1907 and was appointed first degree consul that same year. After Rijeka, he was appointed consul to Tunisia (March 12, 1912), then to Lugano (December 4, 1919) after which he returned to Rijeka as minister in the State of Rijeka on February 2, 1921. He remained in that office until March 4, 1922, which means that he left immediately after the coup d'état against Riccardo Zanella's government. After that, he was minister in Cairo from February 1924 to June 1926, and then held no office. He left the diplomatic corps in February 1927. Danilo I. Massagrande, *Italia e Fiume 1921–1924*. Milano, 1982 p. 23, n. 26. Documents from Caccia Dominioni's personal archives are kept in the State Archives in Milan, (P.A.A.D. – Rivendica Carlo Caccia Dominioni, fond Atti e documenti demaniali). Caccia Dominioni appears repeatedly alongside Michele Castelli throughout the documents.

and foreign Freemasons").

In the conclusion to the letter, the Grand Secretary (of the *Grand Orient of Italy*) requested his "brethren" from the *Sirius* Lodge to notify him of the means they were going to employ to counteract this violent attack.[207]

The dimensions of the conflict between the two Italian orders are obvious from the expressions "Ferra's lodge" and "Ferra's Red Cross," which refer to the followers of Saverio Ferra, the great commander and founder of the *Grand Lodge of Italy* (A. L. A. M., Piazza del Gesù) in 1908. This conflict reflected on the political actions of certain groups in Rijeka, i.e. on the two political solutions to the Rijeka question: the annexationist and the autonomist.

The political groups in Rijeka and their operations can be traced in another undated and unofficial document. The document was probably a report by a supporter of Riccardo Zanella's (the author owns a photocopy thereof), that speaks about the political divisions of the people of Rijeka.

According to the typewriter characters, its author might be Ruggiero Gotthardi.[208]

Gotthardi was the founder of the *Autonomous Democratic Party* and Zanella's opponent. However, at the beginning of 1921, after the signing of the *Treaty of Rapallo,* he returned to Rijeka from Zagreb.

Even though Gotthardi was not member of the Constituent Assembly he did remain, after the coup against Zanella, in touch with the autonomists and the Italian police sent their reports that Gotthardi spent all of his time in Sušak (Kingdom of Serbs, Croats and Slovenes), where he was conspiring with some people.

---

[207] HAR, JU–6, box 393.

[208] An article has been published on Ruggiero Gotthardi. See: Ljubinka Toševa Karpowicz, "La biografia politica d'un autonomista," *Quaderni,* VII/1983. pp. 39–62, idem, "The Political Biography of an Autonomist," in *Argumenti,* Rijeka, 1–2/1985. pp. 27–46. His political biography requires additional research. Based on the list of documents in the Archives of the Italian ministry for foreign affairs, in 1921 Gotthardi's file was as comprehensive as Zanella's, evidencing the need that further research needs to be completed. Ministero degli Affari esteri, Segretaria Generale, *Storia e diplomazia,* Roma, 2008.

After the coup against Zanella, he supported the *National Defense Committee* and its Chairman Attilio Prodam, and the latter sent a telegraph to the ministry for foreign affairs of Italy, in which he claimed to have received the *Autonomous Democratic Party's* proclamation about the events of the previous day, the attitude of which was probably positive.[209]

However, Gotthardi's familiarity with Prodam may be an explanation as to why in the (Gotthardi?) report there is no mention of Prodam. This also explains why the author makes so many suggestions about the future politics of Zanella, when he was already in exile in Kraljevica.

Since the document's preamble mentions the *Conventions of Santa Margherita*, signed on October 23, 1922, we can draw the conclusion that the document was created after that date.

There is another reason why this document is very important. It lists the names of political groups and their options in Rijeka, something that Prodam, probably out of precaution, omitted from his autobiography, to avoid being in disfavor with powerful men. Apart from that, the list of parties includes the *Masonic Sirius* Lodge, which is what it actually was.

The beginning of the document states that, after the attack on Zanella, the foreign fascists (Cabruna, Viola) left Rijeka, leaving the low-ranked, perhaps even the lowest-ranked, fascists behind.

---

[209] (DAR), Rijeka prefecture fund, JU–6, box 133. Prodam's telegraph from Rijeka is in Rome, Telegramma 4645. da Fiume il 4/3/1922. Archivio Centrale dello Stato, fond Consiglio dei ministri, busta 7,10–15–7–1. Zanella's view was that Ruggiero Gotthardi was on the payroll of the ministry for foreign affairs of Italy through the Italian Legation in Rijeka "Congrega massonica" (Masonic brotherhood), Vio and Ossoinack. *La Difesa*, "Gothardi e Superina Jacic," anno V, 10. December 1922, *La Difesa* "Una conferenza diplomatica," April 19, 1923. The article states that in the Italian Legation's offices, Michele Castelli presided over a meeting attended by the following persons from Rijeka: Rugghiero Gotthardi, Andrea Superina, Eduardo Susmel, "pseudoingeniere" Prodam.

The documents states that "The remaining nationalists and fascists fall into two groups as follows":

1. the *Combat Fascio,* supported by a group of avant-garde students and D'Annunzio's scouts, led by Lasini, Antonini and Cartesio. The group has more than a thousand registered members, men and women, with the addition of the members from Turnić and Kantrida (parts of Fiume), who aregetting organized. They have a powerful and efficient organization made up of:

2. former soldiers. It includes: Barbieri, Steve, Morini, Gnatta, Host-Venturi, Giorgio Conighi and another fifty members, former officers. Members of this group are unemployed (scheming) troublemakers, ready to support any kind of disorder. They are in close contact with Castelli, Perata and. . . (name missing from the original document);

3. the "Vedetta d'Italia" group: Hodnig, Rossboch, Olivetti, Chioggia, Colussi, Scrobogna, Giorgi, Antonelli and Carpinelli. Their activity is very limited, since they do not want to have anything to do with the unemployed former combatants, bound only to them by "their spiritual course";

4. Rijeka nationalists: Depoli, Conighi, Papetti, Burich, Susmel, Morini etc. They represent the middle class of Rijeka, and their reach is limited. Mixed with other groups, they have their own ideas about state organization and Rijeka's economy, and their plans were proposed based on amnesty among the citizens of Rijeka. They are bitter enemies of Zanella;

5. extremists: Lasinio, Krall, Lenaz, Marussich. Not considered so far because few are remaining, but they never gave up on their turbulent and terrorist program;

6. the *Italian Republican Party* and *The Italian People's Party* may be considered members of the *National Bloc* and if need be, could unite with it;

7. Soviets: Rora, Alberto Zanier, Blažinić and similar self-interested individuals, ready to unite with anyone who promises profit to them

8. the Communist Party: Mayländer, Quarantotto, Simon and others,

protected recently by the members of the bloc, since they are heavily persecuted by the fascists;

9. the Masonic lodge: Vio, Bellasich, Mini, Ossoinack, Rubinich and others—not to be trusted because they are dangerous and ready to consort with the devil, only to preserve power and money; and

10. the Autonomous Party: still a united bloc, however, as written in the previous report (!), Zanella is losing credibility because of the exacerbating economic situation, due to which pessimism is widespread. This bloc expects Zanella's policy to Italy to be independent and unyielding, given that most citizens of this city consider that the support to Italy should be considered a danger to the interests of the *State of Rijeka*. Since Zanella's policy cannot be openly anti-Italian, and since it is impossible for him to get help from others—whether those are his fellow-fighters, or foreign powers—it seems that it is necessary for him to distance himself from any major political action in the given short period of time, or to make such policies for his own account and in complete secrecy (?) (question mark in the original).

In total, as the anonymous author pointed out further on in the document, the situation in Rijeka is difficult, particularly because the *National Bloc* lacked a recognized and a trusted leader. However, such a situation could not last for a long time, the author claims. The industry needed to start working, the port zone in Sušak needed to be freed and arrangements needed to be made with The Kingdom of Serbs, Croats and Slovenes, which would lead to the strengthening of Zanella's policy in time and the weakening of the anti-Italian element in the city.

"We dare say that the Conventions in Santa Margherita and the application of the Treaty of Rapallo"—as judged by the author—"will only strengthen the autonomist party and Zanella which would make them successful in relation to the Italian government front."

"The disappearance" of Prodam's name from the public and political life of Rijeka after the coup against Zanella is surprising.

After the explanations given in his autobiography, and after the documents that substantiated his claims about the role played by the Freemasonry from Rijeka and Italy in the political events of Rijeka, it is surprising that Attilio Prodam was gone, that he went missing. He was not on the list of those present at the *Italia Nuova* Lodge to which he belonged. This list is dated to 1922.

If indeed he was in Rijeka selling electrical goods, as written in his letter to Mussolini from 1927, it may be concluded that the politics and diplomacy of fascist Italy deliberately "deleted," to the extent possible, testimonies about the terrorist attack against an internationally recognized and sovereign state and its leaders, to whose creation it had contributed. For this reason, the collection of Attilio Prodam's documents and his autobiography have not been widely consulted. It is time that those documents should be more carefully examined, because they represent important testimonies about the creation of fascism and its early articulation in Rijeka.

After the letter of Attilio Depoli, as deputy prime minister of the interim government, sent to the Italian government with a view to appointing a person who would lead the *State of Rijeka* to peace, in September 1923, the Italian government appointed General Gaetano Giardino the military governor for the State of Rijeka.

An issue of the *Bolletino discrezionale* dated January 1, 1924 (again an unofficial and unsigned document) claims: "The *Sirius* Lodge from Rijeka has great influence on actions taken by General Giardino!"

In the historical dynamics that engulfed Rijeka after the dissolution of the Dual Monarchy, many persons had changed; only the influence of the Freemasons from the *Sirius* Lodge remained, according to documents. The reason for this partly lies in their wealth, international position, and consequently the power of its members. "The Fascist Revolution" carried out by marginalized soldiers and certain individuals from the military hierarchy with participation from middle-class citizens, which is obvious from Rijeka's example, did not bring about the change in social structure, but only made the Rijeka Freemasons' connections and informal communication channels more propulsive, helping them to maintain their power.

2. THE *ITALIA NUOVA LODGE* BEFORE FASCISM

A researcher of Freemasonry rarely gets the opportunity to consult the original documents covered by his/her work, which is why all kinds of publications on Freemasonry are generalized and pertain to national Masonic organizations, certain prominent Freemasons and the general political stance of Freemasonry, presented void of any context.

Fortunately, if only to an extent, this is not the case with the *Italia Nuova Lodge* from Rijeka. The State Archives of Rijeka contain several minutes of *Italia Nuova* meetings, confiscated by the Italian police after the entry into force of the 1925 law banning the operations of secret organizations, including the Freemasonry.[210]

Even though only a small number of minutes were preserved, when taken as a whole, their importance is enormous.

Above all, these minutes refute the Masonic thesis that Freemasonry is a charitable and nonpolitical organization, and confirm that a lodge is, or at least the *Italia Nuova* of Rijeka was, a place for discussions and consultations about measures to be taken by its members regarding specific items on the agenda.

Next, considering that at that time, in accordance with the *Treaty of Rapallo*, Rijeka was a state, the minutes reflect the Rijeka Freemasons' attitudes and actions regarding Rijeka's future at a time when fascism had already taken hold in Italy.

Thirdly, since the autonomists and President Zanella had been exiled from Rijeka after the military coup (March 3, 1922), the minutes reflect only the attitudes of former irredentists, who were Freemasons and supporters of Italy's annexation of Rijeka at the time.

[210] (Legge del 26 nov. 1925, n. 2029. Associazioni, Enti ed Istituti operanti nel Regno e fuori i in modo clandestino o occulto).

Unfortunately, the archives contain only some of the lodge's records, leaving much of it lost. These minutes were mostly from meetings during 1923 (twelve), 1922 (four), and 1924 (also four). At the same time, there is no information about the location of the lodge's headquarters, or about the premises it used for its work. Considering that the meetings were also attended by the "brethren" from the *Sirius* Lodge, could it be that they allowed their "brethren" from the *Italia Nuova* Lodge to operate from their headquarters?

The literature—both Italian and Croatian—contains only one mention of the *Italia Nuova* in a note by Renzo de Felice and one made by Amleto Ballarini.

Judging by these data, the lodge already existed in 1919 and belonged to the St. John of Scotland order, i.e. to the Piazza del Gesù Freemasonry.[211]

All minutes have one topic in common, their attitude to fascism, and a common answer—that distance should be kept, and advantage taken of the merits of events that had previously unfolded in Rijeka.

However, fascism imposed itself on everyone, including the Freemasons, both as an ideology, and as political pragmatism.

The Rijeka Freemasons belonging to the *Italia Nuova* Lodge discussed their attitude to fascism in a meeting held on November 24, 1922. Their attitude to it was more conforming at the time, considering the attitude of their Italian "brethren." At this meeting, the "Venerable" (*venerabile*) Guido Lado, a former member of the *Sirius* Lodge, pointed out that in the Masonic ranks, fascism was not viewed as an extremely negative movement, as long as fascists did what was expected of them so that Italy might prosper.

In his speech, Guido Lado vehemently opposed clericalism, but not Catholicism (an old *Sirius* Lodge theme), whose members were organized into the People's Party that had made a noted contribution to the "victory of the national cause."

During the meeting, members of the former *Sirius* Lodge were admitted to the *Italia Nuova* Lodge, but the list of those present does not contain the most prominent members of that lodge.

---

[211] Renzo De Felice, op.cit., Amleto Ballarini, op.cit.

The Rijeka State Archives (Ju–6, box 133) include three lists of the *Italia Nuova* Lodge members. They are, however, undated. The lists contain the names of members, varying between fifteen and twenty-five.

The following are listed as prominent members holding functions in the lodge: The *"presidente"* (!), Secretary Salvatore Bellasich, followed by members De Domini, Prof. Meichsner, Mini Ariosto, Captain Catalinich Adriano (*capitaneria del porto*), Arletta, Alazzeta (*costiera*), Prof. Arrigo Depoli, Gino Lasinio, Righini (*dismissed*), ing. Rubinich (dismissed), Clemente Marassi (*dismissed*), Dr. Curri, and Catarini Italo, totaling fifteen members.

Salvatore Bellasich

It is interesting that Attilio Prodam's name is not included on the list!

Mini Ariosto and Captain Adriano Catalinich were the most senior, being ninth degree Freemasons, whereas Attorney Salvatore Bellasich, the most prominent fascist on the list, was merely a fourth degree Freemason.

The meeting that followed, held on March 7, 1923 was a very important one. In this meeting, comments were made regarding the work of the Kingdom of Italy and Kingdom of Serbs, Croats and Slovenes Border Demarcation Commission. The "Venerable" Guido Lado, having described the state of discussions and "Italy's claim to the port of Baroš," described Dr. Ribar, member of the Yugoslav delegation, as a "well-known enemy of Italy," who was known as such even prior to the war, when he represented Trieste in the Austrian Parliament and was a municipal councilor in Trieste.

This meeting was also important because it was attended by representatives from other lodges: *Sirius* (which had not yet been banned according to the minutes), represented by Nicolo Gelletich; the *Oberdan* Lodge from Trieste, represented by Foti and Condusio; and the *Vedeta di Udine* Lodge, represented by Nave. These were all lodges from the *Venezia Giulia*, annexed by Italy.

In this meeting, a motion to separate the aforementioned lodges from the *Grand Orient* in Rome (Palazzo Giustiniani) was discussed, as was their annexation by the *Italia Nuova* Lodge from Rijeka. The meeting, held on April 11, 1923, was attended by guests from Udine and Panama, and discussions were resumed about the work of the parity commission and the port of Baroš. At this meeting, Clemente Marassi, who was not known to be a member of any lodge, submitted his study and proposal.

Marassi stated that, if the State of Rijeka was not annexed by Italy, municipal statutes should be obtained from German cities, such as Hamburg and Danzig, that were formerly free cities, and from the statute of San Marino, and that the issue should be studied from a technical point of view if Rijeka were to retain its statehood.

After that, "brother" Antonio Alazzeta took the floor to state that he had worked on a similar project with Dr. Antonio Vio and Salvatore Bellasich after the plebiscite held on October 30, 1918, but that the issue of Rijeka is greatly different from the circumstances of the above-mentioned cities, considering the railroad network leading to Rijeka, the legal and customs systems and the foreign currencies circulating in Rijeka. His speech ended with a promise to carry out a study on the circulation of foreign currencies in Rijeka.

He carried out the study and this document is included in the lodge's documentation that was confiscated by the Italian police.

The meeting held on June 27, 1923 was an electoral meeting. Twenty members of the *Sirius* Lodge were present along with twelve members of the *Italia Nuova*, including three external visitors. Salvatore Bellasich spoke for the *Italia Nuova* Lodge, and Andrea Ossoinack for the *Sirius*. The humanitarian and nonpolitical work of Freemasonry was the central theme of the meeting.

The role played by the Rijeka Freemasonry in the signing of the Italian–Yugoslav border agreement, after which Rijeka was annexed by Italy, was also highlighted at the meeting held on January 31, 1924. At the same time, Guido Lado pointed out that Rijeka Freemasonry had always opposed the *Treaty of Rapallo*.

The last minutes of the *Italia Nuova* Lodge meetings are dated February 24, 1924, but we do not know whether this meeting was its last one, or the lodge continued until the law banning it was passed.

At the beginning of 1924, the press, incited by the Rijeka *Fascio*, headed by Host-Venturi, initiated an attack against the *Italia Nuova* Lodge and its operations.

In a special issue of a pamphlet titled *Balaustra*, on November 24, 1924, he declared that fascists were tasked with destroying all old parties and their associates, including all those who monopolized democracy—in short, the entire pre-fascism oligarchy, led by the Freemasonry.

After that, in a report dated November 20, 1925, the prefect of the newly formed *Kvarner Province* notified the Ministry of Interior in Rome—while answering questions about the activities of non-fascist parties—that the *Unione Commercianti e Industriali* was not an enemy of fascism in Rijeka, which was run by Freemasons from the *Grand Orient* order i.e. *Sirius* Lodge, and whose members endeavors were geared towards safeguarding their investments. Fascism's true enemies were the non-organized and weakened autonomists and Riccardo Zanella's supporters, as were the Croats from Rijeka.

Salvatore Bellasich attached a list of the members of the *Sirius* and *Italia Nuova* lodges to this report.

Various lists drafted subsequently confirm the constant interest that the fascists took in members of the Freemasonry, but there was an ulterior motive for this interest. First and foremost was the attack on the Jews, i.e. anti-Semitism. Since the lists of Freemasons included the names of many Jews, the fascists—whose ideological matrix included anti-Semitism—cracked down on the Freemasons for this reason.

However, their fear of the international Jewish operations was motivated by a fear of international socialism, whether as an ideology or as a movement, since both numbered a considerable percentage of Jews among them, and often they were Jewish Freemasons.

The number of Jews in the *Sirius* Lodge was significant, whereas members of the *Italia Nuova* were Italians, officials and merchants. This piece of information may explain the final report made by the Rijeka Prefect dated December 7, 1934, in respect of places of residence in other countries of Rijeka Freemasons belonging to the *Sirius* Lodge.

The few remaining minutes of the *Italia Nuova* meetings paint an authentic picture of the political situation in the State of Rijeka between 1922 and 1924, the change of the social class that formed the backbone of the Freemasonry and the use thereof to rise to power, denouncing the autonomists, Zanella's supporters, and the Croats and Jews as the main opponents of the new regime.

The few documents on this lodge that are available suggest that on January 24, 1923 its motto and simultaneously its goal was *"Resistere per esistere"* (Resist to exist). Since the Free State of Rijeka still existed formally and legally under the *Treaty of Rapallo,* the conclusion may be drawn that the lodge's aim was to obstruct cooperation between the State of Rijeka and the Italian fascist government in their endeavor to abolish the State of Rijeka and have it annexed by Italy.

According to the last minutes, the meeting was attended by fifteen brethren. Only the names of those brethren who held a function in the lodge were listed. Venerable Guido Lado, the Senior Warden (*sorvegliante*) Catalinich, the Junior Warden of the Temple Sparace, Orator Salvatore Bellasich, Secretary De Domini, **Inner Guard** Caccome, Treasurer Miceletti, and Master of Ceremony Desdevich (this name may be wrong).

At the time, the "state apparatus" of the State of Rijeka was in power and was headed by the government consisting of _Rubinich and ten rectors, while Attilio Depoli held the office of prime minister. Considering the goals set by the lodge, its activities were agreed indirectly with the secretary of the *Italian Legation to Rijeka*, Marcello Roddolo, and Michelle Castellli.[212]

Since the *Italia Nuova* accepted some of the *Sirius* Lodge members whose political orientation was different, they mostly remained passive in this lodge. Attorney Salvatore Bellasich, who was not only a member of the *Sirius* Lodge, but Venerable (*venerabile*) of the *Italia Nuova,* was the only one active.

Judging by his biography, Salvatore Bellasich was the most important

---

[212] This intervention was obvious from an attempt made by Attilio Prodam at the beginning of 1923 to return to power. At the beginning of 1923, Attilio Prodam organized, with help from the Dalmatian expatriates in Rome, an orchestrated and determined campaign against the *Treaty of Rapallo* and the *Santa Margherita Conventions*. Consequently, Attilio Depoli relinquished his office as prime minister and withdrew to Trieste. Marcello Roddolo, secretary of the Italian Legation to Rijeka visited him to dissuade him and returned to Rijeka on January 15, 1924. Massagrande, op.cit. p. 116

shadow figure in all of Rijeka's institutions and its government. He conducted a number of secret talks between the Italian and Hungarian governments during the transition and won their trust. It is considered that he, as a person trusted by the Italian government or maybe as a "mole," was charged with infiltrating the *Italia Nuova* in order to secretly monitor its work.[213]

When the law banning Freemasonry was passed, on December 30, 1925, Salvatore Bellasich sent a list of members of the lodge (35), including their occupations, to the prefect of the Italian *Kvarner Province*.[214]

However, Bellasich's natural cautiousness aroused the suspicion of the Italian police. On October 6, 1930 (!), the police rapporteur Basilio Marassi notified the prefect that Salvatore Bellasich, Ferruccio Jellousheg, Mario Serdoz and their wives often met at the *Kafe Budai* in Opatija. He further noted that although their meetings appeared completely innocent, they might be involved with Freemason elements opposed to the government decision replacing the September 20 celebration with the one held on February 11, as indicated in report No. 9734 of October 19 which was received from Police Headquarters.

After both lodges of Rijeka ceased to exist under the law, the issue of the title of the building that was headquarters to the former *Sirius* Lodge remained to be resolved, as stated in a prefecture document dated April 4, 1929.

---

[213] Salvatore Bellasich (1890–1946), was a member of the *Giovane Fiume*. He graduated in law in Budapest. Before Italy joined the war, he was arrested and deported to the Kiskunhalas camp, where he remained until the end of the war. After his return to Rijeka, he was one of the founders of the *Italian National Council*, appointed as secretary. He publicly read the proclamation of the annexation of Rijeka by Italy and was one of the signatories of the invitation extended to Admiral Thaon di Revel. Bellasich became Mayor of Rijeka after the signing of the *Treaty of Rapallo*. At the inaugural session held on October 5, 1921 at the Municipio he spoke as the representative of the "constructive opposition." Following the fall of Riccardo Zanella's government, in 1924, he negotiated with the Hungarian government to transfer the refinery shares to Italy. After Freemasonry was banned, it was rumored that he was still involved with secret societies. Following the fall of fascism in Italy, he was one of the founders of the *Liburnian movement*. After the liberation of Rijeka on May 3, 1945, he went to Florence, and then to Salò, where he died soon thereafter. He was a friend of Atilio Prodam's.

[214] DAR, JU–6, box 133.

7

THE POLITICAL ACTIVITY OF
RIJEKA'S FREEMASONS
AFTER THE FALL OF FASCISM

---

1. THE POLITICAL SITUATION IN RIJEKA AFTER THE FALL OF FASCISM

At the beginning of September 1943, it was clear that Italy would surrender soon. According to the Allied plan for Yugoslavia, the Italian army in the field could proceed in the following two manners: they could either hold their ground and fight the Germans, or retreat, i.e. disband, and return to Italy.

Italy's surrender on September 9, 1943, the questionable central government, the questionable relationship between the *Third Reich* and the immediately declared *Italian Social Republic* (Repubblica di Salò—declared on September 9, 1943), together with the growing and more persistent presence of the partisans around Opatija and Rijeka, jolted Rijeka into political action. Here too the Italian authorities had two options: to remain in Rijeka and await the outcome of events, or to retreat to Italy and wait there.

After the *Italian Social Republic* was created, the *Republican Prefecture of Kvarner* (Prefettura Repubblicana del Carnaro) was established in Rijeka, accommodating the Headquarters of the 61st *Carnaro Legion* of the National Republican Defense.

Following the fall of fascism, the Germans assumed command over Kvarner and Istria, incorporating them into their zone of operations under the name of the *Operational Zone of the Adriatic Littoral*. Hitler made a secret decision on the founding of this zone on September 10, 1943. Its operational headquarters was in Trieste, which was an integral part of the *Italian Social Republic*.[215]

The intelligence service of the partisan units in the Rijeka hinterland monitored the situation closely, which is how a document, written in Italian, describing the distribution of political forces in Rijeka after the fall of fascism, came about. Unfortunately, the document is undated, and neither the institution nor its author are given.[216]

According to the claims made in the document, immediately after Italy's surrender, an autonomy movement appeared in Rijeka. The author of the proclamation was Giovanni Stercich, formerly Riccardo Zanella's secretary, who lived in Sušak, in Yugoslavia, after the annexation of the *State of Rijeka* by Italy. He gathered the surviving members of the former Riccardo Zanella autonomy government and encouraged their activities. One of the heads of the renewed movement was Dr. Blasich, a person whose moral integrity remained uncompromised after the military *coup d'état* against Zanella's government (March 3, 1922).

The German military authorities offered their support to the newly-formed autonomists. However, they declined with an explanation that they were of advanced age and that few surviving autonomists remained.

However, there was talk in their ranks that German support had been refused to avoid collaborating with the German fascists, as they had already fallen victims to Italian fascism.

According to a statement made by Stercich, the partisans also wanted to win them over, but the autonomists refused them as well, believing that it might prejudice the state and legal status of Rijeka after peace was secured,

---

[215] Željko Bartulović, Sušak 1919–1947. Rijeka, 2004 pp. 260–263, 273–275.

[216] Vojnoistorijski institut , neprijateljska arhiva, JNA Military History Institute, enemy units archives. **Belgrade**, Reg.No. 35/2–1, K 903.

i.e. that cooperating with the partisans might jeopardize Rijeka's autonomy. Wishing to remain neutral, they decided to organize themselves and so they established a task force for each department.

They first launched the dissemination of typewritten materials dedicated to renewing the Fiuman spirit and they secretly invited the citizens of Rijeka to have Rijeka banners ready for liberty day. They devoted particular attention to the young people, encouraging them to remain in the city for the time being and to remain passive. The propaganda proved successful among the young people, and this is how two young autonomists came to prominence— Oscar Cecele (from Trieste) and Captain Simicheni (Simičić) Elio. Simičić's involvement attracted objections immediately. He was reproached for being a Freemason and an intimate friend of Attorney Bellasich's.

In his defense, **Simičić stated that he would** be willing to answer before any national court, that his relationship with Bellasich was merely economic because he had helped him financially, and that he was persecuted for political reasons and never a member of the fascist party.

During the twenty-year period since the attack against Riccardo Zanella, the autonomists received moral support from abroad through radio broadcasts from London that they knew were given by Zanella. Still it was Carlo Sforza, a signatory of the *Treaty of Rapallo*, who supported the autonomists the most in his speech dedicated to a discussion on Italy's future political structure. Carlo Sforza's support encouraged Stercich to intensify his actions.

Efforts were directed at the following: (1) initiating a policy reinstituting Rijeka's autonomy, and (2) the means—Rijeka's dock workers and central warehouse workers.

Stercich received a list containing the names of workers of both companies from someone. The campaign to attract workers was limited to these two companies because the fascist syndicates were very strong in ROMSA.

The report mentions other names, but it is interesting that a municipality employee (Dernievi, probably the Italianized variant of the Croatian name Drnjević) was supposed to obtain the 1922 electoral roll, because, according to the autonomist plans, voters from the former electoral roll would be the ones eligible to vote in the future elections.

The document further describes other circumstances in Rijeka after the fall of fascism.

Political views of workers from other industrial companies were taken into consideration, discussions were held on Rijeka's economic independence, and also considered were the dangers posed by the "Croatian element" that might infiltrate the autonomist ranks.

Their attitude to both the Croats and communism was openly negative. They agreed that communism was an ideology employed by the Jews that they were unable to enforce from the "top," so it had to come from the bottom.

The autonomists were generally convinced that, if elections were to be held under the 1922 electoral roll, the outcome would be favorable for them.

An armament plan was drawn up and Rijeka's defense was prepared.

Plans were made to win the young over to take part in the defense, giving them the explanation that they were going to fight the Germans. However, when the young learned of this, they distanced themselves from the autonomist military plan. Still, they won over the soldiers from the barracks commanded by the young Furio Milcevich.

In their discussions, they emphasized that the "fascist Freemasonry" had been and was the enemy, while Stercich maintained that "all sorts of Antoninis, Bellasichs, Host-Venturis, Susmels, Colussis, Violas (Rubinich is not mentioned!) were not members of their movement. They wanted to create a cantonal state like Switzerland, under German protection."

However, in a private conversation, Stercich stated that the Freemasons should not come under harsh attacks, because they did rule the world and mentioned Roosevelt and Churchill as examples.

The autonomist economic plan provided that the factories were to be offered to eminent foreign companies for investments, as was done in 1922, and that should this should fail, the port would be sufficient to sustain Rijeka.

The "international assistance" item clearly demonstrates that the autonomists believed that something would come out of the friendship between Riccardo Zanella and Fiorello La Guardia, and that this possibility would be increased by La Guardia's forthcoming arrival to Italy. It is hard to determine the extent to which this plan was illusory. They probably requested the 1922 electoral roll hoping that at some instance, possibly at the Peace Conference after World War II, its validity would be retroactively recognized. In other words, they hoped that the *Constituent Assembly* of the *State of Rijeka* (October 5.1921)would be legitimized, as an incontestable institution, violently suppressed by a terrorist act.

The partisans from the Rijeka hinterland—mentioned in the document as the forces that offered cooperation to the autonomists against the Germans— probably considered the autonomists their enemies and they were therefore liquidated after the war. This makes the above document's authorship, date, and even the place where it was created all the more interesting. What is also interesting is the fact that the document was written in good Italian, not typical even for the educated political class of Rijeka.

2. GIOVANNI RUBINICH AND THE "LIBURNIAN" MOVEMENT

T he Freemasons and the plan to create a state on Rijeka's soil, the data mentioned in the previous document, all refer to the actions of the so-called *Liburnians*. The basis for their actions and their program are an integral part of a memorandum, signed on March 6, 1944 by Giovanni Rubinich.

The memorandum that we own is a draft document. It includes eight pages of densely written text. The first two chapters are dedicated to the history of the Rijeka *corpus separatum* until World War I. Its borders extended to the area from Labin, via Klana, Kastav, Bakar, Kraljevica to Senj in the east, and to Grobnik and Delnice to the north. The document points out that the relationship with Croatia and Austria was good and that they did not interfere with the natural economic and cultural unity in the aforementioned territory.

Item four of the memorandum describes the situation after the end of World War I and the controversies between the *Italian National Council* and the *National Council of the Slovenes, Croats and Serbs*.

Regardless of whether Rubinich's allegations are completely accurate, he still mentions some circumstances unknown to historians.

Rubinich states that on October 17, 1918, Count San Marzano, an Italian general, commander of Italian allied troops, arrived in Rijeka and exiled the representatives of the *SHS National Council* ("the Governor" as it is written) and ordered the members of the *Italian National Council* to set up a state and elect a government. According to his orders, a government was elected on October 22, 1918. Rubinich was its minister for communications and treasury and its representative in the Italian government. After he "set the state administration in order," Rubinich went to Budapest to define the position of the Hungarian officials in Rijeka state bodies, and then in December 1918, he traveled to Rome, to clarify questions related to the proclamation of annexation with the Italian government.

In his memorandum, Rubinich does not state who were the persons in the Italian government with whom he had discussions, but he claims that the Italian government strongly opposed the annexation of Rijeka because it was contrary to Italy's interests and to the interests of the *State of Rijeka* itself. Therefore, Rubinich negotiated the following conditions with the representatives of the Italian government:

- that Rijeka's Italian character would be guaranteed
- that Italy would help the peaceful economic development of the *State of Rijeka*
- that the port system, comprising docks, warehouses and railways would remain connected, because only in this way could the port remain connected to its hinterland and work successfully.

The second item, i.e. economic security, was resolved by the *State of Rijeka* receiving 300,000,000 lire required for currency conversion, and in order to grant the loan, Italy requested the exclusive privilege of the tobacco factory in Rijeka. According to the testimonies of those Italians who spoke with Rubinich, the reason for this was the fact that the Italian government wanted the Rijeka tobacco factory to manufacture *Makedonija* cigarettes for Italy, with the Rijeka factory retaining an annual amount of 25,000,000 lire, of which 10,000,000 were to go to the *State of Rijeka*, and 15,000,000 to the Italian state. Apart from some other revenues listed in the document, the revenues sufficient to meet all the needs of the *State of Rijeka* were calculated at 24,000,000 lire.

After the agreement had been made, the Italian government sent twenty-three machines for the manufacture of *Makedonija* cigarettes, and an agreement was made with Yugoslavia about the port system. The implementation was supposed to begin when D'Annunzio's march into Rijeka put an end to everything.

After D'Annunzio's departure from Rijeka and Riccardo Zanella's victory in the elections, Zanella did not acknowledge the agreement made by Rubinich in Rome, and the agreements made with Yugoslavia, despite the fact that it was explained to him that he was making a severe mistake. According to Rubinich, Zanella started new negotiations with the Italian government, but the fascists came into power, and they made an agreement with Yugoslavia to share the port system.

"It is a paradox," Rubinich wrote, "that up to October 30, 1918 my proclamation contributed to the creation of an independent state that was definitely Italian, which enabled it to preserve its traditions, and that Riccardo Zanella's inflexibility contributed to the annexation of Rijeka by the Italian government, with severe consequences to Italy."

The Zanella government refugees, as Rubinich pointed out in his memorandum, were forced to live abroad as refugees. After they were successfully repatriated, their leader still remained far away from the city of his birth.

The *Liburnian movement* was described in detail by Mladen Plovanić and we shall rely on his writing further on in this text, since it can be concluded from his text that he relied on documents other than the memorandum, without stating where he had found them.[217]

In the fifth item of his memorandum, Rubinich described the territory of a state that would be called the *Liburnian Confederacy* or simply *Liburnia*.

It would consist of three cantons: Rijeka, Sušak and Slovenian cantons. Rubinich continued to describe the organization of government in the cantons and their cultural and linguistic features that were preserved during fascism.

Each canton would be headed by a prefect or a subprefect, and the confederacy would be headed by its president. Plovanić states that the president was supposed to be German, meaning that the little country would be a German protectorate, as suggested by Rubinich.

Plovanić mentions Stercich's text about how the action propagating *Liburnia* was launched and who took part in it, but he does not mention his source.

According to Stercich, after the fall of fascism, Ruggiero Gotthardi, the former founder and leader of the *Democratic Autonomous Party* and Zanella's opponent was the first one to take out this old project of the *State of Rijeka* and tried to offer cooperation to the "real autonomists," i.e. to Mario Blasich.[218] Since he declined, Gotthardi went to Rubinich's office, and he was happy to accept the suggestion. Since none of "his men" took it upon themselves to do so, Rubinich launched the action propagating the three canton *State of Rijeka*. The action was joined by Salvatore Bellasich, Antonio Vio Jr., Ettore Rippa and Icilio Baccich, who were all Freemasons from both Masonic lodges, except perhaps Ettore Rippa.

---

[217] Mladen Plovanić, Liburnisti I autonomašim 1943-1944, ("Liburnian Autonomists 1943–1944), *Dometi, Rijeka, 5/1980, and 6/1980* pp. 69–97.

[218] The Rijeka Confederacy project presented by Ruggiero Gotthardi at the Paris Peace Conference in May 1919, Archivio storico del Ministero degli Affari Esteri, Rome, fondo Affari politici, Fiume, busta 1046.

Rubinich started visiting the prominent people of Rijeka and Sušak, carrying the draft document with him. He spent the most time with Dr. Fran Špehar, the newly inaugurated (November 2) commissioner of the Sušak–Krk Administrative Command. However, the action soon miscarried.

Even the people who were rumored to have agreed to it, e.g. Dr. Viktor Ružić and Milivoj Korlević, distanced themselves publicly from it.

The failure of the *Liburnians* was the last attempt at a political comeback made by the Freemasons of Rijeka and an attempt at breathing new life into their "little state," in which they would be all-powerful. To make this "historical

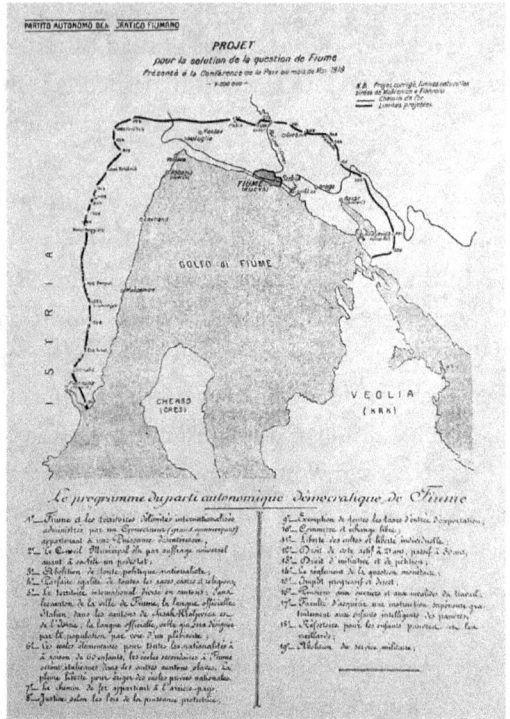

The "Gotthardi" project presented at the Paris Peace Conference in May 1919 as a solution to the Rijeka question.

dream" come true they were even ready to cooperate with their opponents—the autonomists. Zanella's autonomists, even without Zanella's presence, had serious reservations about all issues related to the Freemasons and fascists, who they considered to be one and the same.

However, regardless of the character of the proposed "Liburnian state," regardless of who initiated the proposal, the movement did not have the slightest chance because of the chaotic and complex war situation, in which a political tomorrow was guaranteed to no one. The *Liburnian movement* and its participants, regardless of who they were and how many of them there were, proved that the utopia of a small autonomist state, small even for the standards of the era when fascist empires were falling apart, was unrealistic.

8

CONCLUSION

T he appearance, presence, organization and the features of various Masonic orders in Rijeka reflected the state and legal history of this free city and port. This stands in accordance with the general features of the history of Freemasonry that, based on its statutes, operated in an organized manner and was loyal to the state and its political system.

I

During the first period when Freemasons were present in Rijeka, coinciding with the *Josephinism era*, an independent Dutch (1784), anti-Habsburg, insurgent and pro-French Freemasonry operated in the city. It was therefore **politicized (liberationist-separatist), secret and closed** within a narrow circle of supporters, without any members from Rijeka among them, save a few exceptions.

At the same time, the Hungarian system of *Strict Observance* hid behind the institution of governors who mostly originated from the easternmost part of the Empire—Transylvania. The first of their two lodges, the *Three Eagles*, was founded in 1770. The *Strict Observance* order was reformed in 1778 and named *Drašković's Strict Observance*, since Count Ivan Drašković was its Master and great reformer.

This was a **Templar and occult Freemasonry**, whose organizational seat for the *Provincial Lodge of Hungary* appears to have been in Rijeka for some time.

At the beginning of Joseph II's reforms, The *Order of Strict Observance* supported him, and its members cooperated with the emperor as his counselors. During this period, the Masonic lodge of Rijeka was public and legal.

However, after Joseph II's clash with the Freemasonry in around 1785, regarding the emperor's order that all lodges should be registered and that the names of their members should be made public, the conflict between the Freemasonry and the emperor intensified. The lodges then gradually started operating in secret, which coincided with Joseph II's sudden death in 1790. We do not know who the members of the *Strict Observance order* were. Most likely the first Governor of Rijeka (1776–1783) and the second (1783-1788), third (1788-1791) and fourth (1791-1798) governors were among them. We also do not know how long the lodge operated for after it went underground.

Considering that Count Hund, the founder of the *Strict Observance order* spent some time in Russia and met the Melissino brothers there, we can assume that the order was close to the *Melissino order* on an organizational level. This hypothesis could explain the connection between the executor of the will of the first Russian consul in Rijeka, George Melissino, and Count Antonio Maylát de Szekely (1801–1873), who was the son of the first governor of Rijeka and employed at the time by the Rijeka Magistrate.

Michailo, George Melissino's absent son, a cadet in Russia at the time of the death of his father (1838) who was commander of the Russian Imperial Artillery Guard and a decorated knight, might have been a member of the same lodge.

In any event, the lodges belonging to the *Strict Observance order* in Rijeka, which may even have served as the order's headquarters, were part of a **secret, military, Templar and occult Freemasonry.**

II

At the time of the *Illyrian Provinces*, when the lodges of the Order of the *Grand Orient of Italy* (with its seat in Milan) were being constituted along the Adriatic littoral, a **public, propagandistic, nepotistic, lucrative (French) Freemasonry** was active in Rijeka. Its members from Rijeka were wealthy merchants, officials in the French administration of the city, and members of the city bodies, which made it part of the French administrative system and also made it **public, lucrative, nepotistic and propagandistic.**

III

At the time when the *Gubernium* of Rijeka was reestablished in 1822, up to the 1848 Revolution, the British Freemasonry arrived in Rijeka, beginning with John Leard's return to Rijeka as British consul. This Freemasonry was purely **lucrative**. Its members, beside Leard, were the same nepotistic persons from the time of the *Illyrian Provinces* (Adamić, Sussani, Meynie, Paul Scarpa, and brother Bratich).

IV

The Probable Templar Lodge of *Knights of Malta* in *Kaštel* on Trsat at the Time When Rijeka was a County.

The title of the Great Prior of the *Renewed Priorate of Ireland*, held by the head of the Scottish Templars, and bestowed on Laval Nugent for his services in the battles against Napoleon, suggests that an operative "unit" of the *Knights of Malta* may have operated from *Kaštel* on Trsat. This hypothesis is also substantiated by his son Albert's status as a Knight of Honor of the *Knights of Malta*.

Albert Nugent's political cooperation with the "Illyrians," and mystery visits from unknown "guests" who visited or even stayed at the *Kaštel* on Trsat that was walled-off and closed to the public, suggest that it concerned the fight against the Ottoman Empire in neighboring Bosnia.

The lodge's headquarters might have been in Karlovac, while Trsat was used to negotiate some "dealings."

V

Hungarian Freemasonry at the Time of the Dual Monarchy, the *Sirius* Lodge in Rijeka

The lodge in Rijeka was founded in 1901, when Freemasonry was banned in the Austrian part of the Empire, and weakened in the Hungarian Kingdom.

Its founders were almost exclusively Hungarians from Rijeka, liberal professionals and officials in the state-run *Adria Maritime Society*.

It is symptomatic that until the Masonic temple was built, due to the "lack of space," the lodge operated from the house of a British subject, John Whitehead, a person with a wide international network of connections, particularly with the German military aristocracy. It is interesting that the Master of the *Sirius* Lodge was Swiss, and a bank manager in Rijeka.

In 1905, the Italian Freemasonry established a emulated Masonic and irredentist association named *Giovane Fiume*, whose members were involved in various occasions in political events in Italy, even after the association was abolished (January 22, 1912). The leading members and even founders of the *Giovane Fiume* (Iccilio Bacich, Salvatore Bellasich, Attilio Allazetta) were members of the *Sirius* Lodge, or became members immediately thereafter.

Until 1910, the *Sirius* Lodge from Hungary was predominantly **lucrative** and **less political**. However, when its emulated Masonic political association was founded under the name of the *Autonomous League*, which was a political party, its members, the so called "leaguists," began to conduct a policy that was opposite to the one pursued by the *Autonomous Party*—the "autonomists." The members started cooperating closely with the neoliberal Istvan Tisza's *National Party of Work* (1910) and intensified this cooperation during his presidency (1912-1917).

In the political events that followed, including the changes after World War I that involved Rijeka, the "leaguist" core consisted of a group that later on, until Italy's annexation of Rijeka in 1924, became the ideological and financial agitator and mainstay of Italian irredentism and fascism.

This group, consisting of the *Giovane Fiume* members and members of the *Autonomous League*, shaped by the part it played in the creation of the *Italian National Council* (Consiglio Nazionale Fiumano) and by their role as founders or members of the *Fiuman Combat Fascio* (Fascio Fiumano di Combattimento) confirmed itself as the "Fiuman caste", and was identified as such by the Italian police during the age of fascism. The "Fiuman caste" never explicitly manifested its involvement but was always in the focus of political events, ideologically or organizationally, whether it was by creating or reshaping these events according to their own needs. The personal continuity of the "Fiuman caste" that remained uninterrupted through various state and legal—as well as political—periods in Rijeka, indicates that, in this political game, they were people whose political *habitus* was unquestionable, regardless of the importance of the events that the "Fiuman caste" was involved in, such as a world war.

This personal and interpersonal connectedness and the activity of the "Fiuman caste," preoccupied with maintaining and strengthening their political influence, can be viewed as an independent political variable, and their members as an authentic oligarchic party.

The ties between these individuals, their cooperation, mutual dependence and loyalty were only serving their common goal, while the instruments employed to achieve this goal were nationalist ideology, irredentism and hatred towards opposition political groups centered around different values. The ideological tendencies implemented in Rijeka came from abroad.

Autonomism, anarcho-syndicalism, socialism, irredentism, exulted nationalism, and mixtures thereof, could not shake up the power of the "Fiuman caste," whose foundations were not political—and even less so ideological—but social.

Thanks to the continuous activities of this group, which formally did not exist until the founding of the *Autonomous League*, all political events in Rijeka until its annexation by Italy in 1924, and later on, preserved their local color, something specifically *Fiuman*, often referred to in Italian literature as *campanilismo* (local patriotism). This *campanilismo* separates a political group that practices it from its closer and broader state and legal surroundings.

The politicization of Rijeka Freemasons and the so-called "Fiuman caste," who were identical on personal and ideological levels, manifested itself as Fiuman "liberalism," irredentism and fascism.

VI

Italian Irredentism and Freemasonry. *The Italia Nuova* Lodge and the Merits for the Victory of Fascism over autonomism: ***ideological and politisized.***

Up to the beginning of World War I, and in the period of D'Annunzio's occupation, the main feature of the Rijeka society class structure was the historic heritage of the Hungarian policy conducting model. **This relic, which found its political and historical continuation in Rijeka's politics, though formally altered, is the most interesting political and cultural**

heritage of the long-lasting Hungarian reign over Rijeka, until the city's annexation by Italy, when the more successful individuals belonging to the "Fiuman caste" moved over to the center of political power of the Italian state.

After the fall of fascism in 1943, the remaining members of the "Fiuman caste" in Rijeka tried to cooperate with the German occupation authorities in Sušak and Rijeka, hoping to prolong their "political lives." However, the fall of German fascism and the victory of the national liberation movement were also the end of the "Fiuman caste."

BIOGRAPHIES

OF RIJEKA FREEMASONS
REFERRED TO IN THIS WORK

ANDRIJA ADAMIĆ (1767 –1828), merchant, industrialist and entrepreneur. At the time of the *Illyrian Provinces* he was a member of the French lodge. In our opinion, the theatre owned by Adamić, in which he also lived, housed the Rijeka lodge. There is information to suggest that he was also a member of the lodge in the city of Karlovac where he had business connections. Furthermore, he became a member of the British lodge founded by his friend and associate John Baptist Leard after the French had retreated from Rijeka. Due to several of his father's ships being seized at various Mediterranean ports during the 1789 French Revolution, Adamić spent some time in France, Spain and Turkey. While there, he forged friendships that made him a powerful man in the Austrian Empire, and befriended some politicians, primarily British, and a statesman (Metternich). He provided finance to support Rijeka's growth, funded the construction of the Karlovac-Rijeka road, and built a theatre and a paper mill. He was Austria's and Britain's loyal ally against Napoleon, together with Laval Nugent, whom he helped buy a castle in *Trsat* for a symbolic price. Adamić actively cooperated with the Viennese court in its efforts to rehabilitate the monarchy after the Napoleonic wars.

ICILIO BACCICH (1879 –1945), was the most powerful man in Rijeka in the period between the dissolution of the Dual Monarchy and the fall of fascism. He was a national level fascist. Baccich was the most distinguished member of the "Fiuman caste," a member of the *Giovane Fiume*, and an active member of the *Sirius* Lodge, as a visiting member. His family were fervent irredentists. Baccich was born in Rijeka, and went to high school in Florence. He graduated in law from the famous University of Camerino in 1902. On March 28, 1899, he became a member of an irredentist, emulated Masonic association "Trento-Trieste" which attracted Italian citizens of Austria-Hungary.

In 1899, during the "Trento-Trieste" new administration elections, Icilio Baccich, along with another member, became secretary of the association. He often visited Rijeka, using visits to his family as an excuse.

After Istvan Tisza's government adopted a regulation introducing border police in 1913, Icilio Baccich, at the time an Italian citizen residing in Ancona, was immediately exiled from Rijeka due to "irredentist propaganda." This triggered a turbulent political atmosphere in Rijeka resulting in Dr. Antonio Vio's resignation from the office of mayor on June 14, 1913 because the *Rappresentanza* held him responsible for what happened to Baccich. After this, military rule was introduced in Rijeka, and the governor dissolved the *Rappresentanza* on June 21, 1913. The Hungarian border police arrested approximately one hundred citizens on June 23, 1913. On May 5, 1914, the dissolved municipal administration ordered the Rijeka police not to recognize the Hungarian police. The "Trento-Trieste" association kept a close eye on and responded officially to all these events, which may have been a policy implemented through Icilio Baccich. These events elevated Baccich to irredentist hero status. Italy's neutrality at the beginning of World War I played to his advantage, hence he distributed the propaganda pamphlets *Il problema adriatico e Fiume* (1914) and *Il Quarnero e gli interessi d' Italia nell' Adriatico (1915)*.

After the outbreak of war, he volunteered to join the Italian army and after his brother Ipparcho had been killed, Icilio was sent on a mission to Russia in search of Austrian-Hungarian prisoners of Italian descent with a view to taking them back to Italy.

After the end of the war, he worked in Rijeka on the founding of the *Italian National Council.* Following the founding of D'Annunzio's Italian *Regency of Carnaro*, he was placed in charge of the department of internal affairs and justice. Following the annexation of Rijeka by Italy, he was President of *Carnaro province*. In 1934, he was appointed Senator of the Kingdom of Italy. Following the fall of fascism, he cooperated with the Germans who occupied Rijeka on September 8, 1943. In May 1945, he was arrested by the Yugoslav police.

According to one version of events, a military court sentenced him to death and he was executed on March 3, 1949.

SALVATORE BELLASICH (1890–1946), member of the *Sirius* and *Italia Nuova lodges* and member of *Giovane Fiume*. After completing his law degree in Budapest, he returned to Rijeka and started a law practice. Due to his anti-Hungarian activities, he was imprisoned and taken to the Kiskunhallas camp at the beginning of the war. Following the end of the war, he returned to Rijeka and became the Secretary General of the *Italian National Council* (Consiglio Nazionale Italiano).

During D'Annunzio's occupation of Rijeka, he represented the moderates. After the *Treaty of Rapallo* was ratified, he was appointed Mayor of Rijeka following Riccardo Gigante's resignation. He was always cautious and moderate, which made him acceptable for any political option. Bellasich was assistant to the consul at the Italian Consulate in Rijeka, but his credibility was limited. Following the fall of fascism, he moved to the Repubblica di Salò. He died in Italy.

DR. LAJOS BRAJJER (1865 -?), according to a police report, was a member of the *Sirius* Lodge as of 1905. From 1931, he was a member of the Grand Landlodge of the Freemasons of Germany. As a famous journalist, together with Zbaray, also a journalist, he founded the *Fiumei Estilap*, a new journal in Rijeka. The journal was short-lived—it was published from May 31, 1908 to February 12, 1909.

Since Brajjer was a "Hungarian journalist," D'Annunzio granted him an interview on April 11, 1920 regarding D'Annunzio's emotional relationship with the peoples of the former monarchy.

On March 4, 1923, together with Icilio Baccich, he signed a proposal titled *Considerazione sui traffici marittimi e ferroviari con speciale riflesso al libero sbocco al mare del retroterra*. The date when he became a citizen of the Kingdom of Yugoslavia is unknown.

GIOVANNI DE CIOTTA (Rijeka, 1824 – 1903) Lovran, was one of Andrija Adamić's grandchildren. He graduated from the Military Academy in Vienna. During the 1848-49 Revolution, he fought in Italy, and then served in the army barracks in Venice and Verona. There he befriended de Sterneck, admiral in the Austrian Navy and Count Hadik, majordomo to Archduke Ferdinand Maximilian, who later became the Emperor of Mexico. He left the Austrian Army after Austria was defeated at Solferino in 1859.

He became more politically active in Rijeka after the *Croatian-Hungarian Compromise* (1868), when he became Mayor of Rijeka and Rijeka's Delegate to the *Hungarian Chamber of Commerce* in Rijeka. He remained in office as mayor for the following twenty-five years, until October 30, 1896, when he retired under the excuse of deteriorating health. However, the reason for his retirement was the fact that Hungarian laws were imposed directly to Rijeka, without their prior ratification by the *Rappresentanza,* which Ciotta perceived not only as a reduction of autonomy, but as an abolition of the *corpus separatum* status as well. Although he lived to see the revocation, on April 10, 1900, of the Administrative *Gubernatorial Council* (Giunta amministrativa governatoriale), on account of which he resigned as mayor, he never made a return to public life.

Due to his administrative position, and the enthusiasm that reigned in Hungary during the first years of the Dual Monarchy, he was the key factor in Rijeka's modernization during the *Liberal Party* rule. This made Ciotta not only an associate, but also a close friend of the Hungarian governors in Rijeka, Rijeka's leading entrepreneurs, especially Robert Whitehead and his brother-in-law George Hoyos. He was married to Natalija (1863), Pietro Scarpa's widow, who also was also involved in the city's social life. He owned a remarkable collection of art, primarily paintings by famous painters.

Ciotta became a member of the *Humbolt* Lodge from Budapest in 1871. He withdrew from the lodge in 1894. Of his death, *Hajnal* wrote that Ciotta had not performed any functions of consequence at the lodge, but that he had adhered to the Masonic principles. "He was," wrote *Hajnal,* "leader of the patriotic Hungarian party in Rijeka." His gravestone bearing Ciotta's image in the Hungarian magnate ceremonial clothes does cast him in his true light! After Ciotta's death, "brother" Samuel Mayländer gave a eulogy in his honor at the *Sirius* Lodge.

GUIDO LADO, Master of the *Italia Nuova* Lodge**, was** of a high Masonic degree—eighteenth. He was a civil engineer, and an employee in the municipality. During the *Free State of Rijeka*, he was Chairman of the Chamber of Commerce. Rijeka Freemasons discussed the relationship with fascism in a meeting held on 24 November1922.

During this meeting, Master Guido Lado pointed out that fascism was not viewed as a negative phenomenon in the ranks of Freemasonry, as long as it brought benefit to Italy. During the same meeting, as the Master of the Lodge, he emphasized that the lodge was opposed to clericalism, but not to Catholicism, which was organized in Rijeka as the *Popular Party* (Partito Popolare) and as such gave significant contribution to the "triumph of the national cause." In one of the lodge meetings, he announced that he was going to the Italian Consulate to meet Michele Castelli after his return from Rome, to give him instructions on further actions. This happened during the fascist coup against the government of Riccardo Zanella.

JOHN BAPTIST LEARD (1753 –1831), was a British citizen and a consular officer of Great Britain in Rijeka from 1809 to 1810. He cooperated with Andrija Adamić on timber exports from region Gorski kotar. He was appointed British consul in 1814. For his contribution in the anti-Napoleonic coalition he was made Rijeka patrician in 1823 and awarded himself the aristocratic title of *de Kostel* based on his ownership of the same, which by all accounts he came to own in 1813. In a pompous ceremony, he declared the British St. John of Scotland Lodge open in 1813 in his vineyard at the villa that is now head office of the State Archives. Members of the lodge were famous Freemasons from the *Illyrian Provinces* period. The lodge was probably active until his death. He died in Rijeka, where he lived with his family, and was buried in the family crypt at the Kozala cemetery.

SAMUEL MAYLÄNDER (1866-1925) was a doctor, one of the founders of the *Sirius* Lodge, its member as of 1903, a third degree Freemason, and leader of the *Socialist Workers' Party of Rijeka,* founded in 1903 as a section of the Social *Democratic Party of Hungary,* which was founded in 1890. In the 1902-1903 period, La *Confederazione del Lavoro di Fiume* (followed by *Sedi Riunite*) was founded in Rijeka. After 1918, i.e. after the fall of the Monarchy, as of 1920 it was named the *Camera del Lavoro.*

The latter was founded by D'Annunzio's anarcho-syndicalist secretary, Alceste De Ambris, and was composed of workers and republicans, deserters from *Sedi Riunite.* Samuele Mayländer was opposed to the *Camere Sindacale del Lavoro.* There is no accurate data, although it was mentioned intermittently that he belonged to the *Communist Party of Rijeka,* founded at the beginning of 1919 and led by Albino Stalzer and Simeone Schneider. As a Freemason, he advocated children's summer camps and universal suffrage.

ANDREA OSSOINAC (1876-1965) was a member of *the Sirius* Lodge as of 1909. Rijeka's most powerful man during the liberalism era, he was an industrialist, a politician, and son of a major industrialist in Rijeka, who co-owned the refinery and rice husking plant, one of the largest in Europe.

A graduate in Economics, he studied in London and worked at his father's trading company. At the beginning of his political career, he took part in the autonomy movement, just like his father. When the *Autonomous League* was founded in 1910, he became its member and worked together with the Hungarians.

As Rijeka's representative to the parliament in Budapest, he was a member of the Rijeka delegation that in mid May 1918 made a request to the Prime Minister Istvan Tisza to appoint Ladislao Szapary (a Freemason) the Governor of Rijeka, as he had already been in that office, instead of Zoltan Jakelfa-lassy, the newly appointed governor.

He was Rijeka's last representative to the parliament in Budapest, and gave a historical statement on October 18, 1918 requesting the right of self-deter-mination for Rijeka. In accordance with the annexationist programme, he participated in the Peace Conference of Paris and gave his testimony to Presi-dent Wilson about "Rijeka citizens' desire" to have the city annexed by Italy.

After D'Annunzio's occupation of Rijeka he kept a low profile, at the same time participating, very rarely and under obligation, in the work of the *Italia Nuova* Lodge, although he remained Master of the *Sirius* Lodge.

After Rijeka was annexed by Italy, he moved to Luxembourg.

During World War II he returned to Rijeka, occasionally engaging in po-litical work.

ATTILIO PRODAM (1877-1957) member of the *Giovane Fiume* association in 1907 and 1908. He probably founded *the Italia Nuova* Lodge upon the suggestion of the *Grand Lodge of Italy* (Piazza del Gesù). He was an associate of D'Annunzio's, an opponent to the creation of the *Free State of Rijeka*, and founder of the *Combat Fascio of Rijeka* (Fascio Fi-umano di Combattimento) through which, together with the fascists of Trieste and under the command of Francesco Giunta, he carried out the Fascist coup against the government of Riccardo Zanella, forcing him to sign a statement at the headquarters of the *Combat Fascio of Rijeka* that he would never enter politics again, and exiling Zanella from Rijeka.

He was "removed" from Rijeka's public life because of an assassination attempt carried out with (secret) encouragement from individuals from the Kingdom of Italy's state institutions. He left the Freemasonry on Mussolini's invitation. After 1945, he moved to Rome, where he died.

GIOVANNI RUBINICH (1876-1945) was a member of *the Sirius* Lodge as of 1906. He was one of the few Masonic irredentists who did not belong to the *Giovane Fiume* association, although he lived in Rijeka at the time. He studied architecture in Budapest where he obtained his architecture degree in 1900. After graduation, he returned to Rijeka. His name is included in the list of members of the *Sirius* Lodge indicating that he held a rather high ninth degree position. He was listed as "contractor." The *Italia Nuova* Lodge list contains a note stating that he had been barred.

He began his professional career in 1902 by rebuilding the Women's Eight-year Civil School, followed by the construction of Governor Stefan Wickenburg's villa in 1902. These were followed by the construction of villas for members of the *Sirius* Lodge, for Attilio Prodam in 1903, and a villa for the Master of the *Sirius* Lodge, Artur Steineker, in 1902. He also supervised the construction of the villa for Guido Lado, an engineer and a Freemason (a municipal official, member of the *Sirius* Lodge, as well as Master of the *Italia Nuova* Lodge) and a villa for Antonio Allazeta (a municipal official and member of the *Sirius* Lodge). However, the ultimate proof of recognition of his skills as an architect was the permit to build the temple of the *Sirius* Lodge in 1911 at the expense of the *Consorzia per Costruzione delle Case,* represented by him. He was the author of many other private, state and union construction projects.

With the outbreak of World War I, his career stagnated. Urged by this as well as other reasons, he became politically active, first in the founding of the *Italian National Council.* In the first government of the *Free State of Rijeka,* constituted on January 1, 1921, he was appointed minister for commerce, industry and agriculture. In the attempt to establish the *Constituent Assembly* (Costituente), Rubinich was appointed, along with Salvatore Bellasich, one of the members of the election minority, but the newly elected Riccardo Zanella strongly opposed this. After the coup against the government of Riccardo Zanella in March 1922, he was proposed as resident of the caretaker government together with twenty "rectors."

After Rijeka was annexed by Italy in 1924, on July 20,1929 he passed the state exam, became a *dottore in architettura*, and started working at the construction company of Eduardo Stipanovic in Rijeka. In March 1927, he became a member of the *Sindacato Provinciale degli Ingegnieri della Provincia del Carnaro*, which was led by Carlo Conighi, a Freemason, and member of both the *Sirius* Lodge, and the *Italia Nuova* Lodge. The syndicate was renamed in 1931 as the *Sindacato Provinciale Fascista degli Ingegneri della Provincia di Fiume.*

After the fall of fascism in 1943, he was engaged in recruiting the supporters for the creation of the confederate State of Rijeka and in that capacity, he signed the memorandum on the historical basis of its founding and proposal for its organization. Although the literature identifies it as a proposal made formerly by Ruggiero Gotthardi in 1920, Rubinich's proposition is more superficial and only resembles the one made by Gotthiardi, or perhaps it is merely its pale imitation.

Anita Antoniazzo Bochina, in our opinion an unreliable author regarding statements of a political nature, stated that the partisans killed Rubinich in 1945. According to another author, Olga Magas, Rubinich died of natural causes, and according to the probable year of death, he was 69 at the time.

SOURCES: *Arhitektura secesije u Rijeci, (Secession Architecture in Rijeka),* Moderna galerija, Rijeka 1997 p. 530. Deborah Pustišek, Giovanni Rubinich, katalog Muzeja grada Rijeke, (The City of Rijeka Museum catalogue), 2014
Anita Antoniazzo Bochina, *Il cimitero di Cosala*, Padova, 1995 p. 420.

IGINIO SCARPA (Rijeka 1794-1866) was a politician and an entrepreneur. He was the son of Paolo Scarpa. He continued his father's business and made his fortune trading in wheat. He was Vice-Consul of Denmark in1822, and in 1823 he became Patrician Councillor. In 1823, he was responsible for road construction from Kastav to Sv. Petar (Pivka) and from Kantrida to Opatija (1843), thus creating the conditions for the development of tourism in Opatija.

The construction of *Villa Angiolina* (named after his wife) contributed to this as it was frequented by prominent figures of the Monarchy, including, Ban Jelačić in 1850, and, later on, Serbian Queen Natalija in 1885.

When the *Chamber of Commerce and Industry* was founded in 1852, Iginio Scarpa became its first chairman. In 1854, he was one of the founders of the foundry that was later transformed into the famous torpedo factory. He was made Knight of the Austrian Empire in 1858 for his achievements and was the commissioner executing the will of Georgio Melissino, the Russian consul and later Russian imperial adviser. He maintained friendly correspondence with Melissino's son who was a cadet in Russia at the time.

His portrait, ordered by the City Hall of Rijeka, is part of the collection of distinguished patricians' portraits in the fundus of the *Maritime and History Museum of Rijeka*. The portrait was painted in 1867, after his death. The white gloves in the portrait were supposed to suggest his Masonic membership, but given the fact that the lodges were prohibited in the Hungarian part of the Monarchy after the 1848/49 Revolution, they might suggest that he may have been a member of a lodge, possibly a secret one, outside Rijeka, and even outside Austria.

PAOLO SCARPA Jr., called Paolino, was Commander of the Rijeka Guard in the 1848/49 Revolution. He did not offer resistance to the troops of Josip Bunjevac when they entered the city. We do not know if he was a Freemason, but as he was connected to the structures whose members were members of the Masonic orders (French and British), we can assume (as is usual in the Freemasonry) that he was a member as well.

PAOLO SCARPA (Venice 1765 - Rijeka 1837), was a politician. He moved to Rijeka in 1778. He became a citizen of Rijeka in 1798 and in 1803, during the *Illyrian Provinces*, he became patrician councilor. This was the period of his greatest success. At the beginning of 1812, when the French authorities were to choose between five candidates for *mair* (mayor), they chose Paolo Scarpa. He performed this duty from March 7, 1812 to July 3, 1813. Fearing a shift in political power, as well as his membership in the French Freemasonry, he fled the city. However, as early as 1813 his name appears on a list entitled "former mayors" i.e. a list of members of the lodge founded by the British citizen Leard, in Leard's house, together with Vincenzo de Terzi.

GIUSEPPE DE SUSANNI (Rijeka 1809 –1880) was, according to Attilio Tamaro, a Hungarian aristocrat, and brother of the "serene" counselor who bore the same name. Giuseppe de Susanni was most probably the son of Nicolò Susanni, and was a Rijeka patrician and a gubernatorial counselor. In September 1815, he was the royal delegate to several cities. He was also Rijeka's representative to the Hungarian parliament during the 1848/49 Revolution, and was listed as a member of both the French and the British lodge (1813). He cooperated with John Leard, the British consul, and Adamić on timber exports from Gorski kotar.

ARTUR STEINECKER (1844 –1915) was the British vice-consul from 1880 to 1914, and treasurer of the English Sailors Home Maritime Club situated in John Whitehead's house that also served as the *Sirius* Lodge headquarters. He was Master of the Lodge until his death when Andrea Ossoinack succeeded him in that office. He was one of the most influential bankers, financiers, and industrialists in Rijeka at the end of the nineteenth and the beginning of the twentieth century. Before he moved to Rijeka, he had lived in Gelnica (Hungary), Great Britain, India and Trieste. He often travelled both for business and pleasure. He founded his own banking and trading business— Steinecker&Co.

ANTONIO VIO Jr. (Rijeka 1875-Bolzano 1949), was a lawyer. He was member of the *Sirius* Lodge as of 1909. He graduated in law from the University of Kolozsvar (Cluj). Upon his return to Rijeka he started a law practice. He was a member of the Autonomous Movement with Michele Mayländer and Riccardo Zanella. Then, in 1910, he joined the *Autonomous League.* On May 5, 1911, after Representative Michele Mayländer's death, he became candidate for the *Autonomous League* and the Hungarian Istvan *Tisza's Party of Work*. He was elected representative to the parliament in Budapest with only several votes ahead of Riccardo Zanella.

Since voting was public at the time, we know that members of the *Sirius* Lodge and the Catholics voted for him. On March 15,1912 he went in capacity as mayor to the consulate of the Kingdom of Italy to express his condolences to Consul Dominioni (with whom he would cooperate closely in the future) over an assassination attempt made by an anarchist against the king (the attempt had failed). After Italy entered the war in 1915, the city administration collapsed, because some of the city representatives, especially the younger ones, defected to the Italian Army as volunteers, while the older representatives, including Riccardo Zanella, were sent to the Russian front. Upon the request of Mayor Gilberto Corossaz, the City Council was dissolved and new elections were called. Vio was elected a mayor, so he left his position as Rijeka's representative to the parliament in Budapest to Andrea Ossoinack, Master of the *Sirius* Lodge. Thus, the two most prominent members of the *Sirius* Lodge held the two most important positions in the city—the mayor and the Rijeka representative.

Antonio Vio continued as mayor during the turbulent wartime years. He helped the retreat of the governor and Hungarian authorities from Rijeka. Although the City Council was dissolved on October 29, 1918, Vio remained as mayor and was one of the founders of the *Italian National Council*, together with Antonio Grossich as president, Isidoro Garofolo as vice-president, and Secretaries Salvatore Bellasich and Attilio Depoli.

It was most likely Vio, who accomplished the transition of the *Sirius Lodge* from the membership of the Grand Lodge of Hungary to the *Grand Orient of Italy*.

He withdrew from politics when Riccardo Gigante was elected mayor in October 1919, after D'Annunzio's occupation of Rijeka. He lived in Rijeka until 1945 when he moved to Bolzano.

Apart from Andrea Ossoinack, he was the most prominent Masonic figure of (Hungarian) liberalism. He distanced himself from fascism.

GLOSSARY

According to: Daniel Beresniak, *Symbols of Freemasonry*, Paris, 1997

Like every craft, Freemasonry has its jargon. It uses familiar words but gives them a special meaning, suited to its art and customs. Symbols are universal, but Freemasons link them, organize them and comment on them in their own particular way.

Discussions of symbols often contain terms whose meanings also need to be explained. This glossary explains some commonly used terms and provides information which will come in useful in discussions on the subject of Freemasonry.

APRON: An essential item of Masonic dress, consisting of a rectangle and a triangular bib. An Apprentice's apron is white and a Fellow's is sometimes white with blue edging. At the degree of the Master and beyond, the color and ornamentation of the apron varies. Aprons are generally lined in black, with silver stripes.

ECLECTIC MASONRY: Soon after the convention of Wilhelmsbad in1782, some German Masons, with the celebrated Baron Knigge at their head, conceived the idea of a reform in the system of degrees. It would confine Freemasonry, in its original and legitimate character, to the three symbolical degrees, governed by the English constitution of 1721, and in this way escape from the tyrannical usurpations of the Circles of the *Strict Observance*. The lodges, however, according to this plan, were allowed to select or choose any of the higher degrees, and work them as a kind of amusement or recreation. This innovation did not meet with the success anticipated, and has nearly disappeared. It was never introduced into the United States.

(According to: Robert Macoy, A Dictionary of Freemasonry, New York, 2000, p. 123)

TEMPLE: This word has several meanings in Freemasonry:
- the place where the lodge meets
- the temple of Jerusalem
- a sacred place.

INITIATION: A ceremony which consecrates the admission of a candidate into a lodge. Masonic initiation has kept some of the characteristics of the initiation into the trade which it originated from. In general terms, the initiation rite is a rite of passage from the secular to Freemasonry.

LODGE: Today, a lodge is the physical place where Freemasons meet. This may be a building or location which is specially set aside and arranged for Masonic meetings. The "lodge" is also the term used for a group of Freemasons who work together under a distinctive title or group name.

ORIENT: The light, and therefore power, comes from the East, where the sun rises. Most civilizations of the northern hemisphere have revered the East as the most important point on the compass. The East is the part of the lodge where the master sits.

ORDER OR CRAFT: These terms stand for the brotherhood of Masonry in general. The Masonic order is also known as the Craft. Some Grand Lodges, however, have adopted the term "order," but only when they have an international jurisdiction, for example the Co-Freemasonic Federation of Human Duty and the Order of Memphis. The term "craft" was the corporate term used by the medieval guilds, as well as a synonym for contemporary Masonic associations in Great Britain. In France, the term *"ordre"* (order) is more common.

RITE: A rite is a set of ceremonies observed in a certain order. By extension, a rite is also a moment in a ceremony, for example the rite of entering the lodge, the rite of establishing the officers, and so on. The Masonic rite consists of a set of rituals made up of a varying number of degrees of advancement, the first three of which are Apprentice, Fellow and Master.

The Ancient and Accepted Scottish Rite includes thirty-three degrees, the French Rite seven and the *Memphis Rite* ninety-five.

Rites vary according to their style and teaching. The most commonly observed rites in Europe are: the Ancient and Accepted Scottish Rite, the French Rite, the Rectified Scottish Rite, Emulation Working, and the Memphis Rite.

MEETING: A Masonic assembly.

FREEMASON (MASON): The etymology of this term has long been disputed. There are three possibilities to choose from:

1. *Free-stone Mason*: a term applied to a Mason who sculpted soft stone, as opposed to a rough-stone Mason. With his gavel and chisel, a soft-stone Mason could sculpt more elaborate figures in high or low relief;
2. "Free" meaning the opposite of "enslaved." According to feudal law, people belonged to the overlord of a particular area. Emancipation exempted them from certain obligations towards their lord, such as the duty to stay in one place and serve him. "Free" Masons, therefore, had the right to move and work wherever they chose.
3. "Free" being the status of the trade, rather than the person, with Masonry being a *francmestier* or emancipated trade. According to a book by Ettiene Boileau (1268), stone-cutters were given their freedom, but not Masons, carpenters or plasterers.

MASTER: The most important person in a lodge, where he holds great power. Conditions for the selection of the Master are that he possesses thorough knowledge of Masonic rules, and that he is ethical, and experienced in the workings of Freemasonry. He convenes and presides over lodges' meetings, manages the visits of "brethren" from other lodges, presides over and intervenes in discussions, appoints other bodies in the lodge, opens and closes the lodge, represents the lodge in all meetings together with the Junior and Senior Warden, appoints his deputy, signs the bills and refuses unsuitable candidates.

SECRECY: One of the Freemasons' primary duties. However, there is a misconception that it is related only to the matters of the Order or the Lodge. Secrecy entails silence as well, to keep one from inflicting injustice or harm on a "brother."

TEMPLARISM (Scottish): A form of a Knights Templar system that does not recognize the three symbolic degrees as its foundations, and, as a result, the members need not be Freemasons. The system is composed of two parts: (1) Novice and (2) Squire (a member of gentry) and Knight-Templar. The Knight-Templar consists of three degrees: (1) Knight-Monk, (2) Knight-Commander elected from the ranks of Knights, and (3) Knight Grand Cross, appointed by the Grand Master. Since Templarism differs from the Templar System of Freemasonry, this practice can be considered a Masonic association.

OFFICES AND OFFICERS: The posts held within a lodge and the brethren who fill them: the Worshipful Masters preside over the lodge with their teams, the College of Officers. The Senior Wardens are in charge of the south pillar where the Fellows sit; Junior Wardens are in charge of the north pillar, where the Apprentices sit. The Secretaries are the lodges' memory: taking minutes at meetings, keeping the archives and looking after correspondence. The Orators make sure that the law and rules are respected. It is the Orators who decide whether a vote would be appropriate and, when necessary, give their opinions on the debate. They can contest the Worshipful Master if they think that officer has made a mistake. In addition, they give the speech of welcome to new initiates. The *Hospitaliers* or *Almoners* collect and manage the charity fund. The Treasurers look after the lodges' finances. They collect subscriptions and approve expenditure. The Deacons and the Masters of Ceremonies ensure that the rituals and ceremonies are correctly observed. The

Tylers or Inner Guards watch the entrance and make certain that the lodge is "duly tiled" before work begins, ensuring that no member of the lodge or visitor from another lodge is still waiting outside in the antechamber.

GRAND LODGE: In Great Britain, this term describes a federation of lodges which observe the same rite or the supreme governing body of the Masons. The order has thirty-three degrees.

GRAND ORIENT (ORDER): In France and Europe generally, the term is used for a federation of lodges. The order was founded in 1786 and has seven degrees.

MILITARY LODGES: Were established in larger military formations (regiments, battalions), with the permission of higher command personnel. Civilians who lived in places where lodges were situated or through which the army was passing were not allowed as lodge members, except with the permission of the Grand Master or the Provincial Grand Master.

WORKSHOP: Term given to any organization of Freemasons. According to the degrees or grades, workshops have different names. In the first three grades, which are used in all rites, a workshop can be a synonym for a lodge. At higher grades, there are numerous other terms: lodge of perfection, archi-lodge, college, Aeropagus, consistory, encampment, and supreme council. Other names also exist: court, Court of Sinai, hierarchy or third heaven. The workshop is arranged according to the ritual being enacted, and the brethren wear the appropriate aprons, sashes and collars.

Ljubinka Toševa Karpowicz

APPENDICES

No. 37.

AMERICAN CONSULATE.

Fiume, March 4, 1922.

SUBJECT: Fall of Fiume Free State Government.

THE HONORABLE
THE SECRETARY OF STATE,
WASHINGTON.

SIR:

I have the honor to enclose herewith report covering Italian Fascisti uprising in Fiume and the fall of the Government of the Free State of Fiume.

This report was hurriedly written in order to catch an English steamer leaving tomorrow, thus avoiding the Italian censorship.

I have the honor to be, Sir,

Your obedient servant,

Consul.

Enclosures:
  Reports.

800.

FALL OF THE GOVERNMENT OF THE FREE STATE OF FIUME.

Consul Wilbur Keblinger.

attilio Depoli
Head of Prov. Govt

Fiume, March 4, 1922.

The expected has happened. The Fiume Free State
Government, never too firmly founded, has fallen and its
termination may be said to have been brought about with
the consent, if not the actual connivance, of one of its
creators. The readers of previous reports from this
Consulate on Fiume conditions will have no difficulty
in finding reasons and fixing the responsibility for the
failure of the Free State Government to thrive.

The Free State Government represented the will of the
vast majority of the people of Fiume, as expressed at the
elections held last April. Never since the armistice
has the sympathy for Italy been at such a low ebb as today.
The people are greatly depressed and can see no way out of
their present acute political and economical situation.

The report of February 18, 1922, gave an account of
the increased activity of the fascisti. From day to day
they became bolder and bolder. The arrival of a few arms
for the Fiume Government Police made them realize the
necessity for immediate action before still further supplies
were received and the police organized. The whole matter
was prearranged with the assistance of the fascisti of

Trieste.

- 2 -

Trieste. Several nights ago a fascisti was killed by
one of his comrades in a row over a woman. The fascisti
paper of Trieste admits this fact, but the Fiume fascisti,
supported by the "Vedetta D'Italia" (Italian propagandist
paper) announced he was killed by the Government Police
and a loud outcry was raised to revenge his death. At
5 o'clock on the morning of March 2d a great demonstration
to terrorize the town was made, bombing and small arm
firing over the whole city until about nine o'clock.
The day of the 2d was quiet but on the morning of
the 3d, just before daybreak, the real trouble started
by tremendous explosions of bombs in the neighborhood
and at the Government palace. This was kept up for a
long time. A large number of fascisti had come over from
Trieste under the command of a Mr. Junta, a Deputy to
the Italian Parliament, and it could be seen that everything
had been arranged for a strong attack. An attempt was made
to storm the palace, occupied by President Zanella and
the Government Police. To prevent capture the Government
police returned the fire and the fascisti retreated behind
the walls of adjacent buildings.

I had taken temporary quarters in the Consulate and
was an eye-witness of the entire proceedings. Here is a
rough plan of the scene:

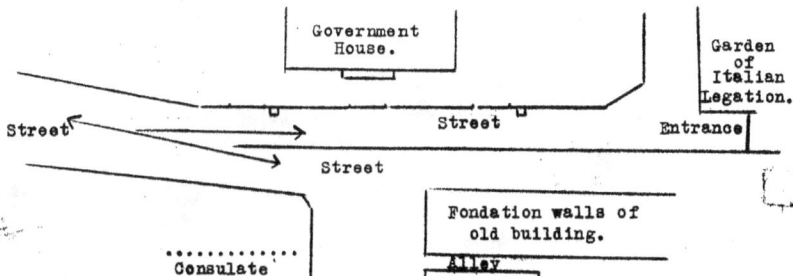

- 3 -

The firing was continuous, in fact enough ammunition
was expended during the day to have furnished material for a
very respectable battle.   A large gun or trench mortar
was placed just under the wall of the Consulate, where
the corner is cut away, and at each discharge the whole
building rocked, much glass being broken in the upper
stories.   All fighting was done from protected places,
none of the attackers, especially the Fiume contingent,
appeared to relish the fight in the open.   The I talian
carabinieri, officers and men, were with the fascisti
encouraging and cheering them on and I personally saw
a number of carabinieri firing on the Government palace.
During the entire morning a small Italian warship, a
subchaser, with a 76 m/m gun, had been unable to get
the range of the Government palace, its misses causing
damage to several buildings. About eleven o'clock a shot
struck the palace and after that many hits were made.
This shelling made the position of the Government police
untenable and the President asked of the Colonel
Commanding the Carabinieri for a cessation of hostilities
and at 12.30 P. M., seven hours from the beginning, the
firing ceased. Two companies of carabinieri ranged up on
the two sides of the entrance to the palace to prevent anyone
from going in, but the fascisti paid not the slightest
attention to them and climbed over the high iron fence
enclosing the building, shouting "Death to Zanella", etc.
In many cases the carabinieri gave them a "foot up".
The Colonel of the Carabinieri protected President Zanella
from injury.

During

- 4 -

During the morning several companies of Italian Bersaglieri came in from Abbazia, but made no attempt to restore order, saying they had no instructions to interfere.

The fascisti and carabinieri and their friends looted the palace from top to bottom, breaking up everything that could not be carried away, especially prizing the new new uniforms intended for the Government Police.

In front of the Palace Mr. Junta made a super-patriotic speech to an assembly largely composed of fascisti, carabinieri and women from the red light district.

A complete list of the killed and wounded has not been given out, but it is known to be considerable, although the protected nature of the fighting prevented any great number of casualties.

The city is sullen and dead and the victors are not singing and yelling in accordance with their usual custom, having accomplished much more than expected and take very seriously their responsibilities. It is believed that most of the Trieste contingent has returned to that place. They were the real force that brought the matter to a focus and they did practically all of the fighting.

The "Piccolo" of Trieste this morning published the following:

"The Ex-President of Fiume, Prof. Riccardo Zanella, was forced to sign within two minutes the following declaration:
    In consequence of the events which occurred today, March 3d, I am obliged to surrender myself to the revolutionary forces and I am turning over the power to the hands of the Committee for the Citizens National Defense, which has been the originator of the movement.   Zanella.

                                    Zanella

- 5-

Zanella wished to turn over the power to the Italian authorities, but the victorious revolutionaries did not consent to his wishes. He was kept a prisoner during the entire afternoon, when at 8 P. M., the revolutionists succeeded in obtaining from him a definite renunciation of power, which was signed in his presence of Dr. Blasich and three members of the revolutionary government.

The text of the resignation:

I, the undersigned do herewith solemnly declare with my present deed to retire for ever from the public life of Fiume, and to make effectively the most ample and unconditioned renunciation to whatever political aspirations, and oblige myself on my word of honor not to take part, directly or indirectly, or through other persons, in the public affairs of Fiume, never and not in any way to try, directly or indirectly, the agitation, propaganda or any other acts of concealed or open hostility against the ideals and national aspirations of Fiume; never to conspire, encourage or aid in any way whatever the propaganda and agitations abovementioned, even if the same will be tried by others or having the purpose of political activity on the part of others.

I recognize that the power exercised by the Committee of Citizens National Defense today constituted is legitimate and sovereign and declare myself to be unworthy to be a member of civil society if I do not faithfully maintain my above obligations.

The following constitute the Revolutionary Government:

Ing. Attilo Prodam (keeper of electrical supply store.)
Cav. Mario Petris (without known occupation).
Ramiro Antonini (has exceedingly bad record.)
Guido Cartesio (has colonial store) is a groceries
Giovanni Amramovich (clerk, apparently Montenegrian.)
Prof. Giacomo Pontevivo (Italian Professor.)

It is interesting to note that none of the persons who was active in previous pro-Italian privosory Governments in Fiume since the armistice has any known connection with the present so-called revolutionary control.

Both the French and English Consuls are in accord with the views expressed in this and previous reports: that it has never been the intention of the Italian Government that the Free State Government should become stable and that the events of yesterday, so well arranged,

had

- 6 -

had either the direct approval of the Italian authorities of that they, as a Government, have no longer control over their troops.

The press reports that President Zanella was taken to Abbazia at about 9 o'clock last night and that his ultimate destination was unknown.

It may be most emphatically stated that the citizens of Fiume, with but few exceptions and they of the worst element, had no part in the proceedings of yesterday.

Telegrams in cipher to the Department and to the Ambassador at Rome were accepted under protest by the telegraph office officials, under direction of the new Committee, but I am not satisfied that they will ever be forwarded.

The Trieste papers of today state that the Italian Government has established a censorship on Fiume mail. The announcement is somewhat belated inasmuch as it has been well known that such censorship has been in operation for many months. The official mail of this Consulate has always been received in such state as to clearly indicate that it had been opened by some unauthorized authority.

It is believed that the pressure being brought to bear in Rome with respect to the concession of certain land in Fiume to the Standard Oil Company of New York by the Free State Government has undoubtedly hastened the fall of the Free State Government.

As a matter of information it may be stated that the Consul remained in the Consulate throughout the seven hours of fighting, there was no way of getting out.

COMITATO DI DIFESA NAZIONALE
FIUME D'ITALIA

N. 1-1922

BANDO

In seguito alla capitolazione del Governo provvisorio avvenuto ieri dopo un aspro combattimento durato dall'alba alle prime ore del pomeriggio

Il Comitato di Difesa Nazionale

dichiara definitivamente decaduti il Governo provvisorio e l'Assemblea Costituente;

assume provvisoriamente i pieni poteri rimessigli con atto ufficiale del Capo del Governo di Fiume;

affida il mantenimento dell'ordine pubblico e la sicurezza dei confini ai RR. CC. e alle Regie Truppe;

invita il Governo d'Italia ad assumere l'amministrazione della Città mediante un suo legittimo Rappresentante che il solo potrà garantire a Fiume l'ordine, la tranquillità e il suo avvenire economico.

FIUME, 3 marzo 1922.

Firmato:

Ing. ATTILIO PRODAM

The National Defense Committee's proclamation on the "collapse of the Provisional Government and the Constituent Assembly"

Архив
Југославије   фонд бр. _100_   фас. бр. _3_   јединица
                                                описа бр. _____

□ Sirius □

„Per aspera ad astra".   Fiume, __ 1912

[handwritten letter in German Kurrent script]

Correspondence between the Sirius Lodge and the Pobratim Lodge from Belgrade

261

Ljubinka Toševa Karpowicz

INDEX

PERSONAL NAMES INDEX

INDEX OF LODGES AND ORDERS REFERRED TO

SELECTED REFERENCES

- Ludwig Abaffy, *Geschichte der Freimaurerei in* Österreich-Ungarn.
- Almerigo Apollonio, "Trieste tra guerra e pace." In *Arheografo Triestino.* 1995, pp. 194-342.
- Maria Arrigoni, *Come gl' Inglesi andarono a Malta e vi restarono.* Milan, 1940.
- Tatiana Bakounine, *Répertoire biographique des francs-maçons russes.* Paris, 1967.
- Amleto Ballarini, *Antidannunziano a Fiume, Riccardo Zanella.* Roma, 1995.
- Eva H. Balázs, "Freimaurer, Reformpolitiker, Girondisten." In *Befördere der Aufklärung in Mittel-und Osteuropa, Freimaurer, Geselschaften, Clubs.* Berlin, 1979, pp. 127-140.
- Eva H. Balázs, "Les Lumières en Europe centrale et orientale." In *L'ère des Lumières et les Josephinistes en Hongrie,* Eva H. Balázs, *Karl von Zinzendorf et ses relations avec l' Hongrie a l'epoque de l'absolutisme eclaire.* Budapest, 1975.
- Željko Bartulović, *Sušak 1919-1947.* Rijeka, 2004.
- Kálman Benda, "Probleme des Josephinismus in den Habsburgischen Monarchie." In *Südostforschungen,* XXV/1966, pp. 38-71.
- Stephan Tull, *Die politische Zielforstehungen der Wiener Freimaurerei und Wiener Jakobiner im 18. Jahrhundert.* Wien, 1993.
- *Bericht der Symbolischen Grossloge von Ungarn über ihre Tätigkeit, Geschäfts- und Kassagebahrung im Jahre 1897.* Budapest, 1898.
- Vaso Bogdanov, *Jakobinska zavjera Ignjata Martinovića [Ignjat Martinovic's Jacobinian Conspiracy].* Zagreb, 1960.
- Ivan von Bojničić, *Die Freimaurerloge "Ljubav bližnjega,"* in *Zagreb.* Zagreb, 1917.
- Andrè Combes, *Le Grand Orient de France au XIXe siècle.* Paris, 1960.
- William R. Denslow, *10,000 Famous freemasons.* 2002.
- Antonella Ercolani, *La fondazione del Fascio del combattimento a Fiume tra Mussolini e D'Annunzio.* Roma, 1996.
- Valentin Erigène, *Napoléon et les sociétés secrètes: le rêve d'un empire universel.* Paris, 1986.
- René le Forestier, *La Franc-maçonnerie templière et occultiste aux XVIII et XIX e siècles.* Paris, Louvain, 1970.
- Vladan Gavrilović, *Timisoaraski sabor i Ilirska dvorska kancelarija 1790-1792 [Council of Timisoara and Illyrian Court Office].* Novi Sad, 2005.
- Giordano Gamberini, *Mille volti di massoni.* Roma, 1975.

- Gaston Grafen von Pettenegg, *Ludwig und Karl grafen und Herren von Zinzendorf, minister unter Maria Theresia, Josif II, Leopold II. und Franz I. Ihre Selbstbiographien nebst einer kurzen Geschichte des Hauses Zinzendorf.* Wien, 1879.
- Silvino Gigante, "Stralcio delle corrispondenza di Lodovico Andrea Adamich col tenente maresciallo Laval Nugent." In *Fiume,* XVIII/1940, pp. 131-171.
- Silvino Gigante, "La guardia nazionale del XLVIII." In *Bulletino della Deputazione fiumana di storia patria,* vol. Fiume, 1913, pp. 177-214.
- Giulio Graton, *Trieste segreta,* Bologna, 1948.
- Manojlo Grbić, *Karlovačko vladičanstvo [The Karlovac Diocese],* book three. 1893.
- Ludwig Hammermeier, "Die politische und Kulturelle Bedeutung der Freimaurerei in 18. Jahrhundert." In *Beförderer der Aufklärung in Mittel und Osteuropa, Freimaurer, Gesellschafte, Clubs.* Berlin, 1979, pp. 69-86.
- Armando Hodenigo – Gian Proda, *La Giovine Fiume. Rievocata nel cinquantesimo anniversario della sua fondazione.* Roma, 1955, p. 34.
- Lajos Horváth, "Riječki zastupnik u mađarskom državnom saboru 1848-49" *[Representative of Rijeka at the Diet of Hungary 1848-49],* Vjesnik Državnog arhiva u Rijeci, volumes XLI-XLII/2000, pp. 127-133.
- Hans Josef Irmeni, ed. *Die Protokolle der Wiener Freimaurerloge "Zur wahren Eintracht(1781-1785)."* 1994.
- Anna Maria Isastia, "Massoneria e fascismo: la grande repressione." In *La Massoneria, la storia, gli uomini, le idee.* Milan, 2004.
- Andrew C. Janos, *The Politics of Backwardness in Hungary, 1825-1945.*Princeton, 1982.
- László Katus, *Hungary in the Dual Monarchy 1867-1914.* NewYork, 2008.
- France Kidrič. "Framasonske lože hrvaških zemelj Napoleonove ilirije v poročilih dunajskega policjskega arhiva". Rad Jazu, book 206. Zagreb,1915, pp. 35-60.
- France Kidrič, "Francusko-ilirska loža Prijateljev kralja rimskega in Napoleona v Ljubljani" *Slovan,* XII. Ljubljana, 1915.
- Danilo Klen, *Tvornica papira Rijeka [Rijeka Paper Factory].* 1972.
- Kuess-Scheilcherbauer, *Zweihundert Jahre Freimaurerei in* Österreich, Wien 1959.
- Eugen Lennhoff, *Die Freimaurer.* Amantea: Verlag, 1926.
- L. Lewis, *Geschichte der Freimaurerei in* Österreich *im allgemeinen.* Wien, 1861.
- *Mackey's Revised Encyclopedia of Freemasonry,* 1969.
- Robert Macoy (1815-1895), *A Dictionary of Freemasonry.* New York, undated, updated edition 1989.
- Danilo I. Massagrande, *Italia e Fiume 1921-1924.* Milan, 1982.
- Teodor Merzdorf, *Keiser Franz I. als Freimeurer.* Wien, 1877.

- Aldo A. Mola, *Storia della massoneria italiana dalle origini ai nostri giorni.* 1994

- Gaetano Morese, "Hrvatska imovina princa Lavala Nugenta u dokumentima Državnog arhiva u Napulju," *[Prince Laval Nugent's Croatian Property in the Documents of the State Archives in Naples].* In *Vjesnik DAR*, 50-52/2011, pp. 61-85.

- Ivan Mužić, *Masonstvo u Hrvata [Freemasonry in Croatia],* VIII updated edition. Split, 2005.

- Zoran Nenezić, *Masoni 1717-2010 [The Freemasons].* Belgrade, 2010.

- Josip Neustädter, *Ban Jelačić i događaji u Hrvatskoj od 1848 [Ban Jelačić and Events in Croatia since 1848].* Zagreb,1994.

- Laval Count Nugent, *Die Abstammung der Familie Nugent* (gotica). Stuttgart, 1904.

- Robert Okay, *The Habsburg Monarchy.* 2001.

- Nicolas T. Parsons, "Custodians of the Future. Scottish and English influences on Hungary in the Reform Age." In *The Hungarian Quarterly,* vol. 39, winter 1998, pp. 96-112

- Hedwig Pavelka, *Englisch-österreichischeWirtschaftbeziehungen in der ersten Hälfte des 19. Jahrunderts.* Graz-Wien-Köln, 1968.

- Mladen Plovanić, "Liburnisti autonomaši 1943-1944" *[Liburnian Autonomists 1943-1944], Dometi.* Rijeka, 5/1980 and 6/1980 pp. 69-97

- Norbert Schindler, "Der Geheimbund der Illuminaten-Aufklärung, Geheimnis und Politik." In Helmut Reinhalter, ed. . *Freimaurer und Geheimbunde im 18. Jahrhundert in Mitteleuropa,*1986. Edition II.

- J. H. Schwicker, *Die politische Geschichte der Serben in Ungarn.* Budapest, 1880.

- А.И.Серков, *Русское масонство 1731-2000.,энциклопедический словарь.* Moscow, 2001.

- Denis Silagi, *Ungarn und die geheime Mitarbeiterkreis Kaiser Leopolds II.* München, 1961.

- Sindarin Thomas, *Freimaurer in Siebenburgen 1749.-1790. Die Loge "ST. Andreas zu den drei Seeblätern in Hermanstadt 1767.-1790."* Leipzig, 1802.

- Attilio Tamaro, "Origini della massoneria a Fiume", *Archeografo triestino,* serie IV.vol. XIV-XV. Trieste ,1948 pp. 355-369.

- Attilio Tamaro, "Episodi di storia fiumana." In *Fiume.* 1933/34.

- Ljubinka Toševa Karpowicz, "Jadran i Sredozemlje u doba Francuza." In *Doba modernizacije 1780-1830 [The Adriatic and the Mediterranean in the French Era, An Era of Modernization 1780-1830].* Rijeka, 2006 pp. 185-199.

- Ljubinka Toševa Karpowicz, *D'Annunzio u Rijeci. Mitovi, politika i uloga Masonerije [D'Annunzio in Rijeka. Myths, Politics and the Role of Freemasonry].* Rijeka, 2007.

- Ljubinka Toševa Karpowicz, "La biografia politica d'un autonomista." In *Quaderni*,VII/1983, pp. 39-62.
- Nevio Šetić, "L'Istrie et Rijeka sous l'administration française et le blocus anglais de la côte adriatique." In *Hrvatske ilirske pokrajine [Croatian Illyrian Provinces]*. Zagreb, 2010, pp. 283-302.
- Jaroslav Šidak "Hotel Lambert i Hrvati," *[Lambert Hotel and the Croats]* in *Studije iz hrvatske povijesti XIX stoljeća [Studies in Croatian XIX Century History]*, 1973 pp. 167-177.
- *Die Ungarische Freimaurerei und das k.u.k.Heer, dritte Auflage.* Wien, 1889.
- Hans Wagner, *Freimaurer um Joseph II. Die Loge Zur wahren Eintracht.* Berlin, 1980.
- Fran Zwitter, "Francuske revolucionarne ideje u zapadnim jugoslovenskim zemljama u vreme Francuske revolucije i Napoleona I." *[French Revolutionary Ideas in the Western Yugoslav Countries in the Days of the French Revolution and Napoleon I]* An outline of the *Collection of papers: Jugoslovenska zemlje i Rusija za vreme Prvog srpskog ustanka 1804-1814. [The Yugoslav Country and Russia during the First Serbian Uprising 1804-1814]*. Belgrade, 1983 pp. 65-88.

INDEX OF ARCHIVES

- Arhiv Jugoslavije (AJ) [Yugoslav Archives], Belgrade.
- Archives of the Ministry for Foreign Affairs (MAE, Archivio storico), Rome.
- Državni arhiv u Rijeci [Rijeka State Archives] (DARI), Rijeka.
- National Archives, Washington DC (NARA), Consular group, Washington.

CONTENT

ACKNOWLEDGEMENT

I n writing and publishing this book I owe gratitude to the many people whose assistance and suggestions made it all considerably easier.

Above all, I owe gratitude to Larissa P. Watkins, librarian at the Library of the Supreme Council, 33°, S. J. from Washington, who not only made it possible for me to avail myself of the publications from this rich library, but also provided useful, professional information regarding Freemasonry.

I owe gratitude to the librarians of the Customer Service Department of the Sveučilišna knjižnica [University Library] in Rijeka, who were always on hand and most obliging in handling my litany of daily requests.

I would like to thank Goran Crnković, director, and the employees of the Državni arhiv u Rijeci [State Archives in Rijeka], who were always willing to assist, both in terms of providing professional advice, and providing access to the material.

I am particularly grateful to the reviewers, University Professors Željko Bartulović and translator Branko Dražić.

I would like to thank Zlatko Moranjak, who coordinated the entire endeavor and those involved in printing the book.

Rijeka, December 2015

The Author

www.ingramcontent.com/pod-product-compliance
Lightning Source LLC
Chambersburg PA
CBHW050646270326
41927CB00012B/2894